Strategic Management

Leadership, adaptability, value creation. These are the skills necessary for tomorrow's managers. Allen Amason approaches the topic of strategic management with these traits in mind. Rather than simply teaching theory and research, he seeks to communicate to students the fundamental keys to how strategy works.

This book is designed to help students think critically and understand fully how to strategically manage their future firms. In so doing, it will enable them to adapt and learn, even as their circumstances change; to apply sound logic and reasoning, even in new and unfamiliar settings. By conveying enduring and fundamental principles of economic and human behavior rather than simply reporting on the latest innovations, this book succeeds in preparing students to excel in the business environment over time, regardless of how it evolves.

To accompany this book are valuable online resources at www.routledge.com/textbooks/amason featuring:

- PowerPoint Presentation Slides for instructors
- Chapter Study Outlines for students with links to articles, videos, and websites that build on the material covered in the book.

Allen C. Amason is Department Head and Associate Professor in the Department of Management at The University of Georgia.

Strategic Management

From Theory to Practice

Allen C. Amason

Routledge
Taylor & Francis Group

NEW YORK AND LONDON

Publisher: John Szilagyi
Development Editor: Felisa Salvago-Keyes
Companion Website Designer: Marie Mansfield
Production Editor: Sarah Stone

First published 2011
by Routledge
270 Madison Avenue, New York, NY 10016

Simultaneously published in the UK
by Routledge
2 Park Square, Milton Park, Abingdon, Oxon OX14 4RN

Routledge is an imprint of the Taylor & Francis Group, an informa business

Typeset in Berling Roman and Futura by Book Now Ltd, London
Printed and bound in the United States of America on acid-free paper
by Edwards Brothers, Inc.

Library of Congress Cataloging in Publication Data
Amason, Allen C.
Strategic management: from theory to practice/Allen Amason.
        p. cm.
1. Strategic planning. 2. Management. I. Title.
HD30.28.A425 2011
658.4'012—dc22   2010030844

ISBN13: 978–0–415–87172–3 (hbk)
ISBN13: 978–0–415–87169–3 (pbk)
ISBN13: 978–0–203–86583–5 (ebk)

Dedication

This book is dedicated to my wife Margaret and to our children, Chase, Jaclyn, Christopher and Yanna. I love you all and I thank you for your love and support.

Brief Table of Contents

Detailed Table of Contents

Preface

Welcome to *Strategic Management: From Theory to Practice*. As a potential reader or adopter of this text, you may ask: Why another book on this subject? Certainly there is no shortage of alternatives, all authored by good scholars who are also knowledgeable in their field and passionate about their work. The answer is that this book is fundamentally different from those others. Moreover, the things that make this book different will also make it an especially valuable tool for teaching and learning. Indeed, students and instructors alike should find this approach novel and accessible.

What makes it so different? Stated plainly, it is a book *on* strategic management rather than a book *about* strategic management. The difference is subtle but important and reflects a basic question that every teacher of this material should ask—specifically, Why do students take this course and what must they take away from it in order to have a successful experience? It is my belief that students expect to leave this course as better strategic thinkers and managers. They want to be able to do the things, to make the decisions, and to deliver the results that will enable their success. In essence, they come to this course wanting to become successful or to become more successful. So this text is organized and oriented in such a way as to help.

Rather than try to convey all that theory has to say on a subject, the book seeks to translate what theory has to say into principles and practices that students need to know in order to accomplish what that they want to accomplish. As mentioned, it is a subtle difference but it is an important one. It reflects an approach that is grounded firmly in theory and research but that is ever so practical in application. It reflects 18 years of experience teaching strategic management, to executives, MBAs, and undergraduates. And it reflects a desire to communicate, in a straightforward and plain-spoken way, a model that has too often seemed overly esoteric and academic to students and executives alike. In essence, the approach is to render strategic management practical by making it accessible and to leverage its utility by leveraging its generalizability. Everything in the book, then, from its coverage to its organization, reflects this philosophy.

Chapter 1 is an introduction built on a simple foundation—namely, that it is all about performance. There is a song by Sean "Diddy" Combs entitled "It's All about the Benjamins." Few books or articles capture the practical essence of our discipline as well as this simple phrase. In business we keep score by measuring performance, and performance is a function of strategy. Of course, strategy and strategic management can mean different things to different people and the study and practice of strategy can involve all manner of complexity and nuance. But tying it all together is the focus and the impact on performance.

Chapter 2 then addresses the question begged by Chapter 1: What is performance? While seemingly simple, the issue of performance has been elaborated and complicated by the myriad different measures that are employed to capture it and by the context in which it is evaluated. Thus, great attention is paid to the technical challenges and trade-offs in performance measurement. Here too, though, the point is to simplify and make accessible and to show performance from a variety of perspectives. Moreover, the discussion is connected to strategic management, to illustrate the responsibility and challenge of the role.

Chapter 3 begins the process of meeting that challenge, and strategic management is presented as a set of "tools" that can help. Covered in this chapter are the principal components of the model. However, the point is not to be comprehensive or exhaustive. Indeed, I intentionally gloss over some fine-grained distinctions and lump together some things that others would prefer to keep separate. I do this because the purpose is to simplify and make practical, to focus on questions of "why" rather than questions of "what," and to provide an overarching framework for the practice of strategy.

Chapter 4 covers the first step in that application—analysis of the environment. While similar in many ways to other texts, this analysis is different in some fundamental ways as well. The first is the way the environment is defined. With a goal of practical accessibility, I define competition as those who interfere with the relationship a firm has to its customers. I define the competitive environment as the sum of those first-order connections that affect the relationship of a firm to its customers. Finally, I cast environmental analysis as the input to the rest of the strategic process. Through the analysis of past, present, and future, environmental analysis must produce the insights that will motivate every step thereafter.

Chapter 5 takes that input and answers the question: Now what? How does a strategist take the output from the environmental analysis and convert it into strategy? The chapter focuses on some common tools for this, such as SWOT, the value chain, and VRIN (value, rarity, inimitability, and non-substitutability) analyses. However, it goes one step further and introduces "competitive profile analysis." This process was developed through years of consulting practice and application and is built on sound theoretical principles. This process, along with all the other material in this chapter, is meant to provide a mechanism for answering the "What now?" question.

Chapter 6 focuses directly on competitive advantage and flows naturally from the issues in chapters 4 and 5. However, rather than discuss competitive advantage as an organizational-level construct, I discuss it as it exists at the transaction level. The point is to facilitate better connection between the "why" and the "how" of strategy. How does the practice of strategy with all of its various models and tools actually connect to performance? The answer is by enabling more and more profitable transactions. This approach also provides a practical measure of competitive advantage that is both tangible and immediate and that links directly to financial performance.

Chapter 7 introduces the concept of multi-business strategy. Viewing competitive advantage at the transaction level focuses attention on environmental conditions and organizational attributes. Those conditions and attributes are specific to individual business units. But what does strategy have to say about diversified firms with multiple business units? Answering that question requires a discussion of synergy and of the "better-off" principle. In essence, a diversified firm should be more valuable than the sum of its individual business units or its corporate strategy will have been unsuccessful. How a firm gains and manages that synergy so as to be better off is the subject of this chapter.

Chapter 8 deals with implementation and marks the final step in the framework. A good comprehension of implementation requires understanding two distinct topics: fit and change. It also requires understanding that the relationship between these things is paradoxical. Designing a firm so that it is tightly fit to the current strategy and the demands of the current environment can facilitate performance in the short term. However, it also limits flexibility and adaptability in the long term. Yet performing well over time requires that attention be paid to both. This chapter, then, is meant to explain both topics in a practical and accessible way, while also introducing the subsequent dilemma and offering insights on how to manage it.

Chapter 9 is supplied almost as an addendum to the larger framework. It is not meant to flow from the previous chapters as the earlier ones did, but rather to derive from the sum of the previous chapters and to show the generalizable nature of strategic management. It does this by comparing similarities in the strategic management framework to issues in entrepreneurship and international business. Some may object to presenting these disciplines as subsets of strategy. But the treatment is intentional and meant to illustrate that, by truly understanding the framework and principles of strategy, anyone can move and work efficiently across a range of contexts and settings.

Chapter 10, the final chapter, is offered both as a summary of the book and as a point of connection between the practice of strategy and leadership. Here, again, the point is not to be comprehensive but to introduce common functions of leadership and to relate them to the framework of strategic management. Governance, which is briefly discussed in this chapter, is presented as a condition surrounding leadership and as an answer to the question: How is leadership structured and delivered in modern organizations? While this approach may not do justice to the complexity and richness of governance, it does serve to make the topic accessible and easily connected to the larger framework of strategy.

The sum total of the book, then, is a straightforward walk through the practice of strategy. Like other books, this one draws from theory and research as it explains the tools, models, and logic of strategic management. However, the language, perspective, and approach are subtly and yet fundamentally different. The result is a text that should be interesting, accessible, and useful to students at every level—undergraduate, MBA, and executive. Moreover, it is an approach that should be refreshingly different and yet still very comfortable for researchers and teachers.

FEATURES IN THE TEXT

To bring the concepts together, each of the chapters ends with a list of **key terms** introduced and some **questions for review**. Additionally, there is a companion website to the book, www.routledge.com/textbooks/amason, which provides accompanying PowerPoint **lecture slides**, as well as **chapter outlines with links** to articles, cases, videos, and interviews. These build on and demonstrate the concepts for each chapter, helping students engage directly with the material and further their understanding of the subject.

Chapter 1

An Introduction to Strategic Management

IT'S ABOUT PERFORMANCE

How is it that some firms can perform so well, while others struggle and sometimes fail? What is it about a firm that allows it to thrive, despite ongoing challenges from its competitors and ever increasing demands from its customers? For example, consider Southwest Airlines, a familiar firm whose story of success has been well chronicled. How has Southwest been able to profit consistently over the past 20 years, while so many other firms in its industry have gone bankrupt, been acquired, or continue to operate at a loss? Or consider Coca-Cola, another well-known firm that is frequently cited for its lasting success. What has enabled Coke to grow so valuable, despite persistent efforts by competitors and substitutes to imitate its products and lure away its customers?

Performance is the crux of business and so also of business education. While different people may hold different definitions of performance, and while some dimensions of performance will matter more to some than to others, performance itself is still the key measure of overall success. Thus, the ability to understand, predict, and ultimately direct a firm's performance is the goal of every business student, every manager, and every investor. Why do investors devote so much effort to the research and study of specific firms and industries? The answer is, because they want to distinguish the exceptional firms from the marginal ones and the marginal ones from the ones that are in trouble. Moreover, they want to do all this before these differences become common knowledge in the marketplace. Why do students study the principles of economics, marketing, management, and finance? Why do managers invest in continuing education and why do they commit resources to the research and analysis of their markets and competitors? The answer in each of these cases is that they want to build firms that perform well and that, like Southwest or Coke, are considered outstanding among their peers. Rather than follow, they want to lead, in the creation of value and performance.

This book is about the quest for performance—about strategic management. Over the years, strategic management has been defined in a number of different ways (see Box 1.1). While these definitions reflect the different perspectives and approaches common during the period in which they were written, they all describe a basic and fundamental phenomenon, the pursuit of superior performance through the creation of superior value. Successful firms create superior value for their customers and are rewarded by those customers with profitable sales. As illustrated in the stories that follow, Southwest Airlines and Coca-Cola are two well-known and successful firms that thrive by creating superior value for their customers, which they are then able to appropriate in the form of revenues and profits. Profits, of course, mean jobs for the managers and employees and returns for the owners and investors. The managers at these firms understand that value creation is the key to performance and so they formulate and implement strategies designed to create and capture value. They understand one of the most fundamental realities in business: real value creation does not happen by accident; rather it is the result of a purposeful and deliberate process.

Strategic management is that process by which managers integrate the firm's functions into streams and patterns of action designed to fit the constraints and demands of the market. To the extent it is done well, the process creates value for the customers, owners, and stakeholders of the firm. As an illustration, the following

---

Box 1.1
Some Prominent Definitions of Strategic Management

■ *The definition of the long-run goals and objectives of an enterprise, and the adoption of course of action and the allocation of resources necessary for carrying out these goals.*

Alfred Chandler (1962)

■ *Strategy is the pattern of objectives, purposes or goals and the major policies and plans for achieving these goals, stated in such a way as to define what business the company is in or is to be in and the kind of company it is or is to be.*

Kenneth Andrews (1987)

■ *The fundamental pattern of present and planned resource deployments and environmental interactions that indicate how the organization will achieve its objectives.*

Charles Hofer and Dan Schendel (1978)

■ *What business strategy is all about is, in a word, competitive advantage ... the sole purpose of strategic planning is to enable a company to gain, as efficiently as possible, a sustainable edge over its competitors.*

Kenichi Ohmae (1982)

■ *Strategy is a set of important decisions derived from a systematic decision making process, conducted at the highest levels of the organization.*

Daniel Gilbert, Edwin Hartman, John Mauriel, and Edward Freeman (1988)

■ *An integrated and coordinated set of commitments and actions designed to exploit core competencies and gain competitive advantage.*

Robert Hoskisson, Michael Hitt, Duane Ireland, and Jeffrey Harrison (2008)

---

stories retrace some familiar ground, outlining the history, approach, and success of two well-known companies. In so doing, they show the importance and the impact of strategic management.

Southwest Airlines

Southwest flies to over 60 cities throughout 38 states spread across the continental U.S. Look over any of its airfields and the only type of plane you'll see is the Boeing 737. Board a Southwest flight and you'll find the seats are first come, first served. While customers often take such things for granted, at Southwest they are the keys to success. Indeed, a careful look reveals a company built for and focused on making air travel easy, inexpensive, and fun.

The company now known as Southwest Airlines was started by Texas businessman Rollin King and lawyer Herb Kelleher. Originally called Air Southwest, the airline began humbly in 1967. It was initially conceived as an intra-state airline connecting Dallas, Houston, and San Antonio, and the company's inaugural flight was made in 1971. Southwest's earliest flights originated from Love Field, in Dallas. Exemplifying the spirit of creativity and fun that still guides Southwest's operations, drinks were called "love potions" and peanuts became "love bites." When the new Dallas/Fort Worth airport opened in 1974 other airlines moved into the larger and more modern home. Southwest, however, remained at Love Field, where it has a virtual monopoly.

The company would take a significant step towards becoming an industry leader when Kelleher assumed the role of company president in 1978. Kelleher was a flamboyant personality who brought much of his free-spirit attitude to the table while setting direction for the company. "Fun Fares" were introduced in 1986, and a frequent-flier program based on the number of flights taken instead of mileage traveled began in 1987. Kelleher took even bolder steps to raise the visibility of the company by personally starring in Southwest's TV commercials in 1992 and arm-wrestling Kurt Herwald, chairman of competitor Steven's Aviation, for the rights to the "Just Plane Smart" slogan.

East Coast expansion began in 1993, with service to Baltimore. The next year saw the purchase of Salt Lake City-based Morris Air, the introduction of a ticketless system, and an internally created passenger reservation system to reduce costs. Growth continued in 1996 as Southwest began service to Florida. Through arrangements with Icelandair in 1996 and 1997, its customers could fly to Europe by way of Icelandair's Baltimore hub. Additional eastern routes were added in 1999, and the following year Southwest placed an order for an additional 94 Boeing 737s to be delivered between 2002 and 2007—its largest order ever.

Despite an industry littered with losses, bankruptcy, and labor strife, Southwest Airlines continues to succeed, as it has now for 30 straight years, by sticking to its tried and true corporate philosophy. Indeed, even after the terrorist attacks of September 11, 2001, Southwest was the only major airline to maintain a full flight schedule and avoid layoffs.

Success like this cannot be explained by accidents of fate or fortune. Rather, there is a discernible pattern to the decisions of Southwest's management. For example, it is clear that the managers realize that customers have options. As a result, flying must be made easier, more pleasant, and less expensive than the alternatives. Southwest's management seems to understand the difference between customers and mere onlookers. Being in the largest and flashiest airports might draw attention, but it can also make life complicated for customers. Southwest's managers seem to appreciate that there are many things beyond their control. Things like fuel costs, air-traffic control bottlenecks, and security delays put a strain on every airline. Knowing that, Southwest emphasizes the things it can control, things like its efficiency and its attitude towards the customer. As a result, the customers continue to fly and Southwest continues to prosper.

The key here is that none of this happens naturally or by accident. Rather, it is the result of thoughtful analysis, careful planning, and coordinated action. In essence, it is the result of strategy. But this is not strategy in the traditional sense; there is more here than formal planning and much more than just policies and goals. Success like this reflects a process that is dynamic and interactive. It focuses on the drivers of customer value, anticipates competitor actions, and adapts as conditions evolve and change. It integrates resources and actions, develops capabilities, and indentifies opportunities and threats. Success like this reflects a strategy that is connected throughout the various parts of the firm and that comes to life through the daily attitudes, actions, and behaviors of the people. It is a strategy that is well conceived and well executed. As a result, it is a strategy that delivers strong results.

The Coca-Cola Company

Rarely in any industry has a single company excelled and led for over 50 years. However, the Coca-Cola Company has bested the 50-year mark and continues as the dominant player in the beverage industry. The Coca-Cola Company surrounds the #2 soft drink, Pepsi, with #1 Coca-Cola classic and #3 Diet Coke, flexing its muscles as the leading choice among carbonated beverages. Other brands under the Coca-Cola umbrella are Barq's, Fruitopia, Minute Maid, Powerade, Sprite, and Dasani. Through their partnership with Danone, Coke distributes Evian in North America and Dannon and Sparkletts spring water brands in the U.S. With some presence in nearly 200 nations, Coke has nearly 300 brands to offer its consumers and potential customers. This impressive list includes coffees, juices, sports drinks, and teas. About 50% of the global soft-drink market belongs to Coke, and overseas sales account for about 70% of the firm's total sales volume.

The thriving enterprise known as Coca-Cola began humbly in 1886 when Atlanta pharmacist John Pemberton invented the now famous soda known as Coke. In 1891, the Coca-Cola Company was purchased by Asa Candler, and within four years the fountain drink was available to quench the thirst of citizens in every state in the nation. Coke became a multinational in 1898 as the young soft-drink giant crossed the borders of Canada and Mexico. A significant part of the company changed hands in 1899, when Benjamin Thomas and John Whitehead bought the U.S. bottling rights and launched a regional franchise bottling system that created over 1,000 bottlers within 20 years. In 1919, Candler's family sold the company to Atlanta banker Ernest Woodruff for $25 million. Later that year, Coca-Cola went public.

Future growth came through product and overseas expansion, and slogans such as "The Pause that Refreshes" (1929) and "It's the Real Thing" (1941) linked the company with the catch-phrase style of marketing. Early evidence of a national love affair with the drink came during World War II. Wanting to help soldiers away from home, the government helped to build 64 overseas bottling plants. After buying Minute Maid in 1960, Coca-Cola began launching new drinks—Fanta (1960), Sprite (1961), TAB (1963), and Diet Coke (1982).

In 1981 Roberto Goizueta became CEO and chairman of Coca-Cola. One of his first major moves was the purchase of Columbia Pictures in 1982, and Columbia earned Coke a profit of about $1 billion when it was sold to Sony in 1989. In 1986 Coca-Cola began consolidating its U.S. bottling operations into Coca-Cola Enterprises. It then sold 51% of this new company to the public. In 2001, Coca-Cola acquired Mad River Traders (teas, juices, sodas) and Odwalla (juices and smoothies), a move that sprang from its desire to strengthen its portfolio in the fast-growing non-carbonated drinks market. At about the same time, Coca-Cola invested $150 million in bottling facilities in China. In another expansion, the company gained distribution rights to Danone's Evian brand in the U.S. and invested approximately $128 million in a joint venture to produce, market, and distribute Danone's bottled water. As a result of all this, Coca-Cola's market value rose from about $4 billion in 1997 to nearly $130 billion in 2009. While no one can predict the future, it is hard to imagine the world without Coke. Indeed, some have estimated that the name itself is among the most recognized symbols in the world, and many employees, executives, and investors have earned substantial wealth through their involvement with Coke.

As in the previous example, this sort of sustained success cannot be accidental. Year after year Coke continues to thrive, despite the changing tastes of the market-place, despite ever increasing pressure from competitors, and despite the ongoing encroachment of myriad new and potential substitute products. Despite all of this friction and drag, Coke remains valuable and profitable, more than a full century since its founding. How does that occur? It occurs through skillful and strategic management. Strategy unifies the various functions of a firm under a common purpose, blending together in the case of Coke a powerful brand, aggressive marketing, and massive distribution capabilities. Strategy provides coherence and purpose, enabling a firm to pursue diversification in its product line and to expand across the globe, while still being focused on its core strengths and advantages. Strategy provides an identity, allowing the firm and its managers to message their value proposition to customers, to investors, and to employees in a way that each understands their contribution to the larger whole. All of this, as evidenced in the example of Coke, contributes to the value of the firm, enabling revenues and profits which can provide a return and be reinvested in further growth and development.

DEFINING STRATEGIC MANAGEMENT

This is a book about strategic management. While Box 1.1 provides some prominent historical definitions, strategic management is essentially a framework for analyzing the environment, for integrating the firm's activities, for learning and adapting to change, and for creating value both in the present and into the future. As discussed later in the book, it is a framework that can be used in every type of organization, large or small, new or old, domestic or international, even for-profit and not-for-profit. It is a framework that can be understood and applied systemically, with discrete components, logical steps, and some simple but powerful models and tools. Beyond all of that, though, it is a framework that, when applied, becomes the process by which managers integrate the firm's functions into streams and patterns of action designed to identify and fit the contours of the environment. Finally, and to the extent it is done well, strategic management is a process that creates value for customers, for owners, and for all the stakeholders of a firm.

While the variety of definitions of strategy has been a source of confusion to some, strategic management is, at its core, a company's manifest plan of action for the ongoing creation and appropriation of value. Strategic management is at once a short-term and a long-term process that involves both plans and actions. It must reflect the immediate realities of the business environment, yet it must also provide impetus for innovation, adaptation, and change. It is most often the province of top management, yet it is also highly relevant and important to each and every employee. Strategic management is, at once, a framework to guide thinking and a process to guide action. Owing to this complex and multifaceted nature, Henry Mintzberg (1987) once described strategic management as being part plan, part ploy, part pattern, part position, and part perspective.

Plan, Ploy, Pattern, Position, and Perspective

Strategic management is certainly part planning. Most texts remind us that the word strategy derives from a Greek military term, *strategia*, which literally means "a plan of action." Strategic management is a high-level cognitive activity, a forward-looking and visionary process that incorporates understanding about the environment, the firm, and the ongoing developments and changes in each. It is the process by which threats and opportunities are identified and accommodated. It is willful and intentional, analytical and creative. Indeed, planning is fundamental to strategic management.

Of course, plans are not always all that they appear to be. They are sometimes more significant for their symbolic value than for their practical value, designed to signal capabilities rather than intentions, and intended to lure a competitor into a poor decision or to create an illusion of strength to mask some vulnerability. In this sense, strategies are as much ploys as they are plans. A ploy is simply an article of deception used to gain an advantage over a competitor, but it can be a powerful and substantial component of a firm's strategy.

Strategic management can also be understood as a pattern. Some strategies are the result of careful planning, but others simply emerge serendipitously from the interactions of the firm's people with one another and with their environment. These emergent patterns are real and significant. Successful firms develop a recipe for success which becomes a consistent pattern of action. That pattern is then instilled and reinforced throughout the company as a part of its culture and standard operating procedures. Think about successful companies like the two described earlier; most follow a consistent pattern in the way they go to market and do business. It is this pattern that is seen by the customers, competitors, analysts, and journalists, and it is this pattern that is understood as the firm's strategy.

But strategic management is also about positioning the firm within an attractive and manageable environment. Granted, such positioning may result from an intentional plan or emerge from a natural pattern. Still, such positions often become the focus and substance of the firm's strategy. Many firms seek positions that allow them to avoid competition. Regulated monopolies, for instance, are protected from competition. While they are constrained by their environments, their strategy is also a function of their protected position. Even in competitive environments, though, a large portion of a firm's strategy is dictated by the realities of its surroundings. Thus, positioning is also a key component of strategic management.

Finally, strategic management is largely a matter of perspective. In other words, firms differ in how they view the world and their place within it. Much as individuals have distinct personalities and characters, firms, too, have distinct perspectives that govern what they do and how they believe they should do it. Some firms are aggressive while others are much less so. Some seek a leadership position in their industries while others are content merely to make good margin, away from the spotlight. Some firms have a reputation for engineering excellence while others are known for their marketing prowess. This collective view of the firm itself, of the environment, and of how the firm should operate within that environment is a large part of strategy.

These five faces of strategy are at once important and accurate. At the same time, they also are at once inadequate and incomplete. At any single moment in time, strategic management may involve them all. Strategy can be a unifying theme that gives coherence and meaning. But coherence and meaning are worth little if they fail to fit the changing realities of the marketplace. Strategy certainly involves the setting of goals and objectives. But goals and objectives are worth little without the skills and resources needed to accomplish them. Strategy is a systematic process for guiding decisions and actions. But a systematic process that cannot adapt and change will inevitably fail. Thus, good strategic management must incorporate all five of these facets. Strategy is, at once, part plan, part ploy, part pattern, part position, and part perspective.

While strategy is all of these things, we should never forget that the end result of strategy is action. Eloquent statements of intention and well-conceived plans are certainly helpful but, day after day, it is action that gives a strategy its life. Look at the mission statements of several high-performing and low-performing firms. What you will find is a remarkable similarity across the two groups. Yet look at the types of actions they take and you will begin to see some significant differences. At the end of the day, strategy is all about action; strategy is all about what the firm really does to produce superior performance. And it is on that ability to produce superior performance that the success of a strategy is ultimately judged.

COMPETITIVE ADVANTAGE

For all of their complexity and in all their various manifestations, all strategies seek the same fundamental thing, **competitive advantage**. What is competitive advantage? It is frequently defined as the ability of one firm to perform better than its rivals. According to this definition, firms that perform above the average for their industry have a competitive advantage. Although popular and appealing, this definition is practically problematic. For instance, who are the rivals against which a firm should be compared? Do they seek to accomplish the same things and do they measure their performance in the same way, such that a fair comparison is possible? What happens if a firm is publicly owned while its rivals are privately owned? How do we compare their performance then? What is the appropriate time period over which to measure and compare this performance? Do we measure performance annually, quarterly, or in some other, more immediate fashion? Does the fact that one firm had greater profit than another in the previous year say anything about its competitive advantage today or in the future? While the ability of one firm to perform better than its rivals is certainly a reflection of competitive advantage, it is not a definition with much practical value.

Competitive advantage also is frequently described in metaphorical terms, as a sporting contest, for example. Defined in this way, competitive advantage is the key asset or ability that allows one team to best another. While similarly popular and appealing, this metaphor can also be misleading because it fails to capture two important characteristics of business competition. The first is that the pursuit of competitive advantage never ends. Consider history and you will find few examples of perpetual success. Even the strongest firms with the most dominant positions, AT&T in the long-distance telephone business, IBM in the mainframe computer business, or General Motors in the automobile business, for example, eventually faltered with the emergence of new technologies and new markets. Unlike a sporting event, where there is a clear beginning and a clear end, the competition in business is ongoing. Because the game never ends, there is never really a final winner. Wal-Mart, for instance, is at the top of the discount retailing business at present. However, history teaches that sustaining this success, in the face of evolving technologies, demanding customers, and emerging new competitors, will be a daunting task. Even Southwest and Coke face the reality of new competitors, new threats, and new demands that must be satisfied over and over again if they hope to continue the legacy of success that they have established.

The second area where the sporting contest metaphor falls short is that, in a sporting contest, the competitors are known. In business, however, new competitors arise constantly. A competitive advantage and the profits associated with it may actually attract new competitors. Vanquish one and two more may arise to take its place. Indeed, few of the major airlines would have seen Southwest as a threat to their business in the early days of its history. Yet today it stands as one of the industry's most successful carriers. Schneider National is the nation's largest carrier of freight in the long-haul segment of the trucking business. Yet some of its most intense competition comes not from other large well-known carriers but from the hundreds of small, relatively unknown independent operators, who enter and exit different markets quickly. The challenge, then, is to sustain competitive advantage in the face of the competition that is known today and the competition that may emerge tomorrow.

This discussion is meant to illustrate that, while the term competitive advantage is often used, it is rarely understood in its fullness. And that is a problem; if strategic management is to be understood as the pursuit of competitive advantage, then we must have a good sense of what competitive advantage really is. Every facet of strategic management, throughout every part of the organization, should point to competitive advantage because competitive advantage is the key to performance. Every goal and objective, every intention and action, every plan, ploy, and perspective, should ultimately point towards competitive advantage, its development, maintenance, and expansion. But what is competitive advantage? How can we define it so that it is practically meaningful to all the various facets of a firm's strategy and to all of those who are involved in a firm's strategic management?

At the Transaction Level

In his 1985 book entitled *Competitive Advantage*, Michael Porter defined competitive advantage as growing "out of the value a firm is able to create for its buyers that exceeds the firm's cost of creating it." While this definition says little about beating competitors or winning games, it nevertheless captures the essence of competitive advantage in a way that is especially meaningful and practical: competitive advantage is achieved in some small measure every time a firm sells a product or delivers a service at a profitable price.

Of course, a lot of firms sell a lot of products and deliver a lot of services at profitable prices. How, then, can such a simple and common action be a measure of competitive advantage? To understand, consider all that is implied by this simple definition. If a customer is to buy a product or service, at a profitable price, it is because she perceives some value in it over and above its cost. For example, when Coke sells a drink, the customer receives value in excess of the price that she pays. That excess is what economists call **consumer surplus**. If the price she pays is also more than Coke's cost in producing the product, then Coke has also earned a surplus, called a profit. The transaction then yields value to both parties.

However, this profitable transaction did not occur in a vacuum. Rather, it occurred in an open and competitive environment, where this customer had any number of other options for her money. She could have chosen to buy a Pepsi or she could have chosen to buy nothing at all, preferring to save her money. By choosing to buy a Coke, she also chose, simultaneously, not to buy from a competitor—at least not in this particular instance. Thus, for the sake of this one purchase, Coke held an advantage over all of the available competition. This advantage is even more significant when you consider that all buyers have scarce resources. In this case, even if our hypothetical customer was quite wealthy, her resources were nonetheless finite. Thus, she can never again spend the money that she spent on that Coke. She may make other purchases, with other resources, at some other points in the future. But, for the sake of this one purchase, the competition ended when she made her transaction, and the advantage in that competition went to Coke.

Why should a text in strategic management begin with such a rudimentary lesson in the economics of a single transaction? Because students, managers, and professors alike are prone to neglect these basics in favor of other, more grandiose issues. Mission statements, globalization, emerging technologies, diversification, and intellectual property—these are the sorts of things that attract headlines and attention. However, while these sorts of issues are certainly important, we should never lose sight of the fact that strategic management is really about competitive advantage and that competitive advantage emerges when a firm is able to create value for customers over and above its costs. What this really means is that strategic management must begin with the customer, and it is in the eye of the customer that competitive advantage must be understood. Much more will be said about this in subsequent chapters. For now, though, it is enough to appreciate and acknowledge that, if customers do not buy a firm's products or services at prices that exceed the costs, then little else really matters.

Moreover, it is through real and specific actions that the firm actually creates products and services that customers want and for which they are willing to pay a profitable price. Thus, competitive advantage emerges and is sustained when a firm's actions create products and services that customers value over and above the available alternatives and over and above the firm's costs. This practical reality often gets lost amid discussions of esoteric terminology and advanced analytical procedures. So it is important to remember that the ultimate arbiter of strategic success is the customer. All else notwithstanding, if customers do not buy the product or service in sufficient volume and at a sufficient price, then the firm will not succeed. Every successful strategy begins with the intent of creating value through individual and specific transactions for individual and specific customers.

The relationships depicted in Figure 1.1 form the basis of competitive advantage and so lie at the very heart of strategic success. The strategy of Harley-Davidson, for instance, is to create value through the making and selling of motorcycles and motorcycle-related products. With our definition, that means providing products and services that customers will value over and above the available alternatives and over and above Harley-Davidson's costs. Implied in this are two fundamental requirements: first, Harley-Davidson must understand the competitive environment in which its products and services will be seen and evaluated; second, it must understand its own capabilities for supplying what customers will want.

Understanding the competitive environment involves asking such questions as: Who are the target customers and what is likely to motivate their purchases? What alternatives exist to buying from Harley-Davidson and what do those alternatives offer? What events or trends in the marketplace or in society might affect the willingness of those customers to buy a Harley in the future? This type of information is essential to understanding how customers will perceive the product in the context of the competitive landscape.

But the managers at Harley must also know something about their own firm. They must know how to produce products that the customers want. They must

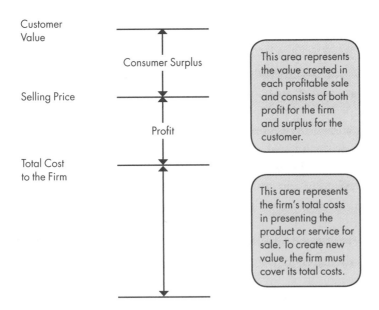

FIGURE 1.1 Competitive Advantage as Value to the Customer

understand the available technologies and the conditions of the labor market, and they must be able to make informed choices about how best to operate. They must recognize the relative costs associated with different levels and means of production, and they must plan for the evolution and adaptation of their own processes that will necessarily have to occur as the market changes. Finally, they must bring all of this information together in such a way that it yields action—action that leads individual customers, acting of their own volition and in their own best interests, to pay a price greater than Harley-Davidson's total costs. When that happens, Harley-Davidson will have competitive advantage. The challenge is simply to do it all over, again, and again, and again, day after day and year after year.

Competitive advantage, then, is best defined as the reason a customer pays a particular firm a profitable price for its products or services. The key is simply this: What is it about your firm's product or service that makes it advantageous in relation to all the other options? Going forward, what is it that makes your firm's products or services attractive in relation to all those alternatives that you can't yet see but that may emerge sometime in the future? By focusing on competitive advantage at this level, strategic management concerns itself with the customer and the competitive environment within which he or she makes purchasing decisions. Alternative suppliers, relative prices, new technologies, reputations for quality and service—these are all parts of the landscape. As such, they are all a part of strategy. But, by focusing on competitive advantage at this level, strategic management also concerns itself with the firm, its capabilities and its resources. Technologies, inventory, engineering and marketing talent—these are all areas in which a firm may exploit a capability to gain advantage. As such, they too are all a part of strategy.

So competitive advantage is about creating value in specific transactions, for specific customers, in a specific competitive context. Understood in this sense, competitive advantage is not simply a state of being. Rather, it is a distinction that has to be earned over and over again, with each interaction. It is defined less by a firm's relationship with its competitors than by a firm's relationship with its customers. It is the source of a firm's success and the target of a firm's competitors. As such, it must be constantly developed, nurtured, and grown because, when left alone, it will naturally erode and decline. Strategic management is about managing this ongoing process of actions that can create and sustain competitive advantage.

STRENGTHS, WEAKNESSES, OPPORTUNITIES, AND THREATS (SWOT)

One of the most commonly recognized terms in strategic management is SWOT. The SWOT framework derives its name from two basic issues that every strategy must address. As explained above, competitive advantage occurs when customers view a product or service as being sufficiently valuable that they actually pay a profitable price for it. To understand this transaction, we must understand the competitive environment in which it takes place. We must also understand the capabilities and resources required to produce the product or service. These two facets of the transaction, the external and the internal, are represented by the acronym SWOT. The S and W represent the internal analysis of the firm, its various strengths and weaknesses; the O and T represent firm external analysis of the environment, its various opportunities and its threats.

There will be much more to say about each of these later. For now, it is sufficient to know two things. First, a SWOT analysis is merely a tool for identifying some key issues. Simple lists of strengths and weaknesses, opportunities and threats, will provide few insights from which to build meaningful strategic initiatives. Yet such lists are an important part of understanding the conditions of the environment and the capabilities of the firm. Second, neither the environmental nor the organizational side of the analysis, alone, can tell the whole story of strategic success. Great products and services do not exist in a vacuum. They are attractive only in a particular context, in relation to specific customers and specific alternatives. By the same token, environmental attractiveness exists largely in the eye of the beholder. What is a threat to one firm may well be an opportunity to another. Good strategy involves analysis and understanding of both the firm's capabilities and resources and its competitive environment. It is important to understand this from the outset, as two major branches of strategic management theory have evolved to address these two different phenomena. **Industrial organization economics** addresses the environment and the competitive landscape of the firm. The **resource-based view** addresses the firm, its capabilities and resources. Both are necessary, but alone neither is sufficient to explain competitive advantage fully. As such, neither alone is sufficient to guide strategy. Rather, good strategic management must be informed by and incorporate both.

When done well, then, strategic management is a framework for managing the interaction of the firm, with all of its weaknesses and strengths, with its environment, with all of its threats and opportunities. Competitive advantage emerges at this intersection of the two. As Hofer and Schendel (1978) define it (see Box 1.1), strategic management is about the interaction of the firm with its environment, with the intent of creating an ongoing stream of products and services that customers will value and purchase at prices in excess of the firm's costs.

COMPETITIVE ADVANTAGE AND FIRM PERFORMANCE

In the strictest sense, management's ultimate responsibility is to enhance the value of the firm. But what does it really mean to enhance the value of the firm? To understand this concept, it is important to realize that the value of the firm, at any moment in time, is a reflection of expected earnings. Coke is a valuable company because the strength of its brand, the size of its market, and the record of its performance leads people to believe that the likelihood of future earnings is great. Because owning a portion of Coke means owning a claim on a portion of those future earnings, increases in expected earnings translate into increases in the value of the firm itself.

Competitive advantage relates directly to a firm's value because it relates directly to earnings. Firms with a strong competitive advantage are in a position to earn more than their competitors and, as a consequence, to be more valuable. Of course, earnings can be affected by any number of different things. A new competitor may arise, imitating your firm's product and thereby reducing your share of the market. A new technology may emerge that makes your service less attractive, thereby making it more difficult to sell. Customer tastes may change, leaving you with a product that was once highly sought after but now is all but forgotten. Demographic patterns may shift, changing the size and nature of your target market. An employee could act negligently, causing harm to others and exposing your firm to litigation and penalties. Someone could manipulate the numbers to make your firm appear more profitable, only to be found out and to undermine the trust of your investors, increasing the firm's cost of capital. In each example, these various occurrences would reduce the expectation of future earnings and so reduce the value of your firm.

Similar scenarios could be imagined where changes within the firm or the environment would enhance the expectation of future earnings and so enhance the value of the firm. A firm could create a new process, allowing it to make a product more inexpensively and so sell it more profitably. A firm could reorganize its board to alleviate concerns that future earnings could be threatened by litigation or poor oversight. A firm could expand into a new market, increasing its revenues and economies of scale. Shifts in demographic patterns or customer tastes could make a firm's products or services much more popular and attractive than they had been heretofore. These sorts of changes would all increase the expectation of future earnings, thereby increasing the value of the firm.

By focusing on competitive advantage, strategic management bears on all of these potentialities and more besides. As explained above, strategic management is concerned with the environment and how changes within it could create opportunities or threats. It is concerned with the firm itself and with the various strengths and weaknesses of its products, processes, people, and technology. Finally, it is concerned with the firm's position within society and how the firm itself is viewed and evaluated by customers, investors, regulators, and employees. Because the ultimate responsibility of management is to enhance the value of the firm, strategic management lies at the heart of managerial responsibility. The value of the firm is a reflection of current and expected earnings, and both of these are a reflection of competitive advantage. Focusing on value creation and on competitive advantage, then, provides a sort of strategic **balanced scorecard** for gauging performance in the day to day. Deliver these two things, and all the other measures of performance that are so frequently tracked and reported will take care of themselves. Thus, the development, maintenance, and ongoing cultivation of competitive advantage are the ultimate responsibility of strategic management and the underlying key to a firm's performance.

THE END OF THE BEGINNING

This is a book about strategic management. As you go through it, you will encounter a number of different topics, frameworks, models, and examples. However, it is important to remember that all of these will point in some way towards competitive advantage. It is also important to remember that competitive advantage results from action. Each framework, each model, each analytical tool should have some implication for action. As you go through the text, stop frequently and ask yourself: How can this impact action? What will actually change, within the firm or between the firm and its customers, as a result of this concept, analytical technique, or way of thinking? How will approaching things in a particular fashion create new value or help the firm to sustain the value it is currently creating? These are the sorts of questions that should demand answers. Too often strategic management is presented in an abstract fashion, as a science or a field of study, interesting in its own right but far removed from the practical details of everyday, organizational life. That is unfortunate because strategic management is the most practical of disciplines. It is the framework through which all of the functions of an organization are integrated; it is the underlying theory of how a firm will pursue superior performance. In that sense, it is the key to a firm's success and the capstone of business education.

KEY TERMS

Balanced scorecard is the name given to a performance measurement framework developed by Robert Kaplan and David Norton. The framework employs a variety of different strategic and non-financial performance metrics, in combination with traditional financial measures, to produce a single "balanced" measure of performance and condition.

Competitive advantage is the reason a customer chooses to transact with one firm over another. It is episodic and best understood through the eyes of the customer.

Consumer surplus is the gap between the value a customer places on a good or service and the price that he or she pays. In essence, it is the difference between the actual price and the price a customer would have been willing to pay.

Industrial organization (IO) economics is an area within the larger field of economics concerned with the competitive forces that affect firm behavior and performance. Established by the work of Chamberlin, Bain, and Mason, IO economics proposes that a firm's performance is a function of strategic conduct, which in turn is a function of industry structure.

A resource-based view (RBV) holds that competitive advantage, and the economic rents or profits associated with it, is a function of a firm's unique and valuable bundle of resources. Such advantage can persist as long as these resource bundles are not effectively imitated or substituted.

QUESTIONS FOR REVIEW

1   Why study strategic management?
2   What is the common theme that runs through the most respected definitions of strategic management?
3   How can strategy be at once part plan, ploy, pattern, position, and perspective?
4   What is the connection between value creation and competitive advantage?
5   What does it mean to say that competitive advantage must be understood through the "eye of the customer"?
6   What is the connection between strategic management, competitive advantage, and overall firm performance?

Companion Website

For a chapter review outline with links to videos and other valuable web resources, please visit the *Strategic Management* website: www.routledge.com/textbooks/amason.

Understanding Organizational Performance

If performance is the crux of strategic management, then it is important to understand performance well. Understanding performance is both simple and complex. While most will readily claim to know what performance is, they will also likely have difficulty defining it precisely. Thus, as we begin this second chapter, it is important to acknowledge three things. First, performance is a multidimensional construct, with a variety of different facets. There are many different ways that performance can be defined and measured, and each of those definitions and measures can produce different indications of how a firm is actually doing. Second, performance is inherently paradoxical. In other words, the pursuit of good performance along any one dimension will often lead to diminishing returns on others. Moreover, there is evidence that good performance in the present can actually produce mindsets and behaviors that can hinder performance in the future. Finally, despite its complexities, performance is still the key to business success and so the standard against which management is evaluated. As such, it pays for managers and students alike to understand what various different measures of performance mean and the implication of each for strategy and the pursuit of competitive advantage.

VALUE AS A MEASURE OF PERFORMANCE

As mentioned in the previous chapter, the ultimate responsibility of management is to enhance the value of the firm. So, would that mean that the most valuable firm is also the one that is performing the best? Unfortunately, it is not that simple. How, for instance, do we measure and compare the value of two firms? Market value, understood simply as the share price times the number of shares outstanding, is a common and popular measure and so a good place to start. The problem is that market price is available only for some firms. **Publicly held firms** have an established market price for their stock. **Privately held firms** have no such established price. How are we supposed to value them? Can we fairly compare a public firm to a private firm, based upon their respective market values?

Estimating value presents other problems as well. What, for instance, does value represent? Fundamentally, value is supposed to reflect the present value of all future earnings. Consider, for example, a small restaurant business. Its various holdings of equipment, inventory, and other assets may amount to $300,000. This value reflects the costs of the equipment, assets, and inventory, less the accumulated depreciation resulting from age and use. The business itself, however, is more than the sum of its tangible assets. Suppose that this restaurant has a great reputation for good food, good prices, and fast service. Suppose that it is also situated in a great location, with lots of visibility and traffic. In that case, the earning potential of those assets may be substantial. Indeed, suppose that this small restaurant generates profits of $100,000 per year. By discounting those profits to their present-day value, at a risk-adjusted opportunity cost of capital of 17.5%, we get a value of $566,091—a substantial increase over the $300,000 figure—obtained from the book value of the tangible assets.

This simple example illustrates several important issues for the determination of value. First, valuation is based principally on future events. A buyer of this restaurant would certainly want to know the history of the business and to find out how well it has performed in the past. However, he would not be buying that history. Rather, what he would be buying is ownership of the profits to come in the future. Anything that affects that future would affect the value of his investment. A demographic shift that produced a change in the traffic patterns around the restaurant might decrease the value of the business. The addition of new menu items that produced new sales but did not require new equipment might increase the value of the business. In both cases, however, these events would occur in the future. Value is thus really a forward-looking measure, and estimates of value are subject to insufficient information, human bias, and outright error.

Notice too that several of the key variables used in the determination of this restaurant's value are subjectively derived. As just discussed, because the value is based upon future profits, there will be some subjection in the process of estimating those profits. How much will the business grow? What sorts of events might occur that will increase or decrease demand and costs? How will the competitive landscape change and what sorts of actions might the owners take to enhance or diminish their competitive advantage? These sorts of issues and the impact that they will have on profitability must be evaluated, assessed, and quantified before they can be used to estimate value. At the same time, the discount rate (of 17.5% in the example above) is a key to calculating the present value of the profits. In this case, a change in the discount rate of 2.5%, above or below the estimate of 17.5%, would result in a change of $158,704 in value, with a 20% discount rate yielding a value of $497,894 and a 15% discount rate yielding a value of $656,598.

The discount rate is meant to reflect the risk of the investment and the opportunity cost of the capital needed to buy and own the business. While there are a number of very good models to aid in the calculation of this discount rate, the value itself is specific to each individual or firm. In this instance, the original owner, with all of his knowledge and experience, would see relatively little risk in the business. As such, he would employ a relatively low discount rate, which would result in a higher value. A buyer, though, would see the business as being much less secure and certain. Thus, he might use a higher discount rate, which would result in a lower value. Each individual, then, might look at the same business, and at the very same stream of profits, and value them differently. So value, while extremely important in assessing a business, is far from being a perfect measure of performance.

PROFITABILITY AS A MEASURE OF PERFORMANCE

Because value reflects profits, many use profitability as the ultimate measure of performance. Indeed, in classical economic theory, to maximize profits, managers are to take whatever actions are available to them, within the bounds of the law and accepted practice, to increase earnings. Unfortunately, though, profitability is as problematic as value, although for different reasons. As such, profitability too fails to measure performance perfectly and fully.

The problems with profitability are threefold. First, profit can be measured both in absolute and in relative terms. Second, while profitability occurs on a continuous basis, it is calculated and reported in discrete increments. Finally, unlike value, profitability is a backward-looking measure; it merely reports that which has already occurred but gives little insight into what is occurring now or what might occur in the future. Each of these problems is discussed below. However, it is important to remember that discussing problems in the measurement of profitability should not be seen as a criticism of profit itself. Firms must create profits; their value and very survival depend upon it. In understanding performance, however, it is important to recognize the strengths and weaknesses of the myriad different ways in which performance is measured and reported.

Profit is important because it is the excess of revenues over costs. As depicted in the last chapter, in Figure 1.1 (p. 12), firms profit as they create products that customers value and buy, at a price over and above the firm's costs. Firms that are creating profits have some measure of competitive advantage in their markets. Customers are choosing, of their own volition, to buy from the firm and to buy at a price that provides the firm with a profit. But, as we expand our view to include many transactions, between many firms and many customers, the picture becomes more complex. Consider two firms, one of which sells $10 million in product and profits $350,000 from those sales, the other of which sells $2 million in product and profits $100,000 from those sales. Which of these two firms is more profitable and which is performing better? It is really difficult to say. The first, while creating more profit in an absolute sense, performed less well in a relative sense. The first firm earned only 3.5% on each dollar of sales; the second firm earned 5% on each dollar of sales. Similar comparisons could be made by looking at profits as a proportion of assets or as a proportion of equity.

For example, suppose the first firm is in a knowledge-intensive industry, where labor costs are high but fixed asset costs are low. Suppose as well that this firm had booked assets of $3 million. That would yield a profit of 11.7% on each dollar of asset. Now, suppose that the second firm was a retail establishment, with a $1 million investment in a stand-alone store and specialized equipment. This firm would have profited only 10% on each dollar of asset. Depending upon how the assets in these two examples are financed, with different levels of equity or debt, we could similarly imagine different levels of return for each dollar of equity. None of these ratios is inherently better than the others. However, they all reflect profit as a percentage of some base, whether that base be sales, assets, or equity. As such, they will all provide somewhat different information and a somewhat different picture than merely reporting profit in absolute dollars.

Another problem arises from the fact that profits are earned continuously; with each sale and with each expense, profit changes, even if only slightly. Yet, when we report profit on a periodic basis, we truncate that continuous, day-to-day activity and report a single number, reflecting activity over a specific and finite period of time. This difference in the nature of how profit is earned and how it is reported can lead to confusion and, occasionally, misrepresentation. For example, confusion can arise over the inclusion of extraordinary events in the calculation of profit. Suppose a firm, which delivers a popular and valued service on which it makes a good profit, experiences a large, one-time expense. This sort of thing happens all the time: a company may overhaul its computer system, it can open a new plant or close an old store, or it may try and fail to expand its product line. All of these sorts of activities would produce expenses that would be significant but non-recurring. Revenues can be affected by similar sorts of events. A firm may sell off a location or win a judgment against a competitor for copyright infringement. In both cases, the revenues realized might be significant, yet non-recurring. Such occurrences are referred to as extraordinary events and can change dramatically the profit of a firm in a single period, without changing any of the fundamental characteristics of the firm's competitive advantage.

Box 2.1
More Profit Than Meets the Eye?

How does an investor decide what companies are the big winners at the end of the year? Bottom-line profit or loss? What about earnings per share? While the final numbers seem to be reasonable means of determining performance, they may not tell the whole story. In the case of MPS Group Inc., a huge overall financial loss and net loss of $5.62 per share met the unsuspecting eyes of investors at the end of 2002. A closer look at the numbers, though, show that a change in accounting practices created this one-time loss in earnings. Without the change, MPS showed a gain of $0.16 per share. The accounting change turned an actual overall net profit into a huge net loss. So, before looking at year-end results, check further up to see if the bottom-line is really telling the whole story.

Adapted from Basch (2003)

Reporting profit on a periodic basis can also provide opportunities for misrepresentation. Why would managers intentionally misrepresent their firm's profit? Because so doing may work to their benefit in the eyes of investors, regulators, or parties with whom they are bargaining. For years, major league baseball has suffered from a highly acrimonious relationship between the owners and the players' association. Part of the acrimony is attributable to the claim by the owners that the franchises themselves are not profitable. The players' association challenges that such claims are merely ploys, on the part of management, to reduce the players' salaries. The owners charge that the players are simply greedy and fail to comprehend the complexity of measuring profit and loss in a major league franchise. Public utilities have similarly sought to understate their profits in the hopes of getting favorable rate decisions from the governing public service regulators. Such firms will argue that, without rate increases, they will have to operate at a loss. The regulators will often respond by saying that the firms are doing a poor job of managing their costs and could be profitable if they would simply do a better job of reducing their expenses. The United States postal service is a classic example of this.

Box 2.2
The Profitability of Major League Baseball

If you listen to the major league baseball owners, the game still affectionately called America's pastime may soon be part of America's past. How could this happen to a game that has held a near sacred spot in the hearts of many Americans for almost a century? After the players' strike in 1994, growth in attendance began to decline. At the same time, players' salaries were skyrocketing, as owners signed free-agent players to record mega-million dollar deals. According to the owners' association, these factors led to financial hemorrhaging so severe that, in 2002, 25 of the 30 teams were losing money. Two teams, the Detroit Tigers and the Tampa Bay Rays, actually needed to draw bank loans in order to make their payroll.

Citing their mounting financial losses, a weak U.S. economy, and a new labor deal that included a luxury tax, franchise owners drastically cut back on the money they offered to free-agent players after the 2001 season. While some superstar players did get big-money, long-term deals, many non-superstars received no offers at all. The average player contract was much smaller, both in dollar value and duration, than in years past. The obvious change in strategy led the players' union to cry foul. While the owners claimed tough economic times and the harsh realities of shrinking revenues and rising costs created this new environment, the union countered that the owners were still doing very well off of baseball but were manipulating the numbers to make it appear otherwise. While the two groups drew their respective lines in the sand, professional baseball readied itself for a battle that could decide the fate of the sport, a battle over whether the franchises themselves were, in fact, profitable.

Finally, managers will sometimes seek to misrepresent their profitability to analysts and investors. Al Dunlap, former CEO at Sunbeam, was accused of this and was fired when the allegations were substantiated. One of the tricks that Dunlap and others have sometimes used is to "book" revenue, which rightly belonged in some future period, in a current period. This can be done in a number of ways: a firm might ship orders early, overloading their customers with inventory but allowing the firm to show the revenue earlier. They might also sell a multi-period contract but recognize all of the expected revenue from that contract at the time of the sale. Both practices are unethical and potentially illegal, because they have the effect of overstating the firm's profits in the current period. Higher profits, or the perception of higher profits, may make the firm look more valuable and so make management appear to be doing a better job. This seems to have been the underlying motivation at Sunbeam, where it was alleged that Dunlap was inflating the firm's value, in anticipation of a future sale. Many of the now infamous ethical scandals in the early 1990s involved similar schemes to overstate earnings for the sake of inflating firm value.

Box 2.3
Accounting for Sunbeam's Earnings

What could be worse than having to promise the Securities and Exchange Commission (SEC) that you will never again act as the officer or director of any public company, while being at the retirement age of 65 and also having to pay a $500,000 fine? This situation confronted former Sunbeam CEO Al Dunlap in 2002 after an SEC investigation into the company's finances during his time as chief executive in the mid-1990s.

Given the nickname "Chainsaw Al" because of his propensity to slash jobs after having being brought in to turn firms around, this was not Dunlap's first brush with alleged accounting scandals. As the president of Nitec Paper in the 1970s, he was also linked to an accounting scandal. Sunbeam brought him on board in July of 1996, and the alleged accounting fraud took place soon afterwards. According to the SEC, in late 1996 Sunbeam created "cookie jar" reserves that it would pull from to improve 1997's results. Other methods used by Dunlap and Sunbeam executives included parking merchandise with a wholesaler and persuading customers to place orders they could later cancel. Approximately $60 million of Sunbeam's $189 million reported pre-tax earnings for 1997 was ultimately traced to deceptive accounting practices, according to the SEC. Dunlap and the other executives hoped to inflate the perceived value of the company in order to gain millions of dollars from its sale.

In June of 1998, Dunlap and former chief financial officer, Russell Kersh, were pushed out as rumors of the allegations started to surface. Sunbeam would eventually file for bankruptcy in 2001, but not before restating earnings for 1996, 1997, and the first three months of 1998 following the removal of Dunlap and Kersh. Phillip E. Harlow, former partner of Arthur Andersen, was the lead auditor for Sunbeam and aided in the scheme by endorsing the inflated financial statements. Arthur Andersen paid Sunbeam investors $110 million to settle a civil suit in 2001. As for Dunlap, he forked out over $15 million in January 2002 to settle the civil suit filed against him by the Sunbeam shareholders.

Following the scandal at Sunbeam, the business world has probably seen the last of "Chainsaw Al." But he will always be remembered for his hack-and-slash management style and the trail of controversy he left upon his exit.

Adapted from Green (2002) and Hilzenrath (2001)

Finally, even when profit is reported accurately and interpreted correctly, it remains a historical measure, reflecting past activity. As such, it is of dubious value for judging performance in the present or for going forward. Profit is certainly an indicator of competitive advantage, good management, and good fit with the environment. However, competitive advantage is based on a number of different things. Changes in customer tastes or in the competitive landscape could render a firm that was profitable in the previous year unprofitable in the current one. Profit is certainly associated with good management, but it would be a mistake to think that the two correspond directly. Some industries are simply less attractive than others. The airline industry, for example, is a very competitive business, with very little overall growth and tremendous cost pressures. As such, it is a business where some very good managers compete over some very small margins. The pharmaceutical business, on the other hand, has seen tremendous growth over the past two decades. With dramatic increases in the amounts spent on prescription and over-the-counter medications, this business has seen rising profits. In comparing these two industries, it is important to understand the structural differences that underlie the differences in profitability.

The point of looking at these two common performance measures is not to criticize them outright—on the contrary, both are essential components of overall performance. Rather, the point is to illustrate the broad and multifaceted nature of performance itself. To be understood properly, performance must be considered over time, from a variety of perspectives, and in its proper context.

PERFORMANCE OVER TIME

One of the most challenging issues in understanding performance is the need to consider it over time. Think of all the firms that were once dominant players in their respective markets—profitable firms with strong reputations and highly sought-after products and services—and that slipped from their positions of leadership. Arthur Andersen, K-Mart, RCA, IBM, Xerox, and Pan American Airways are all examples of firms that once had every advantage but, for some reason, slipped back into the pack or stumbled and fell altogether. How could a firm with all the advantages of K-Mart be overtaken by an upstart, small chain from an unfamiliar town in northwestern Arkansas? How, with all of the market power and money associated with its position in mainframe computers, could IBM fail to take control of the personal computer business when it emerged? How could Arthur Andersen, one of the most respected names in the business of accounting and auditing, stumble to the point of exiting an industry that was virtually synonymous with its name? The explanation will be discussed in detail in Chapter 8. For now, though, these examples should serve as a lesson that, in the business world, the competition never ends. As explained in Chapter 1, the metaphor of a game, with winners and losers, breaks down when applied to business, because, in business, the game never ends.

Danny Miller (1990) has written insightfully on this phenomenon whereby successful firms fall prey to their own complacency, inertia, limited vision, and defensiveness, relating it to the mythical story of Icarus. Icarus was the son of Daedalus, a gifted architect and builder, who was exiled on the island of Crete. To escape the exile, Daedalus fashioned wings, made of wax and feathers, for himself and his son Icarus. But Icarus flew so high that the heat from the sun melted the wax of his wings and, as a result, he fell into the Aegean Sea and died. This mythical story depicts a paradox. Icarus' greatest asset was also his ultimate undoing. The power of his wings allowed him to soar to heights otherwise impossible, yet, in so doing, he died.

Miller brings this fabled lesson to bear on successful companies and argues that the same pattern applies. Successful firms, insulated by the resources accumulated from their past achievements, can grow complacent and cease to exercise the vigilance and drive that made them successful in the first place. They may become so enamored of their own products and services that they fail to continue learning and innovating. They may become so conceited amid the shower of praise from professors, consultants, customers, and writers in the popular press that they fail to consider new and unfamiliar competitors. Finally, they may become so defensive of the status quo that, in trying to protect their current advantage, they fail to invest in the sorts of learning and adaptive behaviors necessary to insure competitive advantage in the future.

By understanding competitive advantage as the continuous pursuit of value creation and appropriation, we can begin to see that performance is ongoing. Competitive advantage does bring profitability, but it is a distinction that must be earned one customer at a time, over and over again. Naturally, firms must perform in the present but not at the expense of the future. At the same time, firms that cannot perform in the present do not last to see the future. This tension between the short and the long term is subtle and paradoxical. Persisting too long in one strategy, even as successful as that strategy may be, can provide an opportunity for new competitors. Good performance is certainly desirable and will often bring with it substantial rewards. Those rewards, however, can dull the hunger, the creativity, and the innovativeness needed to insure performance in the future. Moreover, that performance and the rewards associated with it can attract competition and provide a target on which new competitors can focus. As will be discussed in greater detail later, to perform well over time, firms must learn to be their own toughest competitors, constantly challenging convention, constantly seeking dissenting points of view, and constantly reminding themselves that the contest never ends.

For now, it is enough to remember that virtually all measures of performance are momentary snapshots of an ongoing phenomenon. See Table 2.1, which lists the

Table 2.1
A Changing of the Guard

The Ten Firms with the Largest Market Capitalization

	1980	1990	2000
1	IBM	Exxon	General Electric
2	AT&T	Philip Morris	Microsoft
3	Exxon	IBM	Exxon Mobil
4	Standard Oil, Indiana	General Electric	Pfizer
5	Schlumberger	Wal-Mart	Citigroup
6	Shell Oil	Merck	Wal-Mart
7	Standard Oil, Ohio	Bristol-Myers Squibb	Intel
8	Mobil	Coca-Cola	American Int'l Group
9	Standard Oil, California	AT&T	America Online
10	Atlantic Richfield	Johnson & Johnson	IBM

The Ten Firms with the Highest Revenues

	1980	1990	2000
1	Exxon	General Motors	Exxon Mobil
2	Mobil	Exxon	Wal-Mart
3	General Motors	Ford	General Motors
4	Texaco	IBM	Ford
5	AT&T	General Electric	General Electric
6	Standard Oil, California	Mobil	Citigroup
7	Ford	Sears	Enron
8	Engelhard Minerals	Philip Morris	IBM
9	Gulf Oil	Texaco	AT&T
10	IBM	Du Pont	Verizon

The Ten Firms with the Greatest Profits

	1980	1990	2000
1	AT&T	IBM	Exxon Mobil
2	Exxon	Exxon	Citigroup
3	IBM	General Electric	General Electric
4	Mobil	Philip Morris	Verizon
5	Standard Oil, California	AT&T	Intel
6	Texaco	Du Pont	Microsoft
7	Standard Oil, Indiana	Chevron	Philip Morris
8	Standard Oil, Ohio	Mobil	IBM
9	Atlantic Richfield	Amoco	SBC Communications
10	Shell Oil	Merck	Bank of America

ten firms with the largest market capitalization, the highest total revenues, and the greatest overall profits for the years 1980, 1990, and 2000. While there is some stability, there is also substantial turnover on each of these lists. What is so impressive about this turnover is that it occurred despite the fact that these are some of the best-endowed firms in the world. Those firms on the list in 1980 enjoyed all the advantages of incumbency. They had great name recognition; they enjoyed great bargaining power with their customers and suppliers; they could afford the best minds, the best research, the best locations, and the best advertising. Yet, somehow, they were overtaken by firms with far fewer advantages. What are we to make of this and what is the lesson for strategic managers? It is simply this: although we measure it in discrete increments, success is ongoing. A firm cannot simply perform once and then rest on that success. In time, competitors will adapt and overcome; customers will grow restless and demand better services, lower prices, or both; and markets will adjust their aspirations, taking for granted in the future that which was considered extraordinary in the past. Understanding performance means understanding this temporal dimension; it means understanding that performance occurs over time.

PERFORMANCE FROM A VARIETY OF PERSPECTIVES

In addition to thinking about performance over time, it is important to think about it from a variety of perspectives. As illustrated above, no single measure tells the whole story. Rather, a number of different measures must be considered, simultaneously. Table 2.2 provides a list of and descriptions for a number of various ratios used to measure performance. For any single firm, these measures will provide different information. A firm that is highly leveraged with debt, for instance, may have a high return on equity but a much lower return on assets. A firm with growing sales and substantial profitability may still be performing poorly in terms of cash flow as it fails to collect the money for its sales. Earnings per share would be a function both of the earnings and of shares outstanding. Such measures, though, are of questionable value in the consideration of private firms or firms that are not actively traded. Because no single measure tells the whole story, it is important to use multiple measures and to think carefully about what each one actually reveals.

In addition to the measures in Table 2.2 and the two described at the beginning of the chapter, there are a number of others that are commonly used to assess performance. Three of these, Altman's Z, Tobin's q, and Economic Value Added (EVA), will be discussed below.

Table 2.2
A Sampling of Ratios Used to Measure Performance

Measure	Description	Interpretation
Return on sales (ROS)	After-tax profit / Total sales	Return on total sales; percentage per dollar of sales
Return on assets (ROA)	After-tax profit / Total assets	Return on total investment; percentage per dollar of assets
Return on equity (ROE)	After-tax profit / Total sales	Return on total equity; percentage per dollar of owner's equity
Gross profit margin	Total sales – cost of goods / Total sales	Proportion of each dollar of sales retained as operating profit
Net profit margin	Total sales – total expenses / Total sales	Proportion of each dollar of sales retained as profit
Earning per share (EPS)	Net profit – PS dividends / Common shares outstanding	Profit available for distribution to the shareholders
Price/earnings ratio (P/E)	Stock price per share / After-tax earnings per share	Stock price as a multiple of earnings Indicates anticipated earnings
Cash flow per share	After-tax profit + depreciation / Common shares outstanding	Liquidity to fund operations over and above current costs
Current ratio	Current assets / Current liabilities	Liquidity over and above current liabilities
Debt to total assets	Total debt / Total assets	The proportion of the firm's assets financed by debt
Debt to total equity	Total debt / Total equity	The amount of financing in debt as a proportion of total equity

Altman's Z

Perhaps the most simple and yet powerful of these three measures is **Altman's Z**, which weights and combines the information from five different ratios (some of which are defined in Table 2.2) into a single value, indicating the overall financial health of the organization. The formula itself is:

$$Z = 1.20 \text{ (working capital/total assets)}$$
$$+ 1.40 \text{ (retained earnings/total assets)}$$
$$+ 3.33 \text{ (EBIT/total assets)}$$
$$+ 0.60 \text{ (market value of equity/book value of debt)}$$
$$+ 0.99 \text{ (sales/total assets).}$$

The value resulting from the formula can predict with great accuracy the immi-nence of failure. Firms that produce a value of less than 1.8 on this formula are in great distress and will, in all likelihood, fail at some point in the not too distant future. Firms with values greater than 3.0 are in no distress and not likely to fail. Firms in between, while in less distress than those in the lowest category, are still at greater risk of failure than the highest ranking group. In empirical testing, the formula was found to predict failures accurately nearly 70% of the time and up to five years in advance.

A few observations are in order, though. First of all, this performance measure is no better than the information on which it is based. This is true, of course, of all statistics and measures, but it bears repeating here as all of the values in this formula must come from accounting data provided by the firm itself. While publicly traded firms are required to follow **GAAP** (generally accepted accounting principles) and are subject to periodic review and reporting, privately held firms are not subject to nearly as frequent or vigorous oversight. Moreover, these principles are just stan-dards or recommendations as to how certain situations should be treated. They cannot, nor were they intended to, address explicitly every circumstance for every firm. It is also important to remember that, like profitability, each of these ratios is subject to a form of short-term bias and can be affected disproportionately by non-recurring, extraordinary events. These caveats notwithstanding, Altman's Z is a simple, easily understood, and reliable indicator of financial condition. Moreover, it is easily computed from numbers that are readily accessible. As such, when used well and with the knowledge of its strengths and weaknesses, it can be a very helpful measure of performance.

Tobin's q

This quotient is formed by dividing a firm's market value by the replacement cost of its assets (Lindenburg & Ross, 1981). **Tobin's q** is unique, conceptually, in that it gets at the value of a firm's intangible assets, based upon their earning capacity in the future. Consider, for instance, the example given earlier of a restaurant, with assets valued at $300,000. Recall that this hypothetical firm had a market value estimated at between $500,000 and $600,000—nearly twice the book value of the assets. What accounts for the difference and from where does this value come? As explained, the book value of the assets, in this case $300,000, reflects the costs of the assets to the firm, less any accumulated depreciation. However, those costs are poor indicators of the actual earning value of the assets. Earning value is difficult to assess directly because it is context specific—in other words, it varies from firm to firm and from situation to situation. The restaurant in the example is valuable because of its reputation, its location, and the quality of its product. Change the location or change the way the business is managed and you change the earning value of the assets. Consider the case of a single asset, a laptop computer. The computer may have a book value of $1,500. However, in the hands of a famous and productive writer, that asset would take on much greater value. In the same fashion, a formula for the production of a sweet, dark-colored, carbonated soft drink might have modest value. However, in concert with the legal copyrights to the name Coca-Cola and the marketing and distribution presence to promote and deliver that soft drink around the world, the formula becomes much more valuable. This increase in value, over and above the book value, is intangible and specific to the individual firm. At any moment in time, then, a firm's value is a combination of (1) the actual book value of its assets and (2) the intangible value added to those assets by the managers, people, and strategies of the firm. So, intangible value can be a powerful measure of organizational success and performance.

Calculating Tobin's q requires estimating two values: the market value of the firm and the replacement costs of the firm's tangible assets. Unfortunately, neither value is especially easy to measure with precision. Market value, for example, can be established with the following formula:

> Firm market value = Market value of common shares
> + Market value of preferred shares
> + Book value of total debt (short and long term).

Common shares are easily valued if they are regularly traded. The average number of shares outstanding, over a given period of time, times the average price per share over the same period of time, provides a good measure of the value of the common shares. Valuing other types of shares, such as preferred shares, presents a somewhat larger challenge. When they are actively traded, preferred shares can be valued in the same way as common shares. Preferred shares are not, however, always actively traded. In that event, it's often necessary to consult some other sources of information, such as the Standard and Poor's preferred stock yield index. This index value, in conjunction with the preferred dividend paid on the stock, can be used to establish a value for the preferred shares. More simply, preexisting databases such as Compustat will often report a preferred stock value for firms. The final component of market value is the cost of the firm's debt, including both short-term and long-term obligations. These values are available directly or can be extracted from a firm's balance sheet. The sum of these values provides a good estimate of the market value of the firm.

The denominator in the calculation of Tobin's q is the replacement costs of the firm's assets. Of course, the calculation of this number is highly problematic as it involves estimating the cost of all the firm's assets, in current terms. While a number of procedures have been proposed for estimating these replacement costs, they are all rather cumbersome. Fortunately, research has shown that the book value of total assets is a relatively unbiased estimate of replacement costs (Perfect & Wiles, 1994).

The book value of total assets is readily available from a firm's balance sheet. Using this as an estimate of total asset replacement costs, the calculation of Tobin's q becomes, simply, market value divided by book value. This ratio represents the intangible value added to the firm's assets by its people, its strategy, its unique organizational configuration, and its managerial skill.

As important and powerful as this measure may be, it is important to recognize that it, too, has limitations. The calculation of market value, for instance, is easy enough in the case of large, publicly traded firms. It is much more difficult and much less certain for firms that are not actively traded. Moreover, even among actively traded firms, the determination of market value is subject to daily variation, as the price of the stock rises and falls. Such variation in the share price translates directly to variation in the value of Tobin's q. Additionally, it is important to remember that the book value of a firm's assets reflects the accumulated depreciation of those assets. Firms with older assets will naturally have a smaller denominator and, consequently, a higher q value. Still, taking into account the strengths and weaknesses of the numbers from which it is derived, Tobin's q is a valuable indicator of a firm's performance.

Economic Value Added (EVA)

The measurement of **Economic Value Added** reflects the desire to capture what economists call rents or *economic profit*. Economic profit reflects returns over and above those expected based upon the value of the assets and capital employed. Essentially, it differs from accounting profit in that it takes into account the cost of the firm's capital. EVA is calculated as net operating profit after taxes (NOPAT), less the firm's weighted average cost of capital (WACC). The importance of including the cost of capital into the calculation of profit is that it raises the bar for what constitutes good performance. Without including the cost of capital in the assessment, a manager might invest in marginal projects that produce a return in excess of their direct costs yet ultimately still lose money. Because the costs of capital are real, management should invest only in projects that produce a positive return over and above those costs.

Unfortunately, calculating EVA is more complicated than calculating either Altman's Z or Tobin's q. The first value, NOPAT, is a function of earnings before interest and taxes (EBIT) and the taxes on those earnings. EBIT is equal to revenues—(cost of goods sold, selling, general and administrative expenses, and depreciation). Taxes on EBIT are reported in the company's financial statements. However, when a direct examination of those statements is impossible, or when future taxes are being considered, it is necessary to estimate. Estimating the taxes on EBIT is difficult to do with precision as it involves a number of variables, including interest expense, interest income, and non-operating income. However, a good estimate can be obtained by multiplying EBIT by the statutory marginal tax rate. While this simple approach will not account for deferred taxes or changes in deferred taxes, it will provide a close estimate that can be easily derived. NOPAT is then equal to EBIT less the taxes on EBIT.

The second component of EVA is the weighted average cost of capital. The precise calculation of the WACC is also complicated and so, in practice, is frequently simplified. Calculating WACC involves calculating the cost of the firm's debt as well as the cost of its equity and then weighting each based upon the proportion of capital in the form of either debt or equity.

Estimating the cost of debt is complicated by a number of factors. Specifically, firms may have debt from a number of different sources. A bank loan at an interest rate of 8% is easy to value. However, if a firm also has issued bonds, then the cost of that debt will vary with the quality of the bonds' rating. A rating of A+ might translate to an interest rate of 7.5%, while a rating of B− might translate to an interest rate of 14%. There is also the issue of tax deductibility. If the interest expense is deductible from income, then it reduces the tax burden on the firm, effectively reducing the cost of the debt. Moreover, there are any number of different lease arrangements that also contribute to the total cost of debt that must be estimated. Taking these into account, it is necessary to multiply the after tax cost of the debt by the proportion of debt in that particular form. For example, consider a firm with $1 million in high-quality bonds, on which it is paying 7%, a secured bank loan of $500,000, on which it is paying 7.5%, and lease arrangements on assets totaling $800,000, on which it is paying 8.5%. For the sake of simplicity, assume that all of the interest expense is fully tax deductible. The total amount of debt carried would be $2.3 million and the weighted average cost of this debt (WACD) would be:

$$(.43) \times 7\% \text{ or } (.030)$$
$$+ (.22) \times 7.5\% \text{ or } (.016)$$
$$+ (.35) \times 8.5\% \text{ or } (.030)$$

which equals 7.6%. Recall, however, that this interest expense is tax deductible, meaning that, for a tax rate of 30%, every $100 in interest results in a tax saving of $30. Thus, we would adjust the cost of the debt by 1 minus the tax rate—in this case 70% × 7.6%, for a total WACD of 5.3%.

Calculating the cost of equity is similarly complicated and involves the capital asset pricing model (CAPM). The CAPM is, simply:

Cost of Equity = RFR + FR(E(MRR) − RFR)
Where: RFR is the risk-free rate of return
   FR is firm specific variability, or risk
   E(MRR) is market rate of return.

While appearing complex, this formula can be practically useful. For example, the risk-free rate of return is generally estimated as the interest rate on guaranteed government securities. A good estimate of the market rate of return is the actual rate of return for various stock market indices, like the Standard and Poor's composite index. The calculation of the firm specific risk, referred to as ß or beta, requires regression analysis. The regression formula for beta is:

$R_{i,t} = a + b_i R_{m,t} + e$
Where: $R_{i,t}$ is the actual return on the firm's stock over a set period of time
   a is a constant, equal to $(1 - b)$
   b_i is the estimated value of beta
   $R_{m,t}$ is the market return, and
   e is the error, associated with estimating $R_{i,t}$

Fortunately, beta is provided for most publicly traded companies through various research services, such as Standard & Poor's, so it can be known without actually doing the analysis described above. Still, knowing beta is essential to knowing the value of a firm's equity, because it represents the variance in a firm's stock price as a proportion of the variance of the total market. So, knowing beta allows us to know that a 10% change in the overall value of the stock market will produce a change of beta × 10% in the value of the firm's stock. Stocks with a high beta are risky, and that risk translates into higher equity expenses. Calculating the cost of equity simply involves plugging in the appropriate values. If the risk-free rate of return is 4%, if beta is 1.5, and if the market rate of return is 8%, then the cost of equity is equal to:

.04 + 1.5(.08 – .04), or .10

Conceptually, that means that an equity investor would require a 10% return as compensation for the risk of investing in this firm, rather than in the risk-free instrument.

With the cost of equity and the cost of debt computed, the WACC is worked out simply by adding the percentage of total capital in the form of debt, weighted by its cost, to the percentage of total capital in the form of equity, weighted by its cost. Suppose that our hypothetical firm had total capitalization of $5 million, with 46% of its capital in the form of debt and 54% in the form of equity. The weighted average cost of capital would then be:

.46(5,000,000 × .053) + .54(5,000,000 × .1),
a WACC of $391,900

EVA, then, is simply the NOPAT less the WACC. If this firm had net operating profits of $1,150,000 and a tax rate of 30%, then calculation of EVA would be:

Operating profit	$1,150,000
Taxes	– $345,000
Cost of capital	– $391,900
Economic Value Added	$413,100

Focusing on EVA has some advantages in that it corrects for the biases inherent in the consideration of profit and profit rate. Remember that those firms with the highest profit may not be those with the highest profit rate. As a firm attempts to maximize profits, it may invest in projects that produce revenues in excess of direct cost but that fail to cover fully the cost of capital. As a firm attempts to maximize profit rate, it may under-invest and pass up what could be profitable projects. Focusing on EVA allows a firm to overcome these problems and align the dual desires of maximizing both profit and shareholder value.

Each of these measures has its own advantages and disadvantages. EVA is a very powerful tool for evaluating performance but requires considerable time and sophistication to calculate. Tobin's q is a simple and powerful indicator of success but cannot be applied easily to private firms. Even Altman's Z, while simple to calculate and understand, relies upon data provided by the firm itself and offers limited insight into ongoing performance. Thus there is a need to consider performance from as many perspectives as practical and possible. Along with the ratios in Table 2.2, all of these measures can give us a sense of how a firm is doing, but none of them, alone, is sufficient to tell the whole story.

Unfortunately, many students, professors, managers, and analysts alike become enamored of single performance measures, to the detriment of a better overall understanding. In an insightful and interesting article, Collingwood (2001) documents how firms often alter their strategies, sometimes in ways that actually compromise shareholder value, just to make certain that their quarterly earnings reports correspond to projections and match expectations. As Collingwood explains, given how closely many stockholders and analysts follow the projections and the subsequent performance, executives have begun to manage the process by managing both the projections that make it into the marketplace and the rate at which earnings or losses are reported. By meeting or just slightly beating the expectations of the market, a firm can insure itself of a stable or growing market for its stock. Unforeseen variation, whether over or under expectations, can signal unforeseen problems or raise expectations unrealistically. Thus, companies devote considerable time and energy to the careful development of projections and the management of their activities so as to meet the subsequent expectations. Not only is this effort a drain on organizational resources but it also focuses attention, disproportionately, on short-term results, which may or may not be important to the overall financial health of the firm or the strength of its competitive advantage.

Indeed, in an effort to stem the momentum of this fascination with the setting and meeting of periodic projections, some leading companies, such as Coca-Cola and Gillette, have ceased providing the earnings guidance information that becomes the basis for analysts' quarterly earnings forecasts. Coke made the decision to opt out of this process in 2003. Current chairman and CEO, Douglas Daft, explained the move:

> "We are quite comfortable measuring our progress as we achieve it, instead of focusing on the establishment and attainment of public forecasts . . . Our share owners are best served by this because we should not run our business based on short-term 'expectations.' We are managing this business for the long-term." (Weber, 2002)

Performance is an ongoing and long-term phenomenon. Yet, the success of any effort to manage for the long term is difficult to measure. And so there is the dilemma. It is difficult to measure and value that which has not yet occurred. Yet it is equally difficult to make long-term judgments about performance based only on what has happened in the most recent past. Thus, as has been explained throughout this chapter, performance must be understood and measured from a variety of different perspectives.

PERFORMANCE IN CONTEXT

Industry Benchmarks

The final comment about performance and its assessment relates to the relative nature of success itself. What does it really mean to say that a firm is successful and performing well? Consider the following example. Assume that one firm shows a profit of 10% on its sales while the second firm, with comparable revenues, shows a profit of only 5%. Which of these firms performed best? Well, that depends upon a number of things. For example, the importance of industry was mentioned earlier and a comparison was drawn between the pharmaceutical and airline industries. Pfizer, Merck & Co., and Bristol-Myers Squibb reported profit margins in 2008 of 16.8%, 32.7%, and 25.5% respectively, while the industry as a whole reported a return on total assets (ROA) of 10.8%. During the same period, Delta, American, and Continental Airlines reported net profit margins of –34.2%, –7.0%, and –2.2% respectively, while the industry as a whole reported a return on total assets of –.09%. While these earnings numbers are clearly different, most of the differences are attributable to dramatically disparate competitive conditions in the industries. As a consequence, it is difficult to compare the firms directly. Continental, in relation to the firms in its industry, seems to have performed reasonably well. However, in relation to the firms in the pharmaceutical industry, it has still performed rather poorly. Thus, in assessing the performance of any particular firm, it is important that appropriate industry benchmarks be chosen against which to assess the size of the gain or loss.

Determining appropriate industry benchmarks is easier said than done, however. Consider the airlines mentioned above: Are they representative of the industry as a whole? Although they performed poorly, other airlines have been more profitable. AirTran, Southwest, and JetBlue reported profit margins in 2008 of 1.7%, 4.2%, and 1.8% respectively. The total return on assets for this segment of the industry, the so-called regional carriers, was 1.8%, significantly better than that of the larger carriers. This illustrates two things. First, the way an industry is defined has much to do with the way it is viewed. In considering the airline industry, should we lump together Southwest, AirTran, Skywest, and JetBlue with Delta, American, United, and Continental? That question will be answered in greater detail in later chapters. Asking it now, though, raises an important issue. What is the appropriate industry benchmark for assessing the performance of a firm? For the moment, it is enough to remember that the most meaningful insights can be drawn from comparisons with similar firms. So, when assessing the performance of a firm like Delta, it is important to look at Delta's performance in relation to other similar firms; the more similar, the more meaningful the comparison.

Historical Performance

But industry variation is just one of the several contingencies that should be considered in assessing a firm's performance. An equally important consideration is the history of the firm. For example, Ford Motor Company reported a net profit margin, in 2005, of .08%. While that number is better than the −1.5% margin in 2007, it is well off the pace of earnings in 1999, when net profit margin was 4.5%. When viewed in that light, Ford's modest profit margin looks even less impressive. However, by the middle of 2009, the margin had returned to 2.2%, despite the fact that overall revenues had fallen substantially. Given this variation, what would Ford consider a success?

Just as it is hard to judge a firm's performance in the absence of industry benchmarks, so too is it difficult to judge performance without the context of historical precedent. We need to know both how a firm's competitors are doing and how the company itself has done in the past. Cisco Systems, for example, earned $3.57 billion in 2003 on sales of $18.9 billion, a return on sales (ROS) of just under 19%. But how does this number compare to those in previous years? Well, in 2002 Cisco earned $1.9 billion on sales of $18.9 billion, an ROS of just over 10%. The year before that, 2001, the ROS was negative, as Cisco lost $1.01 billion on sales of $22.3 billion. Thus, 2002 and 2003 represent dramatic improvements. However, looking back even farther, we see that the ROS in the years 1997, 1998, 1999, and 2000 was 16.3%, 16.0%, 16.6%, and 14.0% respectively. What appears to be happening, then, is that Cisco's earnings were simply returning to what might be considered normal before the technology crash in 2000. It is interesting to note that, by the end of 2008, its earnings were $6.1 billion on revenues of $36.1 billion, an ROS of 16.9%.

As these examples demonstrate, history is an important contextual consideration in the assessment of performance. The same amount of profit or the same rate of return can appear completely different when judged in historical context. A firm with consistently rising earnings might see a period where earnings remain relatively flat as a disappointment. On the other hand, a firm with consistently declining earnings might see a period where that decline levels off as a success. Empirical research has shown the importance of past performance to the mental state of the firm's managers and other stakeholders (Amason & Mooney, 2008; Audia, Locke, & Smith, 2000).

After a sustained period of growth and profitability, managers and stockholders may feel entitled to the continuation of such growth. As a result, they may become careless in the assessment of future initiatives and overextend their own expertise and ability. Miller (1990) describes this pattern as the "builder" becoming the "imperialist." Pushed by the expectations of continued growth in revenues and profits, managers will often overreach and make poor investments. Alternatively, success can promote a sense of hubris and detachment among top management, allowing the firm to drift along with its own momentum but failing to learn and adapt with the environment. What this research suggests is that current performance is, in some ways, a reflection of the past. Evaluating performance in the present, then, requires understanding the historical context from which that performance emerged.

Purpose, Values, and Mission

Of course, no consideration of context would be complete without a consideration of the firm's purposes and intentions. Consider, for example, Porsche—an automobile maker, just like Ford. However, Porsche's 2008 revenues of $7.5 billion are a small fraction of Ford's 2008 revenues of $146 billion. Does that mean that Porsche is less successful? Quite the contrary: Porsche's size is a reflection of its basic purpose—to be a small, engineering-oriented maker of high-end sports cars. Porsche's own statement of philosophy explains:

> For Porsche, exclusivity applies in many aspects. Particularly in the fact that for a long time the company has drawn on traditional models. Money alone cannot produce inventiveness. It is far more the pressure of having to prove oneself against the competition again and again. Porsche relishes its role as David amongst the Goliaths in this world.

Ford, on the other hand, has a very different purpose. Its vision and mission statements talk about being a global company, a company able to reach all types of car buyers, with all types of products, in all the regions of the world:

> Our vision is to become the world's leading consumer company for automotive products and services. We are a global family with a proud heritage, passionately committed to providing personal mobility for people around the world. We anticipate consumer needs and deliver outstanding products and services that improve people's lives.

These two companies define themselves very differently. As a result, what is important to one may not be important to the other and what is considered success for one may not be considered a success for the other. Perhaps the most basic yet important contingency to the consideration of organizational performance is the purpose of the firm. Viewed in this light, assessing performance means asking the question, Is the firm accomplishing its own purposes? Is it doing well that which it set out to do? Understanding a firm's purposes requires understanding something about its *values* and *mission*.

Corporate values and missions, which will be discussed in detail in the next chapter, lie at the very root of the strategic process. While basic economic theory suggests that firms should maximize profit, and so shareholder wealth, the reality is that firms are driven by a number of varied motivations. At some point, all firms must earn a profit if they are to survive. But, as the example of Porsche and Ford illustrates, there are many paths to profitability and many different ways of operating that a company may choose to follow. These basic choices are a reflection of the company's values. Chick-fil-A, for instance, states clearly that:

> We exist to glorify God by being a faithful steward of all that is entrusted to us and to have a positive influence on all who come in contact with Chick-fil-A. That's why we invest in scholarships, character-building programs for kids, foster homes and other community services.

This purpose, which reflects the Christian values of the restaurant chain's founder, Truett Cathy, supersedes the profit motivation in a number of tangible ways. For example, all Chick-fil-A stores are closed on Sunday. In real terms, then, the firm is sacrificing 14%, or one-seventh, of its potential revenues and profits for the sake of its corporate values. These values are fundamental to Chick-fil-A's purpose and so form an integral part of how the company defines and measures its own performance.

Starbucks provides another example of values impacting strategy and potentially changing the way performance should be defined and measured. Starbucks states plainly that social responsibility and community involvement is fundamental to its purpose—specifically: "Starbucks is committed to community development through socially responsible investing." The Starbucks Foundation offers millions of dollars in grants to help low-income and at-risk youth. Starbucks offers "Fair Trade" and "Farm Direct" coffees, which are more costly but which provide a greater return to the farmers and so a greater degree of stability to the economies in which the coffees are grown. It invests in a variety of different community programs designed to promote volunteerism and the economic development of underdeveloped neighborhoods. Of course, all of this activity costs real money and so demonstrates the commitment of the company to a value system that supersedes the motivation for profit alone. Naturally, without profit, none of these good works would be possible. Still, the way Starbucks goes about making its profit and the types of activities in which it engages reflect more than just the desire to maximize profit. Rather these things all exhibit a desire to earn profit in a particular way and for a particular purpose. Like Porsche, Chick-fil-A, and Starbucks, all companies have an underlying value system that drives their decision making and affects how they define success and good performance. In assessing the performance of those companies, it is important that we keep those values in mind.

Value systems, like those just described, give rise to the company's mission. These statements of fundamental purpose are also known as credos, principles, or purpose or vision statements. Regardless of the name, however, the mission is the underlying reason that the firm exists. It makes clear the goals and aspirations of the business itself. It articulates the principles upon which the firm's culture rests. It stands as a guiding light amid the turmoil of everyday activity. In his book on corporate mission statements, Jeffrey Abrahams (1999) explains that a mission statement is:

> an enduring statement of purpose for an organization that identifies the scope of its operations in product and market terms and reflects its values and priorities. A mission statement will help a company to make consistent decisions, to motivate, to build an organizational unity to integrate short-term objectives with longer-term goals and to enhance communication.

Mission statements will often make explicit the priorities of the firm. The desires to enhance stockholder value, employee development, community involvement, or customer satisfaction are common to most, if not all, firms. However, not all firms prioritize those various goals in the same way. Ben & Jerry's Homemade Inc., the Vermont ice-cream maker that is now a division of Unilever, Inc., was famous for its commitment to social causes and to its employees. The Ben & Jerry's mission articulated three basic priorities—a product mission, a social mission, and an economic mission. Specifically, it stated:

Ben & Jerry's is dedicated to the creation and demonstration of a new corporate concept of linked prosperity. Our mission consists of three interrelated parts:

Product Mission: To make, distribute, and sell the finest quality, all-natural, ice cream and related products in a wide variety of innovative flavors made from Vermont dairy products.

Social Mission: To operate the company in a way that actively recognizes the central role that business plays in the structure of society by initiating innovative ways to improve the quality of life of a broad community—local, national, and international.

Economic Mission: To operate the company on a sound financial basis of profitable growth, increasing value for our shareholders, and creating career opportunities and financial rewards for our employees.

Underlying the mission of Ben & Jerry's is the determination to seek new and creative ways of addressing all three parts, while holding a deep respect for the individuals, inside and outside the company, and for the communities of which they are a part.

Ben and Jerry's desire was to run their business in such a way that all of these missions were linked and sustainable. The satisfaction of the social mission depended upon the satisfaction of the economic mission, which in turn depended upon the satisfaction of the product mission. Yet the product mission linked back to the social mission, as it was the unique culture of the company and quality of the ice cream that made the product so attractive and so profitable. The satisfaction of this three-pronged mission had demonstrable effects on the way that Ben & Jerry's operated. The company often paid above market prices to its suppliers, reasoning that in so doing it was both contributing to its communities and insuring a sustainable supply of raw materials. It refused to buy milk from dairies that used artificial growth hormone, as part of their commitment to the quality of the product. It also capped the salaries of the highest-paid employees at no more than seven times that of the lowest-paid employees. All of these decisions were reflections of the company's purpose, as articulated in its mission.

The problem at Ben & Jerry's was that not everyone shared this vision of linked priorities. As the firm grew, so did the need for outside investment. Like many entrepreneurs, Ben and Jerry sought that investment through an offering of stock to the public. Unfortunately for the company, many of these new investors were attracted by the prospect of above average returns. As such, these investors favored satisfaction of the economic mission over the others. Thus, as Ben & Jerry's grew, and as the competition in its industry intensified, the company began to get away from its own basic values. Amid the malaise that followed, Ben & Jerry's was taken over by a large diversified conglomerate, Unilever.

The story of Ben & Jerry's can serve as a powerful reminder that not all missions are fully compatible and that different **stakeholders** will define performance in different ways. All firms must make a profit and produce a return over and above their costs if they want to survive. However, many firms, such as Ben & Jerry's, Porsche, and Chick-fil-A, intentionally choose not to maximize volume, profit, or shareholder value and instead choose to try and make money by operating in a way that is consistent with other principles. As a consequence, what these firms view as good performance may be somewhat different than that viewed by others. Provided there is agreement among the various constituents of the firm, that choice is perfectly all right. For our purposes and for the purposes of this text, then, it is enough to remember that performance must be considered in context. All firms do not seek to do the same things, nor do they seek to do those things in the same way. Thus, an essential dimension of performance measurement and assessment is the degree to which the performance definition fits the purposes of the firm.

Before leaving the subject, it is important to make one final comment about missions and mission statements. As discussed in Chapter 1, mission statements are often written for public consumption, designed to sound good and to make the company look good, but to have little tangible meaning and to provide little in the way of specific operational direction. If this is so, why should missions come up here, amid this discussion of real performance? To understand, it is important to acknowledge that there is often a disconnect between what firms say and what they do. In their book on corporate mission statements, Jones and Kahaner (1995) comment on the fact that many firms have at times said one thing, only later to do another. Not all firms invest equal time in thinking through their mission and writing it out for others to see. Even among those firms that do write well-crafted statements of purpose, not all invest equal effort in assessing those missions carefully. In light of this, it is important to remember that, even when there is no formal articulation of a mission and no explicit statement of purpose or direction, there remains some underlying logic, some unspoken principle, that drives the company's strategy and gives coherence to the decisions and actions of its people. It is that basic set of values that must be taken into account when assessing the firm's performance.

TAKING STOCK OF PERFORMANCE

Chapter 1 made clear that performance is the crux of business and of business education. Strategic management, then, is a tool, a systematic framework of cause and effect relationships and associations that, when understood well, can facilitate that quest for performance. Before we can begin to understand the principles and applications of strategic management, however, we need first to understand performance itself. On the one hand, it is a simple idea. Buy low and sell high; maximize revenues and profits and, in so doing, maximize shareholder value. These pithy statements have a clear intuitive appeal. As has been discussed throughout this chapter, however, the reality is that it is never quite that easy. Performance means different things to different people, it can be measured in a variety of ways, and it can change with time. All of these realities must be internalized and integrated into our understanding if we are to make good use of all that strategic management has to offer.

Good strategists understand all of this and so consider multiple measures of performance, depending upon the situation and their goals. Some focus on growth; others focus on profitability; still others focus on stock price or on intermediate measures, like market share, productivity, or asset usage. All of these various measures provide good information that can be useful in the proper context. Some devise composite measures in an effort to distill different types of information into a single measure. Recall that the balanced scorecard was mentioned in Chapter 1. A balanced scorecard takes into account a host of different types of measures in an effort to capture, in a single indicator, the true and overall performance of the firm relative to all of its various stakeholders and interests. While the thought of a single measure of performance that transcends context and setting is appealing, it may not always be practical or even possible. What is possible, though, is better understanding. Good strategists understand the strengths and weaknesses of different performance measures. Good strategists fully comprehend the implications of setting and of the impact of goals. Good strategists focus on performance, but they do so while understanding the importance of viewing performance from multiple perspectives, over time, and in the proper context.

KEY TERMS

Altman's Z is a measure of financial performance that was developed as a tool to identify firms in danger of bankruptcy. The measure itself weights five common financial ratios to produce an index of overall financial health.

Economic Value Added is a measure of financial performance incorporating both accounting measures of profitability and the firm's overall cost of capital. The result is a measure that reflects economic profit or the return over the minimum required by investors.

GAAP, or "generally accepted accounting principles," refers to the set of rules and guidelines that govern how accountants should record and report financial information. The GAAP framework is established and maintained by the FASAB—the Federal Accounting Standards Advisory Board.

Privately held firms are those whose ownership stock is not traded publicly or listed or traded on any public exchange.

Publicly held firms are those whose ownership stock is available to the public and is listed and traded on a public exchange.

A **stakeholder** is an individual or a firm holding a stake in an organization's future and performance. The term usually implies a set of interests beyond those that are purely economic, as would be characteristic of absentee stockholders.

Tobin's q is a measure of financial performance and is the ratio of the market value of a firm, divided by the replacement cost of its booked assets. To the extent that the ratio is greater than 1, it suggests that management and strategy are adding value to the firm's assets.

QUESTIONS FOR REVIEW

1 Why is the value of a firm problematic as a measure of performance? Why would the best-performing firm not also be the most valuable?

2 How could a potential buyer and an owner of a business look at the same resources, the same market, and the same financial history and yet still draw different conclusions about the actual value of a business?

3 Why must strategic managers be so familiar with the specifics of performance and performance measurement? Should technical issues like this best be left to financial specialists?

4 Describe some of the potential problems associated with an over-reliance on various performance measures like profitability, stock price, or market share.

5 Are some performance measures more easily manipulated than others? Why would anyone care to manipulate measures of firm performance?

6 What is the advantage of utilizing more complex measures like Tobin's q, EVA, or Altman's Z rather than simpler, more accessible measures?

7 Why is it so important to consider industry factors and company history in assessing performance?

8 What is a balanced scorecard? Could different companies include different measures in their own balanced scorecard of performance?

Companion Website

For a chapter review outline with links to videos and other valuable web resources, please visit the *Strategic Management* website: www.routledge.com/textbooks/amason.

Tools of the Trade

An Overview of the Framework

Chapter 1 introduced strategic management as the framework of thoughts and actions by which firms pursue superior performance. While accurate and reflecting the complex and multifaceted nature of strategy, definitions like this are not especially helpful to those who would ask, So how does one actually do strategic management? Indeed, students and executives alike are often left bewildered and unsure by the somewhat esoteric nature of strategy. They understand the terminology and grasp the concepts, but they are frequently unable to translate the framework from the conceptual to the practical. As a consequence, strategy remains for many little more than an academic undertaking, a thought-provoking exercise that has little direct connection to the reality of day-to-day action.

Although common, views like this are unfortunate. Strategy is actually all about action. Strategy points towards and culminates in genuine commitments and behaviors that create value for the customer and competitive advantage for the firm. Strategy is a theory of sorts: it is a systematic and organized body of assumptions, principles, and relationships that can help to explain events and predict outcomes. But, as the famous social psychologist Kurt Lewin noted, "nothing is quite so practical as a good theory" (Hunt, 1987), and strategic management is a good theory because it relates so well to practice. In other words, strategy is valuable because it is practical. Understanding strategy can provide insights into why things happen as they do, and those insights can facilitate the prediction of cause and effect.

For example, how likely is it that a potential competitor will encroach on your firm's business? To answer the question, it is necessary to consider the issues in light of some known principles and relationships. Suppose that this competitor had recently expanded its operation and so had excess capacity. Suppose, too, that this competitor was getting pressure from its customers, who were quite large and so had substantial bargaining power because of their purchasing volume. In this instance, you could predict with some certainty that this potential new competitor would need to increase volume, so as better to amortize the costs of the newly expanded facility over a larger number of units. Moreover, in reducing the cost per unit, this competitor could more effectively respond to pressure from its own customers.

Understanding this framework of interactions, the sequence of cause and effect relationships explained by the theory, would allow you to understand and predict the motivations and actions of your competitor and to take substantive, concrete actions to prepare for the actions that he might take. Understanding the environment, the competitors and customers within it, and your firm in relation to these parties can allow you to formulate strategy to increase the strength of your competitive advantage and, along with it, your firm's performance. Because strategic management is all about performance it must also be especially practical. Indeed, to be truly effective, every strategy should be understood at the level at which it becomes actionable. In other words, grand ideas and broad statements about intentions, directions, and strategies are worth little until some action is taken on their behalf.

General Norman Schwarzkopf, architect of the Gulf War victory in 1992, attributes much of this military success to a focus on logistics. The operation "Desert Storm," which pushed the Iraqi army out of Kuwait, succeeded because someone understood the necessary implications of such a strategy for the logistical movement of food, fuel, ammunition, and equipment. In other words, the strategy, while boldly and skillfully conceived, succeeded because a large number of mundane details came together as needed. The point is that the distinction between strategy and tactics is largely illusory. Strategy is simply the aggregation of numerous tactics and actions, and actions and tactics are driven by strategy. Good strategic managers understand that strategy and action are inextricably linked. Thinking about strategy requires understanding the link to action, as well as the reciprocal link from action back to strategy.

This chapter focuses on the nuts and bolts of strategy, the so-called tools of the trade. The word "tools" here is appropriate for a couple of reasons. First, the topics covered in this chapter are not strategy themselves but are the means through which strategy is devised, formulated, tested, implemented, and ultimately made real. Strategic management is an ongoing process, but that ongoing process involves the use of some essential tools. Second, the term "tools" is appropriate because, like real tools, these things are applicable across a range of settings. Every firm is unique. Yet, there are similarities that allow for the application of common tools. Goals and objectives, for instance, are tools of the trade. Every firm has goals and objectives, whether explicitly stated or not. Thus, goals and objectives can be a level starting point for comparing one firm to another. This point was made in the previous chapter in discussing performance. Absent some understanding of a firm's goals, it is hard to evaluate its performance. Yet, because every firm has some goals and objectives, we can compare different firms on their ability to meet their own goals. Every firm exists within an environment. Thus, environmental analysis is a good place to start in the assessment of firm strategy. That assessment is accomplished through the use of some common tools.

The various component parts of the strategic management process, then, are really just means to an end. The end, of course, is competitive advantage and the superior performance that accompanies it. But achieving the end requires diligent attention to the use of each component part, each tool of the trade. This chapter will review briefly some of the basic elements of the strategic management process and discuss how each relates to the practical management of the firm, and to competitive advantage.

Figure 3.1 provides a general overview of the strategic management process. While all of the components are important and necessary, no single one of them is sufficient for understanding the whole. For example, strategic management does begin with the mission or statement of the firm's purpose. However, these are not complete strategies. Indeed, even a good mission statement, if it is unconnected to the other components of the process, will have little or no effect on the performance of the whole. Similarly, analysis and understanding of the environment is essential to success. However, strategic management is more than just environmental analysis. Implementation and processes of learning and adaptation are often

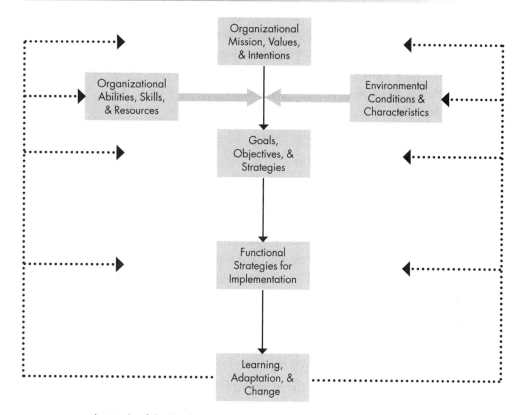

FIGURE 3.1 The Tools of the Trade

cited as the keys to strategic success. Yet implementation does not exist in a vacuum. Thus, every one of these components is dependent upon and related to the others. The key to both understanding and using the strategic management process is the ability to understand each of these components individually as well as collectively.

ORGANIZATIONAL MISSION, VALUES, AND INTENTIONS

At the top of the model is the *mission* of the organization. In the previous chapters, the mission was introduced and linked to the organization's purpose. While there are a number of different names by which this particular tool is known—mission, vision, statement of purpose, value statement, etc.—the idea remains the same. That idea is that, beyond the obvious need to produce a positive return on investment, the organization's mission is the reason the firm exists, the foundational statement of principle by which the firm is guided. For Porsche, it is to be a small, craft-oriented maker of superbly engineered automobiles. For Chick-fil-A it is to be a family-friendly and Christian-oriented provider of chicken-based fast food. Every firm has a mission of sorts, whether it realizes it or not. Some managers are diligent to think through the implications of their mission; others are not. However, every firm is guided by some principle, and that principle is conveyed throughout the firm in subtle ways. Thus, it is important to think carefully and deliberately about the mission and the message that it sends. Consider again, for instance, a portion of Porsche's statement of purpose: "Money alone cannot produce inventiveness. It is far more the pressure of having to prove oneself against the competition again and again. Porsche relishes its role as David amongst the Goliaths in this world."

One clear implication of this statement is that Porsche has no intention of being among the world's largest automobile makers. As a consequence, there are segments of the automobile business in which it simply does not care to compete. In making inexpensive and highly standardized cars, for instance, Porsche would be at a persistent disadvantage vis-à-vis its larger and more automated competitors. Thus, one implication of this mission is the orientation towards unique, high-quality, and customer-focused products. Those products are designed to compete, not on their price, but on the basis of their engineering, styling, and attentiveness to idiosyncratic detail. This is what Porsche believes it can do well; this is what the firm, its managers, and its owners choose to do; and this is what makes Porsche unique and attractive and what enables it to charge substantially more per unit than many of its competitors.

This fundamental mission also serves as a guidepost to Porsche employees and other stakeholders. Whether making decisions about new products or markets, new technologies or manufacturing methods, or a new inventory or financing system, all operational decisions are tested against this philosophy. Where an action is inconsistent with the mission, it is rejected. Similarly, investors understand that Porsche will never have the lowest labor costs, the quickest development cycle, or the fastest assembly line. Those sorts of characteristics, while desirable for many companies, are inconsistent with Porsche's basic philosophy.

Another example would be the Minnesota Mining and Manufacturing Company, better known as 3M. In 2003, 3M operated in over 60 countries, with total sales in excess of $18 billion. Yet, as large and successful as it has become, 3M still takes care to remain faithful to a set of principles developed in 1948. In that year, William L. McKnight, president and soon to be chairman of the board, laid out a set of principles that remain the foundation for the company's operations:

> As our business grows, it becomes increasingly necessary to delegate responsibility and to encourage men and women to exercise their initiative. This requires considerable tolerance. Those men and women to whom we delegate authority and responsibility, if they are good people, are going to want to do their jobs in their own way.

Mistakes will be made. But if a person is essentially right, the mistakes he or she makes are not as serious in the long run as the mistakes management will make if it undertakes to tell those in authority exactly how they must do their jobs.

Management that is destructively critical when mistakes are made kills initiative. And it's essential that we have many people with initiative if we are going to continue to grow.

These principles have been elaborated into a detailed set of value statements, conduct guidelines, and operational and performance metrics, all of which are designed to promote sustainable economic growth and community involvement that transcends the technological, demographic, and cultural changes which are bound to occur over time and over the range of many different markets. 3M is dedicated to innovation. That dedication reflects the belief that customers, markets, technologies, and economies are in a state of constant change. The only way to remain fit to these changing conditions is to change as well. The problem is knowing how to change and when. To understand that better, 3M makes use of its 60,000 employees. Each employee brings to the table his or her own unique interests, experiences, skills, and understandings. As such, collectively, this group of people represents tremendous potential for experimentation, learning, and development. Thus, 3M seeks to engage their efforts with selection, socialization, compensation, and promotion systems designed to encourage creativity, innovation, and new product development. Employees are encouraged to spend paid time creating, and they are rewarded when their creations succeed as new products. But, just as importantly, they are not punished for their failures. Consistent with its basic principles, 3M appreciates that finding those few truly successful innovations means enduring any number of failures. Thus, it commits to the process of innovation by cultivating a culture where creativity and invention can thrive.

What really makes these principles effective tools, however, is not just the quality of the values they depict but also the closeness with which they are linked to real and practical actions. In the Porsche case, the value of being a small, quality-oriented firm translates directly into specific operational tactics, focused marketing practices, and real performance measurement implications. The consistency between the values and the practices reinforce for its employees, managers, owners, and other stakeholders the type of firm that Porsche intends to be and the types of strategies that it intends to pursue. Similarly, 3M's basic philosophy of innovation and creativity has real and practical implications for the firm's hiring and socialization practices, for its compensation and promotion systems, and for its measures of individual productivity. Again, for this corporate philosophy to be meaningful, it must show up and have a real effect on action. To the extent that it does, it is a

Box 3.1
Post-it Note Story

Success can come from well-thought-out, carefully crafted plans. However, with a little innovation and creative thinking, people can sometimes turn a failure into a triumph. Such was the case in the creation of what is now recognized as one of the most famous and widely used office supplies, the Post-it note.

The birth of the Post-it started in 1968, as the failed experiment of 3M scientist Spencer Silver (Corey, 1990). While attempting to develop a super strong adhesive, Silver came up with a film which had relatively little sticking power but which retained its weak bonding capacity, even after repeated applications. The weak substance was simply filed away until another 3M colleague, Art Fry, found a use for the failed experiment. Fry sang in his church choir and needed something that would stick in the pages of his hymnal more reliably than just a bookmark. He combined the weak adhesive with bits of paper and *voilà* the Post-it note was born.

That is not all there is to the story, however. Fry was able to commercialize the idea thanks to a 3M policy called "bootlegging." As a company whose historical success had been driven by innovation, 3M started the idea of bootlegging to stimulate creativity. It encourages its researchers to spend up to 15% of their paid time working on whatever projects they choose. The Post-it note is not the only brainchild to emerge from this innovative policy. Scotch Tape, surgical masks, and countless numbers of other inventions owe their creation to the "bootlegging" of 3M researchers and scientists.

Indeed, if the bootlegging policy was not in place at 3M, the argument could be made that the company would not be around today. While that may or may not be true, it was the combination of Fry's creativity and 3M's policies supporting innovation that gave the world the little pieces of yellow paper all have come to love as the Post-it note.

Adapted from Post-it Note History (n.d.) and Corey (1990)

meaningful part of the strategic process. To the extent that it does not have an effect on action, then it is at best a waste of time and at worst a potential source of cynicism and resentment.

THE SWOT FRAMEWORK

Organizational Abilities, Skills, and Resources

The SWOT framework and analysis will be familiar to and popular among most business students and practitioners. The acronym is formed from the words strengths, weaknesses, opportunities, and threats. The logic of the analysis is simple yet deceptively powerful. Competitive advantage emerges when a customer sees value in a product or service and so pays the firm providing it a profitable price. As explained in Chapter 1, the value that the customer sees is a reflection of two things. First, the options available within the environment—the customer can buy the product from your firm, buy a substitute product from a competing firm, or buy nothing at all. The attractiveness of the product, the attractiveness of the substitutes, and the attractiveness of doing nothing or doing something entirely different is a reflection of the environment. There is also the issue of how the firm and its products are received. Given the other alternatives, what is it about your firm that makes it attractive? Is it truly a better product or is it merely a less expensive one? This determination reflects the unique qualities of your firm as they affect this particular purchase. The SWOT framework captures both of these components. The strengths and the weaknesses deal with issues internal to the firm, its qualities, skills, abilities, and resources. The opportunities and threats deal with issues external to the firm, the characteristics of the environment and the nature of environmental change.

To really understand the strengths and weaknesses side of the SWOT analysis, it is important to understand why strengths and weaknesses are important. To help with this, we need to return to the definition of competitive advantage supplied in Chapter 1. Recall that competitive advantage is the value a firm is able to create for customers over and above the costs of creating it. Defined this way, competitive advantage is achieved momentarily every time a firm sells a product for a profitable price. The competitive advantage is then the reason that the customer saw this particular firm's product or service as being advantageous or desirable over and above all of the other available options. For example, when a customer chooses one hotel over another, he or she does so for a reason. That reason is at least a part of the hotel's competitive advantage. When an airline chooses a vendor for its in-flight food and drink service, it does so for a reason. That reason is at least a part of the vendor's competitive advantage. To understand competitive advantage, we must understand what advantage customers see in particular firms. The attributes and abilities that lead to those advantages, then, are the strengths of the SWOT analysis. Alternatively, the absence of the sorts of attributes and abilities that lead to perceptions of advantage are weaknesses.

Unfortunately, students, managers, and academics alike conduct SWOT analyses yet fail to apply these criteria fully. As a consequence, they end up with little more than unorganized lists of characteristics that firms may use to describe themselves but which have little or no connection to real competitive advantage.

Some examples here would probably be useful. Consider Wal-Mart, one of the largest and most profitable companies in the world and the clear leader in the business of discount retailing. What are Wal-Mart's strengths and weaknesses? To answer the question, we need a sense of the firm's competitive advantage. To get that sense, we have to ask ourselves, What is the value that Wal-Mart creates? For most of us, the answer to that question is the ready availability of a wide variety of staple goods, at the lowest possible, or nearly the lowest possible, price. We go to Wal-Mart because we expect that it will have the goods that we want and have them for as low a price as anyone else. As such, Wal-Mart creates value by providing us with products quickly, reliably, and inexpensively, thereby saving us time and money. But what strengths allow this? Well, to do what Wal-Mart does, a firm would have to be large, so as to buy in bulk, at discount prices, and to be able to carry a wide array of items. It would have to be able to move those items around efficiently, so as not to add costs unnecessarily. It would need a substantial infrastructure in procurement, inventory, and logistics as well as a host of good locations to make the purchase of these products convenient. All of these attributes—size, inventory and logistical infrastructure, as well as the number and location of the stores—would be strengths of Wal-Mart, strengths that lead to competitive advantage. But, more importantly, these strengths would be just as essential to any firm seeking competitive advantage in this market. Moreover, the absence of such strengths would represent weakness.

Consider, for example, K-Mart, the principal rival to Wal-Mart for many years. K-Mart filed for bankruptcy in 2003, all but conceding the market of discount retailing to Wal-Mart and Target. Just as an assessment of strengths and weaknesses can help us to understand Wal-Mart's success, so too can it help us to understand K-Mart's decline. First, we must begin again with a consideration of competitive advantage in this particular environment. People choose to go to Wal-Mart, rather than K-Mart, for any number of reasons. Perhaps price or availability, or the convenience of knowing that returns will be accepted—all of these are component parts of a competitive advantage in this particular industry. Strengths, then, are the attributes or capabilities leading to these value-creating activities or perceptions. Unfortunately for K-Mart, its capabilities were deficient in many of the key areas needed for competitive advantage.

Although it was large, and so had substantial buying power, K-Mart was not especially good at managing the flow of goods through its stores. This logistical weakness led to higher costs and reduced availability. K-Mart was not especially good at tracking the sales of products from its stores. As such, it was unable to restock items that were selling quickly or to eliminate items that were selling poorly. It did not have good locations. As it was the older of the two chains, K-Mart suffered as demographic changes shifted traffic patterns away from its stores. As that occurred, what was once a strength increasingly became a weakness, as the value of the K-Mart stores declined and as the inability to reposition them quickly created opportunities for its two new rivals.

The point of this is that strengths and weaknesses cannot be judged in a vacuum. Rather, certain attributes and capabilities are strengths because they lead to competitive advantage in specific markets. At the same time, the absence of certain attributes or capabilities in specific markets is a weakness when it inhibits the attainment of competitive advantage. Actually doing a SWOT analysis then requires understanding the value of specific attributes and capabilities in their proper context. It is not enough simply to list various characteristics on which firms may differ or various capabilities that a firm may or may not have. Rather, the "analysis" in SWOT analysis requires discerning the **key success factors** of a particular market and then assessing the firm's position relative to those factors. Where firms have much of what is needed, they are in a position of strength; where they have little or none of what is needed, they are in a position of weakness.

Environmental Conditions and Characteristics

To judge the strength or weakness of various organizational attributes in their proper context requires understanding something about that context. Thus, the other half of a SWOT analysis, the analysis of the environmental opportunities and threats, is just as important as the analysis of the firm's strengths and weaknesses. Indeed, so important is the subject that all of Chapter 4 is dedicated to the analysis of the environment. For now, however, a brief overview would be helpful.

Effectively analyzing opportunities and threats is a two-step process. In the first step, the environment must be clearly identified. The reason for defining the environment is to narrow the focus of the analysis. Not all aspects of the environment are equally important to all businesses. Fluctuations in international currency markets, for instance, are more relevant and important to firms that do business in multiple countries. The price of labor is more important to those firms that employ large numbers of people. Changes in population patterns may be more important to those who sell retail than to those who sell wholesale. The environment must be defined clearly and carefully or the environmental analysis will quickly become unwieldy and virtually meaningless.

To facilitate the process of careful and clear definition, it is important to view the environment as a series of concentric circles (see Figure 3.2). At the center of the circles is the firm itself. As will be discussed later, a firm is like an organism; it is an **open system** that must exchange resources with its environment if it is to survive and grow. Thus, the next ring, just beyond the boundary of the firm, holds that set of actors with whom the firm interacts most regularly. This part of the environment has been referred to as the competitive environment or the industrial environment. In this group are those firms that supply products which customers see as substitutable, the customers who buy or who might buy the products or services supplied by the various competing firms, and the primary suppliers to a firm's industry. Thus, Microsoft and Intel would both be a part of Dell's competitive environment because both supply basic components that Dell needs in its pursuit of competitive advantage. Beyond the industrial environment is a circle representing what is called the general environment or the macro-environment. In this circle are all manner of potentially important forces, the effects of which may be broadly felt but are difficult to influence. For example, the general state of the economy is a macro-environmental force that can impact a firm's performance. Yet the state of the economy is difficult to affect. Changes in technology or in demographic patterns are also macro-environmental forces. These sorts of forces or conditions collectively make up the general environment in which firms must operate and with which they must contend (Castrogiovanni, 1991).

Finally, it is important to remember that every firm has a slightly different environment. Even for two firms as similar and as commonly thought of as Coke and Pepsi, the environments are slightly different. Why? Well, because Coke is a part of Pepsi's environment but is not a part of its own. Likewise, Pepsi is a part of Coke's environment, yet it is not a part of its own. So it is important that the environment be defined carefully and on a firm-by-firm basis.

With the environment defined, the SWOT analysis turns to the identification of opportunities and threats. Here again, though, care must be taken or the analysis will become little more than a list of observations, unrelated to any particular

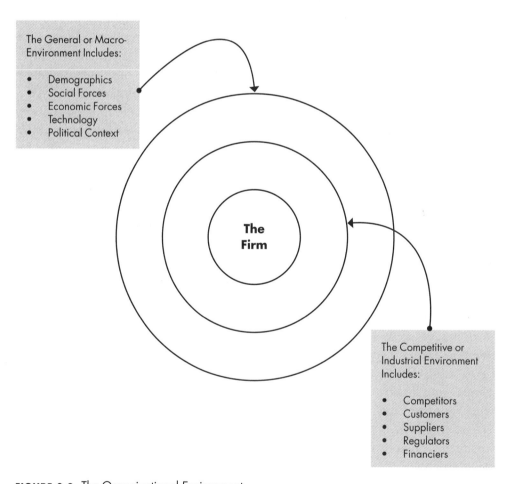

The General or Macro-Environment Includes:

- Demographics
- Social Forces
- Economic Forces
- Technology
- Political Context

The Firm

The Competitive or Industrial Environment Includes:

- Competitors
- Customers
- Suppliers
- Regulators
- Financiers

FIGURE 3.2 The Organizational Environment

business or environment and irrelevant to the formulation of strategy. As with the assessment of strengths and weaknesses, analysis of the environment should relate directly to competitive advantage. As competitive advantage is the reason a customer chooses one particular product or service, environmental analysis needs to focus on the context in which that customer's choice is made. Opportunities are instances for firms to gain new competitive advantage, either by attracting new customers or by getting additional business from existing customers. Threats are hazards to competitive advantage, forces that might interfere with the existing relationship between the firm and its customers or between the firm and customers that it would like to pursue.

Again, an example would be helpful. Delta Airlines, based in Atlanta, is one of the so-called major U.S. air carriers. Over the years, Delta has been profitable and unprofitable, as the state of its environment has changed. How might we assess the environment of Delta? Well, we would begin with a definition of the first concentric circle, the industrial or competitive environment. Delta's industrial environment includes its customers and potential customers and the other major carriers, such as American, United, and Korean Air, as well as a host of other regional carriers, like AirTran and JetBlue, which fly overlapping routes. In Delta's industrial environment are its principal suppliers, such as Boeing, Airbus, the airline pilots' union, and the suppliers of jet fuel. With this portion of the environment delineated clearly, the analysis then turns to the relative **bargaining power** of these various groups. What options, other than buying from Delta, are available to customers? How much control does Delta have over its supplies and suppliers? How loyal are customers to a given carrier and what costs are associated with switching from one carrier to another? What is the position of the competition and what resources do they have for competing with Delta? It is through the systematic assessment of these issues that the most immediate opportunities for and threats to Delta's competitive advantage are assessed.

With the industrial environment assessed, attention then turns to the second concentric circle, the macro-environment. For Delta, the macro-environment involves such forces as the general economy and the various demographic trends that relate to dispersion of the population and of business. The macro-environment would include the governmental entities that regulate the airline industry (the FAA), the security of airports and the screening of passengers (the TSA), and the various local governments that own and operate the major airports that Delta serves. All of these entities or forces have the potential to impact Delta greatly. An obvious example of this would be the events surrounding September 11, 2001. When terrorists flew United Airlines jets into the World Trade Center towers, as well as into the Pentagon, they effected tremendous change on Delta. The attacks deepened an emerging worldwide recession. They worried the traveling public to the point that air traffic was substantially reduced and prompted the creation of the Transportation Safety Administration (the TSA) to oversee airport security, the additional costs of which were borne largely by the airlines and by their customers. Thus, these macro-environmental events changed the nature of Delta's industry and so affected its competitive advantage.

Other examples could also be given for how changing actors, forces, and events could affect the nature of the relationship between Delta and its customers. For instance, the entry to the Atlanta hub market of discount carrier AirTran substantially limited the price that customers were willing to pay. Similarly, dramatic increases in fuel costs have forced Delta to raise ticket prices or begin charging baggage fees. These things affect the nature of Delta's competitive advantage by affecting the attractiveness of flying, in general. Each of the above examples illustrates the importance of the environment to competitive advantage. Thus, all of these various forces, events, and actors should be carefully identified and their potential effects thoroughly considered as part of any SWOT analysis.

More will be said about the assessment both of strengths and weaknesses and of opportunities and threats in subsequent chapters. This was merely an overview. The key point should not be missed, however, that a real analysis of SWOT goes beyond the simple listing of various characteristics. Indeed, few of the tools of strategic management have the potential to be so powerful, and yet are so often underused, as the SWOT analysis. When done well, it can provide the key to understanding strategy. As such, it is worth the time to do it well.

GOALS, OBJECTIVES, AND STRATEGIES

From this point forward, the strategic process becomes increasingly deductive. In other words, while the consideration of the mission and purpose, the development of competencies and resources, and the definition of the environment are all largely **voluntaristic**, or the result of self-determination and free choice, the act of actually forming strategies from these other parts of the process is more **deterministic**, or the result of structured analysis. To illustrate what this means, let us return briefly to the example of Delta Airlines. Delta's vision statement reads:

> We are dedicated to being the best airline in the eyes of our customers. We will provide value and distinctive products to our customers, a superior return for investors and challenging and rewarding work for Delta people in an environment that respects and values their contributions.

As currently the largest airline in the world, with one of the most far-reaching route structures, Delta has committed itself to the execution of this vision on a worldwide scale. However, commitments such as this are discretionary. In other words, Delta's management chose, at some point, to be a high-value carrier, providing a full range of services across an international route structure in an effort to be distinctive and desired in the eyes of its customers. But those choices were discretionary; they were made voluntarily. Thus, they are referred to as voluntaristic decisions. Similarly voluntary was the development of the firm's various strengths and weaknesses. Delta chose to headquarter in Atlanta. It chose to develop an inventory of over 500 aircraft and over a dozen different aircraft models. It chose to grow through acquisition, having acquired most recently Northwest Airlines—another major worldwide carrier. It also chose how to advertise and market itself and what sort of reputation to try and create in the minds of its customers.

With these various strengths and weaknesses in place, and with the environment and its various opportunities and threats identified, the process of actually forming strategies and setting goals becomes less discretionary. The decision to compete worldwide, through a vast "hub and spoke" route system, placed Delta in direct competition with a number of other large carriers. The presence of that competition and the similarity of the products and services offered by Delta and its competitors provide customers with a number of alternatives from which they can choose. What that means for Delta is that, if it hopes to maintain competitive advantage, it must respond either with lower prices for comparable service or with new and improved services at comparable prices. It is free to try new initiatives such as better seating, better in-flight entertainment, different pilot training programs, or different vendors for fuel and supplies, for instance. However, the success of those initiatives is a function of how they are actually received by the environment. Customers may or may not be willing to pay more for the extra services. New training programs or vendors may or may not have the desired impact either on costs or on reliability. Competitors may or may not imitate Delta's changes. The success of any company action is determined at least partly by the conditions of the environment. Delta may choose to set its own goals for market penetration or earnings, for instance, but its success in reaching those goals will be determined by its own actions as well as the reactions of the marketplace. Success, then, is a function of how specific strategies and actions fit within the environment.

What should emerge from the SWOT analysis is a set of reasonable objectives, along with the necessary plans for reaching those objectives. For example, based upon its own SWOT analysis, Delta may choose to pursue more intermediate-distance routes. These routes may reflect an opportunity in that they are currently underserved by other carriers. Moreover, Delta, with its fleet of diverse aircraft, its extensive reservation infrastructure, and its large staff of flight and ground crews, is highly capable of expanding into new areas of service. It may set as a goal the establishment of a number of new routes or the generation of some amount of revenue from these new routes over the next several years. It might also undertake a strategy of aggressive pricing on these new routes, so as to dissuade other competitors from entering the market. Delta might invest in new aircraft, designed expressly for intermediate-distance flights, to further its ability to defend the new market from competition. These goals, objectives, and strategic actions would all reflect the analysis of the SWOT and the desire for Delta to mold its offerings to fit the opportunities in the marketplace.

But are there specific ways in which goals should be stated? Should managers worry about confusing goals and objectives with strategies? Are there specific periods of time over which goals or objectives should be set? The answer to these questions is, no not really. Over the years, many teachers of strategy have sought to make all sorts of fine-grained distinctions between goals and objectives, to set specific time limits on the horizon over which plans should be made, and to distinguish goals from strategies. While some of these distinctions may reflect important principles, others serve little purpose. Indeed, after more than 30 years of this effort, the result is a myriad of confusing terms, definitions, categories, and rules that hinder real understanding. Thus, for the purpose of this text, goals and objectives are synonymous and any strategy for achieving goals and objectives can be either good or bad, under given circumstances. There are no specific periods of time over which plans must be made, and the strategic process includes both the setting of goals and the taking of actions necessary for accomplishing them.

There are, however, general principles that govern the establishment of goals and objectives as well as the formulation of plans and strategies. The first of these, as mentioned already, is that goals and strategies should flow from the conclusions of the SWOT analysis. To be effective, strategies must fit the environment for which they were fashioned. In other words, strategies should be developed around specific opportunities, to accommodate specific threats, and be built upon specific organizational resources. While general notions about being the first or being the best are fine, they are not likely to lead to real competitive advantage because they lack specificity. A good way to test for specificity in the setting of objectives and the formulation of strategies is to ask what will change as a result of them—specifically, Who will do what differently? Then ask, How will these new actions create value for customers? Well-designed objectives and well-formulated strategies will lead to actions that create value for customers. In the example above, Delta will begin flying new routes; it will reposition some people, or perhaps hire some new ones; and it will shift some assets or, again, buy some new ones. And all of this activity will have the effect of providing a new travel option to customers who lack that option currently.

The second general principle is that goals, objectives, and strategies should be specific in the short term but general in the long term. At the heart of this principle is an idea called **logical incrementalism** (Quinn, 1980), which reflects the reality that, over the course of time, conditions in the environment, as well as within the organization itself, may change. Thus, in setting goals and in articulating strategies, managers should be specific in the near term, where those specifics can be supported with good data and analysis. Yet, in the long term, where data are uncertain and analysis is based largely on conjecture, goal setting and strategy making should be more general. The question will be asked, of course, What is the long term? The answer depends upon the business and the business environment. Some firms exist in relatively stable environments and can foresee several years clearly. Others exist in highly uncertain environments, where it is difficult to see much of the future at all. Just how long the long term really is will vary from firm to firm and from setting to setting. However, the principle remains the same: as firms can see and anticipate future events more clearly, they should be similarly more specific about their goals, objectives, and strategies. As they are less able to see and anticipate future events clearly, they should be more general as to their goals, objectives, and strategies.

Failing to follow this principle can lead to two problems. First, if goals, plans, and strategies are too imprecise in the short term, then they will have little or no effect on company actions and performance. As discussed earlier, strategy is important because it is so practical. Strategies, then, matter and have their desired effects only to the extent that they change the way things get done. Towards this end, strategies with a short-term focus must be articulated clearly and directly and should be oriented around distinct and direct short-term objectives. If, on the other hand, goals, plans, and strategies are too specific in the long term, they may cause the firm to commit to courses of action that might well become burdensome or seem, at some point, out of date. Even more problematic, committing too much too early might lead a firm to make poor decisions because of the lack of information. Thus, it is important that firms do not commit too much too soon but, instead, reserve the option to change for as long as that option exists.

The last general principle to keep in mind is that all of the parts of the process—the environment, the organization, the goals, objectives, and the strategies—are tractable. All are subject to change, over time. Environments change, some more quickly than others, but all do change. To stay fit to them, firms must adapt and change as well. New resources must be acquired and new skills learned, new capabilities must be developed and outdated capabilities shed. The organization itself must be viewed as a means to an end, not an end unto itself. Visions and missions, strengths and weaknesses, strategies and goals—all can and must change with time if the firm is to survive amid a changing environment.

IBM has learned this lesson as it has twice had to remake itself, adapting to new environmental conditions, developing different competencies, and acquiring new skills. As it made these changes, it developed new goals, objectives, and strategies for how best to take advantage of its new strengths and weaknesses and its new opportunities and threats. IBM was once a dominant force in the mainframe computer business. Changes in the environment led to a shift away from mainframe computing to personal computing. To fit itself to this new environment, IBM had to restructure and retool. It had to acquire the new strengths needed to create value in this new environment. With a new and different set of strengths and weaknesses, opportunities and threats, IBM had to develop new strategies and set new goals and objectives. Even having made these changes, the company could not rest. Just around the corner was another set of dramatic changes. As the personal computer industry grew, so did the intensity of the competition. Indeed, so intense was the competition that IBM chose to shift its focus again, this time away from hardware manufacturing altogether, to concentrate on software and consultation services. With this shift came another new environment, and with that environment the need for still newer competencies and skills.

Remember, then, goals, objectives, and strategies are simply the solution to the set of variables presented in the SWOT analysis. They are the answer to the question, What now?, which should be asked once the environment and the firm's resources are well understood. Thus, they should relate back to the firm, its resources, and the context of its environment. In addition, they should be articulated directly, where they are needed to guide immediate action, and generally, where they are meant merely to set general direction. Finally, they should be revisited and reassessed regularly and revised whenever necessary, so as to keep the firm well fit to its ever changing environment and focused on what really matters, which is the creation of value for the customer.

FUNCTIONAL STRATEGIES AND IMPLEMENTATION

More than any other tool, functional strategies and implementation relate directly to customer value. Yet, for all of its importance, this tool is often overlooked or treated cursorily by strategy texts. Part of the problem is terminology. Just what is implementation? Is it really strategy or is it simply the process through which strategy takes life? Are functional strategies synonymous with implementation or is one the plan while the other is the execution? As before, debates over these sorts of issues create more confusion than understanding. So, for the purposes of this text, implementation is a fully participating part of strategy. Moreover, implementation of strategy takes place through a series of interrelated functional strategies, which detail how the specific work of the organization will be done.

Perhaps the easiest way to view implementation is to think of it as that part of a strategy that customers really see. It is the physical manifestation of the strategy, the end result of the analytical process. In many ways, then, implementation is the strategy as it emerges in the real world. Consider, for example, the firm Marks & Spencer. Marks & Spencer is synonymous with retailing in Great Britain. A large, well-established firm, selling a multitude of items from groceries to clothing, through a network of locations across the country, it is an integral part of the consumer goods environment in Britain. It is also a firm that is in trouble. Increasingly, Marks & Spencer is under pressure from above and below. Newer, larger, and more efficient competitors are stealing away the most elastic customers. By offering products that are comparable or very nearly comparable, for lower costs, these new competitors are taking away some of the historical customer base of Marks & Spencer. At the same time, smaller high-end stores offering a narrow range of highly specialized products are chipping away at the more inelastic customer base. These competitors offer a mere fraction of what Marks & Spencer offers. However, because of their specialization, they can provide greater customization and service. As a result of these competitive pressures, Marks & Spencer is losing customers, losing market share, and seeing its return on assets decline.

The question for strategic management is, What should be done about this? Rather than try to answer that question completely right now, think for a moment about what must happen for the situation to change. For the market erosion to cease, customers must see actual prices fall, actual services increase, or some combination of lower prices and greater service. Only when these conditions become a tangible reality will market share and revenue rebound. For return on assets to increase, Marks & Spencer must, somehow, increase turnover with its existing asset base or maintain its existing turnover on a smaller asset base. What that really means is achieving more sales through the existing stores or the closing of less productive stores, so as to reduce the asset base used in generating the current levels of revenue. In either of these cases, solving the problems of Marks & Spencer must involve changing the way that things actually get done. Implementation, then, is the process of connecting the intent of a strategy to the actions required to bring those intentions to reality.

On its face, this sounds pretty straightforward. In reality, however, it is actually quite complicated. First of all, there is more to implementation than just the things that customers see. For example, Wal-Mart's competitive advantage lies in its ability to offer a tremendous range of products, conveniently, and at costs as low as, or lower than, its competitors. Customers know that many of the things they need can be found, found easily, and found inexpensively at Wal-Mart. That is what they care about and that is what they see. Yet, what enables this availability and the low prices is an advanced logistical and inventory management system that insures rapid turnover, minimizes carrying costs, and provides for near immediate replenishment of the store shelves. These systems are largely invisible to customers. However, it is through the working of these systems that Wal-Mart's competitive advantage is realized. Implementation, then, includes all of those things that must happen to produce that which the customer sees.

Of course, herein lies another of the vexing problems for strategic management. One of the reasons that implementation is so complicated is that just about everything affects just about everything else. Staying with our example, consider the inventory and logistical system that supports Wal-Mart's competitive advantage. Could its competitive advantage be imitated through the replication of this system? Many have tried but few have been successful. The problem lies in the fact that the implementation is more than just the computer hardware and software, more than just the warehouses and trucks. It is also the human component and the know-how of making it all work. It involves the right people, motivated by the right compensation system, supported by the right training, and communicating in the right time frame. It takes the right equipment and the financial wherewithal to get that equipment into the proper alignment. It includes the critical mass of throughput necessary to provide economies of scale and a network of suppliers conditioned to work with Wal-Mart's systems. Like putting together a puzzle, implementation requires more than just the right pieces; it requires putting those pieces together correctly. Any breakdown along the chain, any missed pieces in the linkage between the concept and the customer, and the implementation will fail and the competitive advantage suffer.

To borrow a phrase from Thomas Edison, functional strategies and implementation are more perspiration than inspiration. Whereas the analysis of the environment, the crafting of missions, and the formulation of strategies is a creative and cerebral endeavor, implementation is about really doing the work that brings the strategy to life, as it was intended. It is tedious and detailed work, work that often happens behind the scenes and with little fanfare. Yet, in every instance, the real success of strategy hinges on the implementation. For Wal-Mart, the key to success is the ability to continue supplying a vast array of goods inexpensively. For Delta, the key to success is the ability to continue flying passengers reliably and less expensively than its competitors. For Porsche, the key to success is the ability to produce cars that are seen as well engineered, well built, and able to perform better than others. For every company, the key to success is the ability actually to do those things that produce value for the customers.

In Chapter 8, we will discuss the linkages between specific functions and specific types of strategies. For now, however, it is sufficient to remember that implementation requires real action and the expenditure of real resources. To be successful, those actions and expenditures must be consistent with the nature and intent of the strategy. From the customer's point of view, then, implementation is the strategy. And so, fit between implementation and strategy is the key to strategic success and to competitive advantage.

LEARNING, ADAPTATION, AND CHANGE

As mentioned in Chapter 1, business is ongoing. It is less like a single game than an entire season. But even calling it a season fails to capture fully the fact that, in business, the contest never really ends. Rome was the greatest political and military power that the world has ever known. With an empire that spanned the known world and stood for centuries, Rome was and remains in a class by itself. Yet, for all this power, its empire eventually fell. Chrysler, the third of the so-called big three in the U.S. automotive business, was a large and profitable company for many decades. Yet it too declined, being acquired and then sold off and eventually filing for bankruptcy. McDonnell-Douglas, K-Mart, Wachovia, and Northwest Airlines—all are examples of firms that were once large and profitable leaders in their industries but are now either shadows of their former glory or gone altogether. The lesson in these examples is simple but profound: in business, the competition never ends. Those firms that fail to adapt, that fail to change, that fail to learn and evolve with their environments are doomed to eventual mortality. Thus, the key to strategic success long term, to competitive advantage that is truly sustainable, is the ability to learn, to adapt, and to change as necessary.

The final element of our model, then, is a "tool," or series of tools, designed to enable ongoing learning and adaptation. At this point some might ask: Is learning, adapting, and changing really a strategy or is it quite the opposite? After all, having a strategy suggests purposeful intent, a plan for how to get from point A to point B. How then can we reconcile the mandate to learn, adapt, and change with the whole process of planning? The answers to these questions are complicated and will take some time to answer. Chapter 8 of this text will be devoted to them more completely. For now, though, it is important to understand that learning and adaptation are as fundamental to the strategy process as any other element, as important as a mission statement and as practical as implementation. Thus it is essential that managers attend to these tools as regularly and as genuinely as they would any other.

The way they do that is by never being satisfied and never becoming complacent. Miller (1990) compares managerial behavior in successful firms to the paradox of the mythical figure Icarus. Managers, prideful of their own success, complacent and buffered from the shocks and jolts of a competitive world, unwilling to risk their positions of leadership for all but the most promising of undertakings, lose touch with their customers and their markets. As such, they fail to see the signs of impending change. They fail to listen when customers say that they want something different. They fail to understand how competitors can deliver better products at lower prices. They fail to grasp the promise of new technologies or to understand why strategies that worked before are working no longer. As they grow successful, these managers lose the motivation, the will, and the time to learn and to take risks, often with catastrophic results. The key to avoiding this paradox is to do those things necessary to keep the drive, to maintain the hunger, and to avoid the trappings of success that lead to complacency and risk aversion. Of course, maintaining that hunger is easier said than done. Indeed, in some ways it is contrary to basic human nature.

Thus, mechanisms that can help must be institutionalized, integrated throughout the structure, culture, and decision-making practices of the firm. Six specific mechanisms will be discussed briefly here and in greater detail later. These are (1) minimal consensus, (2) minimal contentment, (3) minimal affluence, (4) minimal faith, (5) minimal consistency, and (6) minimal rationality (Hedberg, Nystrom, & Starbuck, 1976). Minimizing anything is another of those concepts that has grown increasingly unpopular in the nomenclature of the day. In this instance, however, doing only that which is necessary, committing only that which is required, could be the key to sustaining competitive advantage.

The first of these principles, minimal consensus, focuses on the propensity to emphasize agreement above all else. Dissent can be healthy, as it forces consideration of assumptions and the examination of points of view long held. To sustain competitive advantage, a firm must remain vigilant and sensitive to divergent points of view and alternative sources of information. Thus, the premature or overzealous pursuit of consensus, while seeming beneficial in the short term, can be detrimental in the long term. The ability to tolerate, and even encourage, open dissent without losing control and falling into acrimony is a key to avoiding the trap of complacency and the paradox of success.

Minimal contentment focuses on that tendency to allow things to go on as they always have. The greater the contentment of the firm's people, the stronger the contrary force must be to effect some change. Thus, in a firm of talented people backed up by substantial resources, minor signals that something is changing can be overlooked or misinterpreted. Such was the case at IBM in the early 1980s. Despite the evidence of the growing popularity of personal computers, IBM was reluctant to acknowledge this new technology. That reluctance was, at least in part, a reflection of its contentment as the market leader in mainframes. With less contentment, people are more willing to experiment, more willing to complain or to raise a red flag. Thus, contentment, while essential in some measure, becomes hazardous when it inhibits sensitivity to negative feedback and stifles the motivation for change.

Minimal affluence is an especially difficult concept because all organizations seek to earn as much as possible. Indeed, strategic management is about the pursuit and increase of competitive advantage, and competitive advantage relates directly to earnings. However, earning money and holding on to money are not one in the same. Indeed, in addition to maximizing their earnings, firms may seek to maximize their inventory of earnings—in essence, their affluence. The problem is that such stocks of **slack resources**, as they are called, can buffer the organization from the very sorts of feedback it needs to promote adaptation and change. A modest decline in sales might be met with muted concern by a firm with a deep well of resources. For a firm that is on the brink of profitability, however, a decline in sales would set off urgent alarms. The point is to maintain a sense of imperative sufficient to encourage vigilance and the prospecting for new opportunities.

Minimal faith relates to the confidence that firms have in their own plans. Planning is a necessary reality for any organization. However, planners can sometimes forget that some things are truly unpredictable; some things simply cannot be anticipated, and so all plans must be subject to change as events warrant. As many firms learned on September 11, 2001, even the best-laid plans are subject to random jolts and unexpected shocks. These unforeseen events need not be negative, however. Pascale (1984) tells the story of how Honda adapted to unpredicted shifts in the motorcycle market to gain acceptance of its small bikes when the sales of the larger bikes slumped. Seizing that opportunity required scrapping the initial plan and quickly developing a new one—a new one built on different assumptions and different facts.

Minimal consistency, in a strange sort of way, is really about minimizing the costs of inconsistency. Because a firm must stay fit to its environment, and because that environment will inevitably change, change on the part of the organization is inevitable as well. However, change costs money and can be a source of substantial discomfort. As such, change is often avoided, put off, and delayed until the need becomes so great that a revolution takes place. Revolutions can be costly to undertake and difficult to control. Yet, paradoxically, the only way that they can be truly avoided is by assuming numerous and regular evolutionary changes over time. By enabling such small, evolutionary changes, a firm can prevent the revolutionary changes that it so wants to avoid. But embracing evolutionary change requires foregoing a measure of consistency.

Minimum rationality is the final principle, and it too often seems contrary to traditional wisdom and thought. Indeed, the pursuit of rationality appeals to our desire for certainty and control. It can lead us to over-objectify subjective phenomena, to value known commodities too highly, and to discount risky ventures too sharply. Unchecked, rationality can become a straight-jacket, limiting the range of organizational motion and the scope of a firm's vision. It can lead to a focus on processes and procedures, on measures and methods, to the detriment of other more important issues. Peter Drucker addressed the pathological pursuit of rationality in his famous distinction between "doing things right" and "doing the right things." Managers must take care to remember that long-term success comes more from doing the right things than it does from doing things right. Thus, managers must take care not to overemphasize rationality and not to cut off creativity by insisting that things be done by the book.

The key to avoiding the paradox of success and to sustaining competitive advantage is the institutionalization of principles like these. Each should be instilled at every stage of the strategy process and promoted throughout the organization so as to prevent calcification around any particular mindset and to encourage ongoing adaptation, learning, and change.

CONCLUDING THOUGHTS AND CAVEATS

One of the biggest stumbling blocks to understanding in the study, teaching, and application of strategy is the tendency to allow these tools to become more important than the trade itself. Many students, teachers, and managers alike become so fixed on the form of the process, so absorbed in the details of the analysis, that they lose sight of competitive advantage, of the customer, and of the reality strategy is meant to create. Peter Drucker has said that the real purpose of a business is to create and keep customers. Regardless of how a firm measures its performance, a growing stream of satisfied customers will always translate into good returns. Thus, these tools, and the whole process of strategy, are valuable only in so far as they facilitate the creation of satisfied customers, what we are calling competitive advantage. Towards that end, then, it is important to close this chapter with some additional thoughts and caveats.

Starting from Scratch is the Exception

It is rare indeed that this process starts *tabula rasa*, with a blank slate. Almost always there are processes, investments, and people already in place. In these instances, creating new strategy means initiating and managing change. While change is problematic in its own right, the issue here is broader than the need to deal with change. Winston Churchill once said "we shape our buildings, thereafter they shape us." The "building" that is the organization is both an instrument of and a constraint on strategy. Firms must work with what they have; they must make use of their own resource base, broad or narrow as it may be. Whatever the future holds for Delta, in the near term it will remain in the airline business because it has so much invested in an asset base that ties it to that industry. While divestment of those assets is possible, it is surely not easy, nor could it likely be accomplished quickly and without substantial loss. Thus, any strategy that Delta formulates must take into account its substantial assets in place.

But assets need not be tangible to constrain the strategic process. Firms invest great effort in selecting, hiring, and training their people to fit a particular strategy. While this can aid implementation, it can also serve to constrain the ability of the firm to adapt and change. The shift from a product-based to a service-based company, for instance, involved a considerable and concerted effort by IBM to develop new human resources and to divest itself of some old ones. While IBM's people were very good, the things at which they were good were not the things needed for the new strategy. Thus, the formulation and implementation of the new strategy hinged on the ability of the firm to shift away from some resources and into others.

Even in those rare instances where strategy making can be initiated from scratch, in the establishment of a new firm, for instance, there remain constraints. The skills, talents, and biases of an entrepreneur, for example, constrain and govern the strategy. The strategies of new firms are especially susceptible to pressures wrought by the availability of resources. Whereas a new firm might desire to grow through the traditional means of raising finance and then using that finance to fund its investment, the realities of the marketplace and the limits on the capital the firm can raise may necessitate a different strategy, such as franchising. Moreover, whatever these initial trade-offs and decisions, they set precedent and become the constraints on the strategy process in the future. This is a phenomenon known as **imprinting**. Founders imprint upon their organizations a particular strategic image, and that image continues to characterize and constrain the firm well into the future.

Thus, at any point in time, the strategic manager must contend not only with the firm, its intents, its strengths, and its weaknesses, not just with the various opportunities and threats in the environment, but they must do so while working with the resources at hand. To borrow an old phrase, they must play the cards as they have been dealt. Over time, resources can change, old assets can be sold, and new assets acquired. However, all of that takes time. Thus, the strategy process almost never begins from scratch.

Whose Job is Strategic Management?

The second caveat relates to involvement. Just whose job is strategic management, really? On the one hand are those who would say that strategy is the province of top management. The CEO and the top management team are the ones best positioned to think strategically, to see the big picture, and to prescribe direction. As evidenced by the number of studies on CEOs and top management teams, this view seems to dominate the scholarly literature on strategy. While partially correct, this view overlooks the fact that the CEO and the other top managers are often isolated by the organizations and bureaucracies that surround them, cut off from direct customer feedback, from regular interaction with the environment, and from day-to-day knowledge of the firm's operations. As such, they are often unaware of many things very near the heart of their own competitive advantage.

On the other hand are those who argue for an egalitarian process. Viewed from this perspective, strategy making looks rather like an episode of *Oprah*, with a facilitator rather than a leader, with broad and inclusive sharing of ideas, and with consensus on and commitment to the outcomes being as important as the outcomes themselves. The object of this approach is both to engage the diverse and specialized expertise of people throughout the organization and to create a sense of buy-in to the final strategy. The problem with this approach is in the execution. Such broad and inclusive processes are slow and cumbersome. Moreover, without some means to resolve conflicts, these processes can produce acrimony and resentment, which can hinder implementation later on.

The best answer to the question of involvement, then, lies somewhere in between these two extremes. Strategic management does involve seeing the big picture and thinking ahead. It does involve looking beyond the current state of affairs and past the provincial lines of specific units or departments. It also requires, on occasion, leading people in directions that they might not have otherwise chosen. For all these reasons, the responsibility for strategic management falls disproportionately and unavoidably on top management. Yet, top management is rarely, on its own, able to know everything that must be known, to foresee everything that must be foreseen, and to decide everything that must be decided. There are simply too many variables and too much complexity for the process to rest in the hands of just a few.

As a result, there must be participation throughout the organization. For example, as discussed earlier, implementation is the process through which the intentions of strategy become real. Those involved with implementation are often invaluable sources of information about what really works and what does not. Competitive advantage is really about creating value for customers. Thus, those involved directly with customers are often invaluable sources of information about technological and demographic trends, as well as about competitor actions and customer preferences. Engineers, designers, logistics managers—all can be tremendous sources of information about the possibilities and constraints of a new strategy. Indeed, strategy is made better when the process includes information from all of these various specialties and functions. The challenge for top management is to create a process that seeks and gets all of this diverse input but that does so without stifling the real work that all of these various people are charged to do.

Herein then lies what Hamlet would call "the rub" of participation. The issue of involvement is fundamental to the process because changing who participates will very much change the nature of the strategy. Yet, involvement is often decided in an ad hoc fashion and based upon dubious criteria. Those who are most important to the process may sometimes be those with the least amount of time to spare. Broad and diverse participation is important, but not everyone needs to participate on every decision. It is very likely that the best practices and minds will be distributed throughout the organization. However, a relative few of those minds will be tasked with thinking about the organization as a whole. Thus, the issue of involvement represents a challenge of balancing many important but competing criteria. A streamlined and quick process has advantages but it may sacrifice comprehensiveness and depth. A centralized and focused process may offer advantages but it might neglect some possibilities and alienate those charged with implementation. These trade-offs are inevitable, just as the responsibility for resolving them falls inevitably on top management. Still, in deciding who participates, whether that decision is made implicitly or explicitly, management shapes the nature of the strategy and so affects the nature of the competitive advantage.

Intended versus Realized Outcomes

Strategy does not always emerge as expected. Events intervene, conditions change, people adapt, learn, and grow, and all of this variation affects the way strategy works. As mentioned earlier, Richard Pascale tells the story of Honda's growth in the U.S. in the early 1960s. Honda had analyzed the U.S. market carefully, with the goal of selling its largest bikes to American motorbike enthusiasts. Unfortunately, the Japanese engines were ill-equipped for the longer distances and higher speeds common on the U.S. highways. As a result, the motorcycles broke down. For a domestic firm this might not have been a tremendous problem, but for Honda it was a disaster. Honda had been limited by its own government to a mere $250,000 in working capital. Thus, it could hardly afford to import the parts necessary for the required repairs. So, to save money and stretch its funds, it began importing larger numbers of smaller motorcycles, some of which were used by the Honda employees themselves. With this exposure, Honda was able to sell small bikes to consumers who might otherwise never have bought a motorcycle. With this growing new segment of the market, Honda was able to distribute its products through outlets such as Sears, which heretofore had never carried motorcycles.

The rest, as they say, is history. Honda grew, along with this new market, ultimately to a position of dominance in the U.S. market. However, more than the result of brilliant planning and execution, Honda's success was attributable to its flexibility, its sensitivity, and its ability to learn, adapt, and change.

It is important to understand that strategy can emerge differently than intended and still be considered successful. Indeed, in many cases the success of a strategy may actually depend upon its changing. Henry Mintzberg (1987) distinguishes between deliberate and emergent strategies and likens the strategy process to the creation of clay pottery. The strategist, or the potter in Mintzberg's analogy, starts with a set of raw materials, a general idea of where she wants to go and what she wants to accomplish, and a talent for shaping the materials according to her desires. The process itself, however, is more organic than mechanistic, as the strategy emerges from the interaction of the strategist's intentions, observations, and experiences. In this sense, strategies are formed in process, as opposed to being formulated *a priori*.

This metaphor may be useful to some while seeming overly ethereal to others. The point, however, should not be lost. The strategy process, with all of its various components, is meant to be an adaptive mechanism, to keep the organization fit to its environment. Plans should be made and direction should be set. However, those plans should be revisited often, as conditions and competencies change and as feedback is received from the field. New insights should be sought and standing assumptions should be challenged. Simple things, like the definition of the target market, the competitive appeal of the product or service, or the relative strengths and weaknesses of the competition, should be examined regularly and regular input should be sought, and listened to, from throughout the organization. Ralph Waldo Emerson once said that a foolish consistency is the hobgoblin of little minds. Competitive advantage, not consistency, is the object of strategic management. As such, it is important to remember that strategies may often emerge differently but even better than intended.

The Process is Often Messy

In many ways, models like the one presented in Figure 3.1 do a disservice to students of strategy. The disservice comes from the fact that the process of strategy is not nearly so neat and linear as is suggested by this and other similar renderings. Indeed, the actual practice of strategy is considerably messier, with every step in the process affecting every other step. Missions and statements of purpose are often influenced by an awareness of what is possible and popular at the time. Strengths and weaknesses and opportunities and threats are difficult if not impossible to separate and assess independently of one another. Implementation many times is far removed from the more deliberate stages of the process and so often looks more ad hoc and reactive than it does purposeful and strategic. These realities notwithstanding, however, texts like this one continue to present strategy as an orderly and linear series of steps that start at one end and finish at the other, while being governed all the while by a common and overarching logic.

The disconnect between this common depiction of the process and its actual nature is really a matter of perspective. There is an old saying, attributable to Otto von Bismarck, that the making of laws, like the making of sausage, is a process best viewed from a distance and by its end result. The same could be said of strategic management. The process is messy and, at times, hard to understand. There are all sorts of fits and starts, attributable to both external and internal causes. It is a very human process and so is subject to all manner of human limitations and biases. Politics, self-interest, misunderstanding, and serendipity all play a role and all influence strategy as it emerges. As a consequence, especially in large firms, it is difficult to pull together and explain all of the various analyses, strategies, and functional efforts that produce a particular set of outcomes. Yet, somehow, at least in firms that perform well, all of this complexity comes together to place consistently on the market products and services that customers value. Thus, the complexity notwithstanding, there are some essential elements of strategic management that, when viewed from a distance, stand out and that make a difference to organizational performance. Those essential elements are represented in Figure 3.1.

Each of these tools is an essential component of strategy. Each is necessary but none alone is sufficient. They all must work in concert and all must point towards and produce some demonstrable effect on customer value. For many organizations, that is where the process breaks down. Thinking through the messiness of implementation during the formulation of strategy is difficult and uncertain, yet it is altogether necessary. Revisiting the mission periodically to see if it still fits the reality of the environment in which the firm is operating is time consuming and tedious. Yet it must be done if the firm is to avoid stumbling into the future, following without question the path that it is currently on (see Box 3.2). Taking time actually to listen to and learn from feedback is complicated. Taking sales people away from selling to talk about what they are hearing from customers or pulling consultants off of their projects periodically to have them share with one another some of the new best practices that they are learning often means absorbing real costs or sacrificing real revenues. Yet how else is the firm to gain information first hand about the market and the ever changing opportunities and threats within it?

Box 3.2
The Calf Path

This poem, by Sam Walter Foss (1858–1911), has been a source of amusement to many. In addition to being amusing, however, it offers an important lesson on human nature. For students of strategy, it is essential to recognize the tendency just to continue doing things as they have been done before.

Strategic management is about managing change. It is about adapting with and staying fit to an environment that is constantly changing. It is about continually learning what is working and what is not and adapting in such a way that you control your destiny, rather than your destiny controlling you.

Thus, this poem, and the lesson it offers, can serve to remind us all to keep one eye on the day-to-day details of ongoing operations, while keeping the other focused on the direction in which those operations are taking us. It is in the managing of this tension, between the long term and the immediate, between the deliberate and instinctive, between the analytical and the reactive, that strategic management really adds its value.

> One day, through the primeval wood,
> A calf walked home, as good calves should;
>
> But made a trail all bent askew,
> A crooked trail as all calves do.
> Since then three hundred years have fled,
> And, I infer, the calf is dead.
> But still he left behind his trail,
> And thereby hangs my moral tale.
> The trail was taken up next day,
> By a lone dog that passed that way.
> And then a wise bell-weather sheep,
> Pursued the trail o'er vale and steep;
> And drew the flock behind him too,
> As good bell-weathers always do.
> And from that day, o'er hill and glade,
> Through those old woods a path was made.
>
> And many men wound in and out,
> And dodged, and turned, and bent about;

And uttered words of righteous wrath,
Because 'twas such a crooked path.
But still they followed—do not laugh—
The first migrations of that calf.
And through this winding wood-way stalked,
Because he wobbled when he walked.

This forest path became a lane,
That bent, and turned, and turned again.
This crooked lane became a road,
Where many a poor horse with his load,
Toiled on beneath the burning sun,
And traveled some three miles in one.
And thus a century and a half,
They trod the footsteps of that calf.

The years passed on in swiftness fleet,
The road became a village street;
And this, before men were aware,
A city's crowded thoroughfare;
And soon the central street was this,
Of a renowned metropolis;
And men two centuries and a half,
Trod in the footsteps of that calf.

Each day a hundred thousand rout,
Followed the zigzag calf about;
And o'er his crooked journey went,
The traffic of a continent.
A hundred thousand men were led,
By one calf near three centuries dead.
They followed still his crooked way,
And lost one hundred years a day;
For thus such reverence is lent,
To well established precedent.

A moral lesson this might teach,
Were I ordained and called to preach;
For men are prone to go it blind,
Along the calf-paths of the mind;
And work away from sun to sun,
To do what other men have done.
They follow in the beaten track,
And out and in, and forth and back,
And still their devious course pursue,

> To keep the path that others do.
> They keep the path a sacred grove,
> Along which all their lives they move.
> But how the wise old wood gods laugh,
> Who saw the first primeval calf!
> Ah! many things this tale might teach—
> But I am not ordained to preach.

Recognizing that the strategy process can be a little messy is key to realizing its value. Order and cleanliness, like consistency, can be a hobgoblin in the mind of the strategist. Reality will never look as sterile as the picture in Figure 3.1. The process will never be as orderly as a textbook's table of contents. Yet it is in learning to use all of these tools and how to manage the complexity inherent in their use that they become truly valuable.

KEY TERMS

Bargaining power refers to the competitive relationship between suppliers and buyers of any good or service and relates to the ability of either party to exert power and influence over the other. The concept and its application to strategic management will be discussed extensively in Chapter 4.

Deterministic theories of management view a firm's performance as being largely attributable to factors and forces within the environment. The role of management in this view is simply to assess these forces and respond to them appropriately.

Fit is a concept based on the open systems view, where strategic success is linked simultaneously to the strategy, the characteristics of the firm, and the environment. In this view, any combination of strategies, resources, and conditions can yield competitive advantage, when properly aligned.

Imprinting refers to the patterns an organization takes on and repeats over time, without special intent or effort. These patterns may reflect principles of the firm's founders or practices that were instrumental in some early success. Regardless, though, they become part of the routine set of accepted practices or actions within an organization.

Key success factors are the drivers of success within a particular industry, environment, or setting. They are the things that are essential for competitive advantage, in relation to specific sets of customers and specific competitive conditions.

Logical incrementalism is a concept linking the specificity of strategic actions to the certainty of a particular setting. The idea is to set long-term goals in general terms, so as to allow for flexibility and adaptation, but to move forward through incremental and small steps, minimizing commitment and risk and increasing opportunities for learning.

Open systems theory views success as the result of interdependence between the conditions of the environment and the characteristics of the firm. All open systems, whether organizations or organisms, survive by acquiring inputs, performing some value added transformations on them, and then returning them to the environment in the form of outputs.

Slack resources are resources held by the organization but are in excess of what is needed to satisfy immediate needs. Slack is typically either unabsorbed and available in the form of cash, receivables, or excess credit, or absorbed and held in the form of excess capacity, excess inventory, or redundant capabilities.

Voluntaristic theories of management, in contrast to deterministic theories, view a firm's performance as being largely a function of specific actions and resources. The role of management in this view is to leverage unique characteristics and assets, so as to be distinct from the competition.

QUESTIONS FOR REVIEW

1   What does it mean to say that strategic management is "good theory" because it is so practical?

2   What is a mission statement and what two purposes do such statements often serve?

3   Many scholars and managers alike have debated the similarity and distinctions between missions, visions, and statements of purpose. What is the common theme running through all of these various statements?

4   The SWOT framework really consists of two distinct parts; what are they and how does each inform the other?

5   Describe the different forces operating within the macro- and the competitive environments. What value does it add to make the distinction between the two?

6   How does the principle of fit affect strategic management? Does understanding fit appear to make success easier or more difficult to achieve?

7   Is implementation an integral part of the strategic process or simply the execution that comes after the strategy? Whatever your answer, why is this so, and is that as it should be?

8 What is the connection between implementation and those parts of the strategy that the customer sees and the strengths and weaknesses identified through the SWOT analysis?

9 Why are learning, adaptation, and change so important to strategic success? After all, should not good strategy be about precise planning?

10 What is the distinction between intended and realized strategies and how might a real manager use these concepts to be more successful?

Companion Website

For a chapter review outline with links to videos and other valuable web resources, please visit the *Strategic Management* website: www.routledge.com/textbooks/amason.

Chapter 4

Analyzing the Environment
Assessing the Opportunities and Threats

Having detailed in the previous chapter the various "tools" of the strategic manager's trade, we look here in detail at one of those tools, the analysis of the environment. In terms of immediacy and importance, the environment is probably the single most significant driver of strategic success. Indeed, many have argued that conditions within the environment actually determine the appropriate strategy for the firm. This belief reflects a deterministic view of the strategic process (Bourgeois, 1984; Child, 1972). Recall from Chapter 3 that this deterministic view simply means seeing strategy as a series of known cause and effect relationships, where strategy is developed analytically in response to external forces, and where strategic success reflects the quality of that analysis and those responses.

The academic debate between determinism—the view that strategic success is a function of analytical precision and fixed cause and effect relationships—and voluntarism—the view that strategic success is a function of creativity, innovation, and the exercise of strategic choice—is not a matter of great practical importance. However, the tension between these two philosophies does belie a comparable and important tension between two practical strategic philosophies, proaction and reaction.

A cursory browsing of the business section at the local bookstore will reveal any number of books on proaction, leadership, taking the initiative, and being first. A relative few would include much on the importance of reaction. Indeed, the subject of reaction is largely ignored. Undoubtedly, there is something satisfying about being first. Especially in business, we tend to celebrate leaders rather than followers. However, the reality is that leading is an imprecise science that often entails great risk. Sometimes it is better to wait, to allow others to do the basic work of research and development, and then simply to react quickly to the emerging changes in the marketplace. Thus, well-timed and appropriate reaction is an important part of strategy. Indeed, in some instances, reaction may be the very key to survival. At the same time, there are instances where being first can yield clear and sustainable advantages. In these cases, a firm would do well to accept the risks and step out ahead of the competition and, sometimes, ahead of the accepted wisdom.

But how is a manager to know the difference? When is it appropriate to act and when is it appropriate to react? Answering these questions requires knowing and understanding a great deal about the environment. Unfortunately, most people do environmental analysis only to understand the present. What is the size of the market? What are the attributes of the competition? What are the costs of the raw materials or what is the status of pending regulation? These are all important questions, without doubt. However, they are limited in that they look only at static conditions. In essence, questions like this ask: What is the state of things right now? Certainly the current state of the environment is important. However, good environmental analysis should provide more than just an understanding of the present. It should also provide insight into how the current environment evolved and how that ongoing evolution affects the future. The philosopher Søren Kierkegaard once said, "Life can only be understood backwards, but it must be lived forwards." For strategists, the implication is that the knowledge of how the environment is moving forward is best discerned in understanding the patterns of the past.

Doing good environmental analysis involves following a series of steps. First, the environment must be accurately defined. Many firms have suffered because of poor definition of the environment. The next step involves analysis of the current conditions. This step employs the "five-forces" model (Porter, 1980). Like the SWOT analysis, the Five-forces model is at once simple and yet extremely powerful. A thorough and deep understanding of the five forces and the factors that govern their interaction can yield substantial insights. The third step in the analysis is to consider how the various forces at work in the environment have been and are continuing to change. Two additional models, both of which will be discussed later, provide further guidance in understanding environmental evolution and the sorts of conditions that will emerge in the future.

DEFINING THE BUSINESS AND THE ENVIRONMENT

The process begins with one of the models presented in Chapter 3—Figure 3.2 (p. 56). The environment is best thought of as a series of concentric circles, with the firm itself at the center of the rings. This representation reflects the view that organizations are open systems. The open systems view holds that firms are interactive and dynamic systems, embedded within other, larger, interactive and dynamic systems (Boulding, 1956; von Bertalanffy, 1950). Viewed in this way, a firm looks like a biological organism. Like living organisms, firms engage in three fundamental processes: input, transformation, and output (see Figure 4.1). And, like living organisms, firms survive and prosper as they fit themselves into and interact successfully with their environments.

For example, for a firm to be successful, its capacity for transformation must match the available inputs. A company that makes windows and doors, for instance,

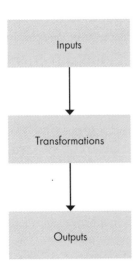

FIGURE 4.1 The Firm as an Open System

must have access to raw materials like wood, aluminum, plastic, and glass, and those materials must be available at a reasonable price. It must also have the necessary capital for plant, equipment, inventory, and working capital. Without access to these necessary inputs, the firm would have difficulty surviving. There must be sufficient demand for the firm's outputs, its products and services, and that demand must come at a sufficiently high price for the firm to sustain itself. A firm cannot survive for long if there is no demand for its products or if that demand exists only at prices below the firm's costs. So, just like a living organism, the firm must be able to interact successfully with the environment to obtain its inputs and to derive a return on its outputs.

Complicating matters, though, is the fact that interaction with the environment is more than just a dyadic exchange. Competitors affect the conditions under which firms obtain their inputs and distribute their outputs. As the story of Coke and its shift away from sugar as a sweetener illustrates, important inputs are often sought by many competitors, and that demand can affect their price and availability. Similarly, to have sufficient demand, at a sufficient price, the firm's products and services must be seen as being unique and desirable over and above the available options. What that means is that the firm's products and services must either be comparable to, but less expensive than, the competing alternatives or be considered qualitatively better than the competing alternatives. Competitors then threaten the firm's viability by interfering with the relationship that it has with its suppliers (inputs) and its customers (outputs).

Understanding the firm from this perspective means knowing something about the firm itself, as well as about its suppliers, customers, and competitors and the overall context in which all of these various groups interrelate. Thus, Figure 3.2 serves to remind us of two very important points. First, each firm exists within its own unique environment; no two firms, no matter how similar, share exactly the same environment. Good environmental analysis, then, must be done specifically for individual firms and with a specific eye towards the relationship between the firm, its customers, its competitors, and its suppliers. Second, each environment includes the various actors that affect the firm's survival and success. As a result, thorough environmental analysis begins with the identification of these various actors.

Identifying these actors requires understanding what the firm really does. In other words, defining the environment begins with defining the business. Abell (1980) proposes that businesses generally define themselves along one of three dimensions—customer groups, customer functions, or dominant technologies. Some firms, for instance, service particular groups of customers. Wholesale building products firms, for example, service contractors almost exclusively. They sell many products and provide a host of different services, but they do so specifically for a particular group of customers. Medical supply businesses are another example of this orientation. They carry a range of products and offer a number of different services. Yet they do this all just for hospitals, medical practices, and outpatient clinics. Other firms satisfy a particular function. Wal-Mart and Target sell to virtually everyone; they do so because they satisfy a function—the supplying of stable goods that are nearly universal. Grocery stores, like Kroger or Albertson's, banks and financial services firms, utility companies, and cell phone providers all tend to define themselves in terms of the function that they provide. Finally, some firms define themselves in terms of the technology that they build or employ. Caterpillar, for instance, makes diesel and natural gas engines for all sorts of large industrial machine applications, and General Electric makes turbines for engines and power plants. Anyone who has need of these products or technologies is a potential customer. In that sense, then, it is the technology itself that drives the definition of the business.

With the business defined, two questions arise. First, who are the customers? Second, what other options do these customers have for these products or services? For Caterpillar, the customers are firms in transportation, construction, mining, power generation, and a host of other businesses. The various options for these firms include not just other makers of diesel and natural gas engines but also alternative types of suppliers. For example, a firm that makes no engines at all but rather reconditions older engines would be a potential substitute for and so a competitor to Caterpillar. For a cell phone provider, such as Verizon, the customer is just about every individual and business interested in mobile communication. The options available to these customers comprise other cell phone providers as well as other communication technologies, such as two-way radios, internet-enabled mobile messaging services, and pagers. For a medical supply company, the customers are physician practices, hospitals, and outpatient clinics. The various suppliers to these customers include other specialized supply firms as well as any firm providing the products and services that hospitals and medical practices buy. Indeed, warehouse distributors or large pharmaceutical firms might also offer alternative sources of supply to these customers and so be competitors to specialized medical supply firms.

The common theme across all of these examples is substitutability. Substitutability, in the eye of the customer, is the key to defining a business's competitive environment. Defining the business allows the firm to identify its customer. Identifying the customer and suppliers of substitute products and services allows the firm to identify its competitive environment. The importance of substitutability goes back to the open systems view of the firm. For the firm to thrive, it must fit well within its environment. Competitors are threats to the firm because they can disrupt the flow of inputs and outputs into and out of the firm. Who are the competitors? They are the firms whose products and services lure away customers. They are the firms whose products and services are the benchmarks, in the mind of the customer, against which a firm's products and services are compared. Identify the customer and you will identify this group of firms. Identify this group of firms and you will identify the competitive environment.

ANALYZING THE COMPETITIVE ENVIRONMENT

The competitive environment, the first circle beyond the firm in Figure 3.2, is the most immediate and important part of the environment. As such, it is where most of the time and effort in environmental analysis is spent. It is especially important because interaction of the actors in the competitive environment directly affects the bargaining power of the firm in relation to its customers and suppliers. This can be understood through a simple example. Consider the case of someone selling a house. As the seller thinks about a price, she considers the attributes of the property—its size, its age, its condition, and so on. But, more than any of these issues, she also considers the nature of the market. Is the house in a popular area or neighborhood? How many other houses are for sale? What is the ratio of buyers to sellers? How motivated are the sellers to get out and how motivated are buyers to get in? In popular areas, like resorts or dense downtown districts, properties can sell at extraordinary premiums even if they are in poor condition. In less attractive, low-traffic areas, properties can sell at a heavy discount even if they are in excellent condition. Thus, in pricing her house, our hypothetical seller wants to know her market. Will she have a large number of bidders? If so, then she can likely ask and wait for a high price. Or will she see relatively few bids? If so, then she will likely have to take whatever price she can get. Are there a large number of comparable properties on the market? If so, then she may be motivated to get out before the price declines. Are there a large number of buyers moving into the market? If so, then she may be motivated to wait while prices escalate.

This simple example illustrates the importance of bargaining power, and bargaining power relates directly to the economic concept of **elasticity**. Elasticity is about having options. Do customers have options to the firm's products and services? Can they afford to "walk away" from the deal? If so, then they have great elasticity and bargaining power and the burden on the seller is much greater. However, when the buyer has few options and is unable to walk away, the balance of bargaining power shifts. In these instances the burden is on the buyer, as the seller can now name the price and terms.

The concepts of elasticity and bargaining power are potent and relate directly to competitive advantage, profitability, and overall success. Indeed, because of their importance, these concepts lie at the root of many well-known business practices. **Branding**, for instance, is a popular term in marketing circles. Branding seeks to promote a high degree of familiarity, recognition, and respect for a particular brand in the mind of the customer so that, when thinking of a particular product, the customer will think only of that brand. For example, a customer who wants a small electronic device might think first of the Sony brand name and so seek out only a Sony product, excluding other options. The effect would be to increase Sony's bargaining power by limiting the options, or the perceived options, available to the buyer. By building a strong preference for its brand, Sony is able to affect its bargaining power in relation to its customers, making them less likely to consider the products of other suppliers. As a result, Sony is able to increase its returns.

Other firms may, through regulatory means, try to limit customer options. Cable TV companies, local phone service providers, and power generation firms have all benefited from their status as protected monopolies. While they are subject to considerable regulation and oversight, they are also protected from direct competition. As a result, customers are often left with limited options for cable or power service. In the absence of options, these customers have little or no bargaining power. Indeed, it is to prevent these sorts of suppliers from abusing their bargaining power advantage that such firms and their prices are so carefully regulated. Other firms benefit from legal limitations on competition as well. Companies in the pharmaceutical and biotech businesses often get patents for their products and processes. These patents protect the firms by limiting the ability of competitors to make and sell comparable products. With few if any comparable products available, customers must deal with the patent holder. As a result, the holder of the patent has great bargaining power and great ability to sell more and to sell at a premium price.

Bargaining power relates directly to competitive advantage and is a large part of understanding profitability. Firms with much bargaining power are often able to sell more and at a higher price. Firms with little bargaining power must often work harder to make sales and will often sell less or at a lower price. Thus, understanding bargaining power and the various forces that govern it is a key part of environmental analysis.

THE FIVE-FORCES MODEL

Fortunately, a considerable amount of time and effort has been devoted to understanding bargaining power. From this work has emerged a simple, yet powerful tool, the Five-forces model (Figure 4.2), developed by Porter (1980), which depicts competitiveness or profit potential as resulting from the interaction of five forces: the bargaining power of sellers, the bargaining power of buyers, the availability of substitute products, the threat of new entrants, and the rivalry among existing competitors.

Bargaining Power of the Seller

The bargaining power of the seller relates to the attractiveness and availability of particular products and services in relation to available options. Returning to the earlier example, Sony is considered a maker of reliable, high-quality electronic equipment. That perception translates into bargaining power for Sony. Customers

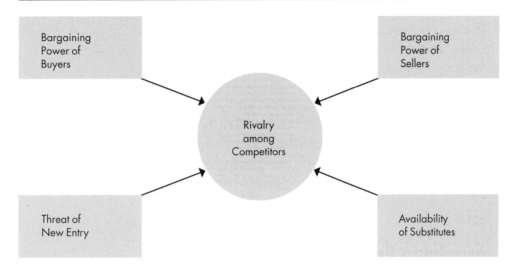

FIGURE 4.2 The Five-Forces Model

can pay Sony's price or they can settle for something else, but buying from Sony likely means paying a premium price. Quality, then, or perceived quality, produces bargaining power for the seller. Bargaining power for the seller can also relate to the absence of competition. Airline ticket prices are generally higher on routes that are served by only one carrier, for instance. The importance of the product or service also relates to bargaining power. For example, buyers rarely choose a surgeon based on cost. Because of the importance of the service, customers will generally want the best available provider. To get that provider, they may end up having to wait longer for their procedure, having to pay more for the procedure, or both. Quality, exclusivity, prestige, or importance of the product or service can all shift bargaining power away from the buyer and to the seller by limiting the ability of the customer to walk away and go elsewhere.

Of course, the ultimate example of seller power is a **monopoly**. Where there is only one provider, the seller can sell at a substantial premium. But monopoly conditions can exist even when no true monopoly is present. As mentioned, there are regulated monopolies, such as cable TV, local telephone services, and residential power distribution. But there are also pseudo-monopolies, conditions where customers feel that they have only one option, even when other options are in fact present. Coke benefits from such an effect in many areas, as some consumers prefer Coke, regardless of the presence or price of the various alternatives. In the minds of these customers, Coke has **monopoly power**, despite the presence of competition. Microsoft benefits from a similar effect. So strong is the desire for the Windows operating system and the associated Microsoft applications on the part of end users that computer makers such as Dell and HP have no choice but to purchase Microsoft software for installation on their machines. The effect is to give Microsoft monopoly-like power, which translates into tremendous revenue and profits.

Firms such as Aramark and Ticketmaster create monopoly-like conditions through licensing agreements which give them exclusive rights to sell concessions or tickets at large sporting and entertainment venues.

The key to understanding the bargaining power of the seller lies in understanding the needs of the buyer and the available options. When buyers have strong needs but few options, or if they believe that they have few options, the power to bargain or negotiate the terms of the sale shift to the benefit of the seller. Relating this back to the example of our hypothetical home seller, when her home is one of just a few available in an attractive area that is expected only to grow more attractive, she has great power with which to negotiate the sale.

Bargaining Power of the Buyer

Buyers and sellers represent opposing sides of the same relationship. For there to be a buyer, there must be a seller, and for there to be a seller, there must also be a buyer. Thus, when we see bargaining power shifting to the seller, it is necessarily shifting away from the buyer. To understand the bargaining power of the buyer, simply think about those forces that affect the power of the seller, but think about them in reverse. For example, just as selling a product that is highly important to the buyer will provide the seller with power, so will selling a product that is relatively unimportant translate into power for the buyer. Products like chewing gum, pencils, paper clips, or blank CDs are inexpensive, readily available, and rarely of great and immediate importance. Thus buyers are rarely in a position of needing them urgently or having to get them from just one supplier. That availability, coupled with a lack of intense need, provides the buyer with great bargaining power.

Buyers can also increase their bargaining power by purchasing in bulk or by ordering in advance. Both serve as inducements to the seller and so might allow the buyer to negotiate better terms or prices. Having great bargaining power is especially important to firms such as Wal-Mart or Target. These firms use their size and volume to negotiate low prices along with favorable payment and shipping terms from their suppliers. Indeed, understanding bargaining power and the importance of volume buying can shed light on the workings of many different industries like groceries, steel, or automobiles. In all of these industries, firms need the ability to negotiate low prices from their suppliers. One way to accomplish that is by being large enough to buy in bulk.

Buyers can also increase their bargaining power by developing alternative sources of supply. In the earlier example, Coke increased dramatically its bargaining power in relation to the sugar suppliers by demonstrating the efficacy of high fructose syrup. Similarly, for firms like Dell, Compaq, and HP, having the option of using

AMD processors increases their bargaining power in relation to Intel. Many firms actively seek out and cultivate new sources of supply, not necessarily because they are unhappy with their current providers but because so doing gives them enhanced bargaining power over their providers.

Box 4.1

Coca-Cola Switches from Sugar to High-Fructose Corn Syrup

In late 1980, Coca-Cola announced that it would begin substituting high-fructose corn syrup for 50% of the sucrose or sugar used in the making of Coke. The change came after a two-year period during which the company gradually increased the corn syrup used in some of its other beverages, such as Sprite, Mr. Pibb, and Fanta. Eventually Coke switched to 100% corn syrup in all of its drinks. Soon afterwards, other soft-drink makers followed suit and did the same. Why would Coca-Cola and these other beverage manufacturers move away from sugar? To understand, it is important to view the move in the larger context of the competitive environment.

During the 1970s, global demand for sugar grew at an astounding rate. Naturally, this led the price to increase dramatically as well. That price reached its all-time high of 72 cents per pound in 1974. In addition, by 1980 nearly half of the U.S. domestic sugar supply was imported. As a result, prices became increasingly volatile, as supplies became subject to disruption by a range of various natural and geopolitical forces. As a consequence, sugar consumers were increasingly put at risk and forced to pay higher and higher prices to insure a steady supply. In the meantime, the producers of corn syrup were experiencing steady growth (25% per year) as they marketed their product as a good and reliable substitute to the increasingly expensive sugar.

In an effort to lower production costs and to provide stability, Coke made the decision to begin testing the high-fructose corn syrup in some of its less popular products. Once management was convinced that corn syrup was a suitable replacement, the company began using it in all of its products. Of course, this reduced dramatically the worldwide demand for sugar and prices fell sharply. Initially, the producers of high-fructose corn syrup had trouble meeting all of this demand, not only because of Coca-Cola but also because of the other beverage makers that followed Coke in making the same decision. However, suppliers soon adapted and other new suppliers entered. Even to this day, most popular beverages are made with high-fructose corn syrup.

Adapted from "Corn Refiners Expand to Meet the Shift to Fructose,"
Chemical Week, December 17, 1980

Availability of Substitutes

Bargaining power is all about options. To the extent that buyers have options, they are able to exercise greater elasticity in their purchasing. To the extent that buyers have few options, they are less elastic. In and of itself, elasticity is neither good nor bad. Sellers prefer that their customers come to them first and foremost. Buyers prefer a range of options and the ability to select from among multiple suppliers. Understanding the dynamics of elasticity, though, is important to both buyers and sellers, as both seek to get the best deal and to maximize their returns. Thus, the availability of substitutes is a key component of bargaining power.

The problem is that substitutability lies in the eye of the beholder. Are Coke and Pepsi substitutes? That depends upon who you ask. Some would say absolutely; others would not think of drinking anything other than their favorite. Thus, just because two products "look" alike does not mean that they are truly substitutable. Indeed, substitutes need not look like the product or service that they are substituting. Natural gas is a substitute for electricity, ceramic tile and hardwood can substitute for carpet, and the internet is a substitute for newspapers and magazines. Substitutability lies in the eye of the one doing the substituting. That is why it is so important to look at competition as being any force that disrupts the relationship between the firm and its customers and suppliers.

Of course, there is one potential substitute for just about every product or service. That substitute is the option of doing nothing at all. Staying home is a substitute activity for going out to a movie or for dinner. Keeping an automobile one more year is a substitute for buying a new one. Driving is a substitute for flying and making coffee at home is a substitute for purchasing from Starbucks. Understanding substitutability requires getting inside the mind of the customer and asking what options he or she has. What alternatives does the customer consider in the decision to purchase or not to purchase? As that customer sees more alternatives, as he or she identifies more products or services that will substitute, so will his or her bargaining power increase.

Threat of New Entrants

New entrants, or the threat of new entrants, play an interesting role in affecting bargaining power. New entrants to an industry can offer alternatives to customers, reducing the bargaining power of the sellers. The entrance of AirTran, formerly Value Jet, into the Atlanta market, for instance, had a substantial impact on the bargaining relationship between Delta and its customers. Many years ago, the entrance of two new long-distance carriers, Sprint and MCI, reshaped dramatically the bargaining relationship between AT&T and its customers, setting in motion a series of events that would reshape the entire telecommunications industry. New entrants can have a profound impact on both buyers and sellers.

The effect of new entrants can be felt even before entry occurs. Indeed, the mere threat of new entrants can be a powerful force. Economics tells us that new entrants are encouraged by the prospect of profitability. During the 1990s, when fuel was cheap, Mercedes, BMW, Accura, and Nissan all entered the SUV market. The attraction for these firms was the profit that other firms such as GM and Ford were at the time making from these vehicles. A multitude of "reality" television shows followed the initial success of shows like *Survivor*, *The Real World*, and *The Bachelor*, endeavoring to capitalize and make money off of this trend in the viewing market. The potential for profit provides an incentive to new entrants. Those new entrants, in turn, provide options to customers, increasing their bargaining power and reducing the profitability of the sellers.

As a consequence, firms will often try to deter new entry by making the market appear less attractive. This is called **contrived deterrence**, and it affects the bargaining relationship between buyers and sellers. To deter new entrants, a firm may build overcapacity and, in so doing, reduce its own profit. If that overcapacity deters new entrants, however, it may well be worth the cost. A firm may intentionally sell below the highest possible price that it could charge. Coca-Cola does this in many places. While it could likely reap higher profits from those who strongly prefer it, raising prices could open the door for Pepsi, or for some other drink maker, to gain market share. Thus, Coke leaves its prices below full potential to deter the competition.

As these examples illustrate, where there is the potential for new entry, there is increased bargaining power for the buyer and decreased bargaining power for the seller. Alternatively, where there is little potential for new entry, there is decreased bargaining power for the buyer and increased bargaining power for the seller. Thus, in analyzing the environment, it is important to assess the potential for entry. When is it difficult for new firms to enter the market? It is difficult when there is some legal or structural impediment. Patents and copyrights are legal barriers to entry. Licensed monopolies, such as exist in cable television, retail electrical power, and some local phone service markets, are all barriers to entry. **Switching costs**, the cost to the buyer to change from one provider to another, can be a barrier to entry. Brand preferences, shared usage, network connectivity, and distribution channel saturation can all be barriers to entry and so forces that can deter a competitor from entering. That deterrence translates into increased bargaining power for the seller.

The key to understanding the threat of new entry is remembering that new entrants represent potential new alternatives, new options that increase the bargaining power of the buyer. Thus, industries lacking the sorts of barriers discussed above are unable to prevent or deter new entry and so will likely see bargaining power gravitate towards the buyers and away from the sellers.

Rivalry among Competitors

The last of the forces is rivalry among the existing competitors. Even in those instances where there is little threat of new entry, existing firms may still compete fiercely by offering substitute products, by offering inducements for customers to switch suppliers, and by working to convince customers that their products or services are better than the available options. This sort of competition, called rivalry, impacts bargaining power directly, shifting it away from the sellers and to the buyers.

But what leads to rivalry? Essentially, rivalry reflects the balance of supply and demand. When there is more demand than supply, rivalry will be relatively low because firms can grow by selling to new customers. On the other hand, when there is more supply than demand, rivalry will be relatively high because firms can only grow by inducing customers to switch from one provider to another.

Thus, mature markets, where sales growth is slow or non-existent, generally have higher rivalry than growing markets. Mature markets, with stagnant or slow-growing demand, are typically populated by large firms with substantial capacity. These firms often have low marginal costs and so great incentive to increase volume. Such increases, however, come at the expense of competitors, who retaliate in their own defense. Substitutability is often high in mature markets, as customers frequently see little meaningful distinction among the products and services of the leading firms. Moreover, many of those firms have invested heavily in the specialized plant and equipment necessary to compete effectively. Those investments become exit barriers, locking the firm into the particular business, despite its marginal profitability. Indeed, firms in mature markets, where high exit barriers exist, will sometimes find it necessary to operate at a loss, simply to create positive cash flow. Recall that firms can operate at a loss for so long as marginal revenues are higher than marginal costs and can continue to generate positive cash flow by slowly cannibalizing the value of their assets. High levels of investment in fixed and specialized assets then often create exit barriers and low marginal costs, both of which lead to intensified rivalry.

Taken together, these five forces can provide an excellent picture of the competitive conditions within a firm's environment. Where customers feel that they have options, and where firms are motivated to increase volume, the exercise of elasticity will lead to lower prices, provide inducements for the buyers, or both. Where customers do not perceive that they have options, and where firms are less motivated to increase volume, there will be less elasticity and so higher prices, lower inducements for customers, or both. Notice, then, that competitiveness also relates directly to profit potential. Where there is greater competitiveness, the potential for profit will be low. Where there is little competitiveness, the potential for profit will be higher.

The implication of all this is clear: firms should carve out a market space that is defensible, where competition will be low, and where customers will have little opportunity to exercise elasticity. This implication, however, is just the tip of the iceberg. Indeed, many have criticized this model by asserting that it offers little more than the simple prescription to find non-competitive positions within the environment. The problem, though, is that ongoing change in the environment makes such spaces very rare and such prescriptions worth little. There are few niches that are not subject to competition over time and few positions that can be defended indefinitely. Thus, the Five-forces model is often criticized for not being sufficiently dynamic. Such criticisms, though, fail to comprehend the full potential of the model. Indeed, understanding the five forces and how they change over time can provide powerful insights into the nature of market evolution and environmental opportunities and threats. Thus, the next section extends the concepts of bargaining power and competitiveness by exploring how they change over time.

COMPETITIVENESS AND THE LIFECYCLE MODEL

Figure 4.3 will be familiar to most students of business. It is called the industry or product lifecycle, as it depicts the common pattern by which the market for given products evolves and changes over time. To appreciate its utility, it is important to understand some of the model's basic features. First, there are two axes: the horizontal axis is time and the vertical axis is sales volume. Second, the function itself is a curve, upward sloping in the beginning, flat or nearly flat at the top, and then tapering off at the end. Finally, this curve is generally divided into stages. Some schemes will use four stages, others will use five. However, the progression of stages

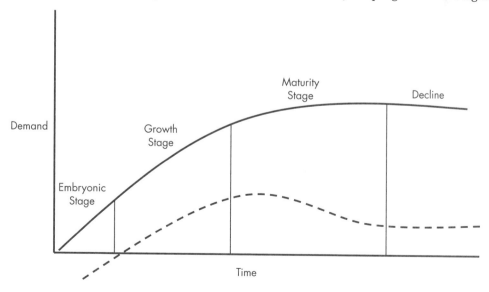

FIGURE 4.3 The Product/Industry Lifecycle

always follows the same pattern. First, there is an initial, startup phase, during which time the new product is introduced. Second, there is a growth phase, where product/industry standards begin to emerge, standardization in manufacturing and delivery begins to proliferate, and acceptance and demand grow. Then, there is some sort of maturation period, where supply catches up with demand, where overcapacity begins to emerge, and where the growth in sales volumes begins to flatten. Ultimately, there is some period beyond maturation, where growth becomes negative and volume actually declines. Over the course of this lifecycle, both sales and profitability follow a predictable pattern. In Figure 4.3, the solid top line is sales and the dashed bottom line is profitability.

Understanding this basic pattern of relationships provides a powerful tool for analyzing environments. Indeed, combining this model, and an awareness of the changes that it represents, with the Five-forces model, outlined above, can provide a vivid picture of emerging opportunities, potential threats, and the evolution of environmental conditions over time. Thus, rather than thinking of these two models as distinct analytical tools, it is better to see them as providing different but complementary pieces of information that, when combined, provide a more complete picture of the environment, how it has evolved, and how it is evolving.

To illustrate, consider any new product or industry. In its infancy, it would be described as being in the embryonic or introductory stage of development. Digital video recorders were in this stage of development just five to ten years ago. Typically, in very new environments, there is very little bargaining power on the part of the sellers. After all, the customers must be convinced of the product's utility and value. They must be sold on the fact that this new product is worth the investment in effort, time, and money. Given this position of general indifference, customers will have substantial bargaining power. They may try the product or not, but most will generally require some sort of inducement before buying. Sellers, as a consequence, will generally have to offer some sort of promotion if they are to increase their sales volume. Given little knowledge and understanding of the product, substitutability is hard to measure. Some will see no need for the product at all while others will see it as a one-of-a-kind solution. Still, given the newness and the variety of forms in which the product or service may come, the availability of substitutes will be difficult to determine. The threat of new entry will still depend on a number of things, like the accessibility of the technology and requisite resources. At the same time, it is difficult to determine exactly what constitutes new entry at this stage, as industry standards have yet to emerge clearly and potential substitutes have yet to materialize. Many firms, with many somewhat similar products, may be undertaking similar developmental activities simultaneously. Thus, other firms might have already "entered" but simply have not yet been recognized. Finally, given this lack of clarity about the product, the general indifference on the part of customers, and the potential variety in product features and service models, there is not likely to be great rivalry among competitors.

However, as the products gain acceptance and become more popular in the marketplace, these conditions begin to change. First, as the customers perceive value in the new products and services, bargaining power begins to shift, away from the buyers and towards the sellers. Whereas they had formerly been indifferent, customers now demand the product. As the product proliferates, it gains further acceptance, and so creates more demand. This acceptance and rapid growth in demand leads to an imbalance of demand and supply, with more of the product being demanded than can be supplied, which increases bargaining power for the sellers and decreases bargaining power for the buyers. Of course, one reason that sales of the product are growing and one reason that bargaining power increasingly favors the sellers is that customers have few available substitutes. Even if many firms are making and selling the product, there may be few available given the high demand. Such an imbalance of supply and demand, however, will inevitably attract new entrants, who seek to fulfill the unsatisfied demand. Indeed, even in cases where the technology is proprietary or where there are physical or legal barriers to direct competition, competitors will try to adapt and imitate elements of the new product, so as to capture some of the demand.

Finally, in the face of this growth, rivalry among the competitors will generally be low. With more demand than they can satisfy, firms are not likely to offer inducements to attract new customers, nor will they likely target one another's customers and prompt any sort of competitive retaliation. Instead, during these periods of rapid growth, firms typically concentrate on expanding their own capacity to meet the unsatisfied demand and working to position themselves as a desirable brand.

So long as there is more demand than supply, there is easy money to be made. However, the prospect of those "easy" profits will continue to attract competitors and to provide an incentive for firms to increase capacity. Thus, inevitably, supply catches up with demand and a balance is reestablished. It is at this point on the curve that sales begin to flatten, sales growth actually declines, and the industry begins to mature.

That maturation brings with it some new challenges. As supply catches up with demand, sales growth slows. Slowed sales growth prompts efforts at innovation in terms of product features, marketing efforts, packaging and delivery services, and so on. These efforts are aimed at stimulating demand so that it returns to the growth seen in previous periods. However, these new efforts cost money, and such new expenses often reduce overall profitability. Thus, as sales growth slows, maintaining volume becomes increasingly expensive. In addition, as firms seek to stimulate demand, they will begin to target the customers of their competition. Whereas previously there was sufficient demand for the suppliers to grow their sales without having to compete head to head, slowing demand prompts direct competition. Competition leads to rivalry, increased perceptions of substitutability, and decreased bargaining power for the sellers. As a consequence, profit margins begin to decline. As profits decline, efficiency becomes increasingly important. Customers, who are now very familiar with the product, will have several options for obtaining it. As such, they will have more bargaining power than in previous periods. As they demand lower prices, better services, quicker delivery times, and more features, so do they put downward pressure on the profits of the suppliers. As a result, these firms must become more efficient and find ways to reduce their costs, sell more products, or eliminate some competition. In light of the pressures associated with this stage, it is common to see some firms succeed and others fail.

This stage of the cycle is often called the shakeout or consolidation stage, because it is during this time that the number of firms declines, while those remaining grow through the consolidation of the industry's demand. It is important to note that the forces underlying this process are the same five forces discussed earlier. Changes in supply, demand, and the nature of the marketplace cause fundamental shifts in the balance of bargaining power between buyers and sellers. In the face of the resulting decline in sales and profits, some firms fail while others sell out to their more successful competitors. The result, though, is the consolidation of the demand and assets into the hands of a smaller set of larger competitors. As illustrated by the case of the banking industry, consolidation produces an industry with fewer but larger firms.

An industry that has substantially consolidated is said to be mature. Those firms that survive the consolidation are typically large, efficient, and able to operate on slim profit margins. Because of their size and level of investment, they typically have high barriers to exit and lower marginal costs. Customers in these mature industries are generally well informed about and somewhat elastic with respect to the products or services. Thus, mature markets are generally very competitive such that it is difficult for firms to maintain high profit margins.

There is, however, opportunity in mature markets. As industries consolidate, the number of suppliers declines, which eliminates some competition. Indeed, many firms will acquire their competitors as a part of this process for the express purpose of limiting competition. Moreover, the surviving firms, being larger, generally have greater bargaining power over their suppliers. That bargaining power and scale may translate into lower costs and greater operational efficiency. Given the size of the firms in mature markets and the modest opportunities for growth and profitability, there is generally little threat of entry from new firms.

Ultimately, as industries continue to evolve, they may become so consolidated, efficient, and competitive that it becomes virtually impossible to make profits. That segment of the airline industry populated by the major carriers such as United, Delta, American, Continental, and US Air may have reached this point. Substitutability is so easy, imitation is so quick, marginal costs are so low, and barriers to exit are so high that there is virtually no opportunity for sustainable profit. Such industries are said to be **empty core** markets or industries (Button, 2002). Empty core markets exist where substitutability is so easy and the bargaining power of the sellers is so low that there is little prospect for sustainable profit (Sjostrom, 1993).

Box 4.2
Consolidation in the Banking Industry

In 1980, there were 14,434 commercial banks insured by the Federal Deposit Insurance Corporation in the U.S. By 2003, that number had fallen to 7,769. During this same period, the total assets of those banks increased by more than 400%, from $1.8 trillion in 1980 to $7.6 trillion in 2003. No doubt by the end of 2010 the number of banks will be even lower, and yet the average value of the assets held by each of those banks will be much larger. What accounts for this pattern? Consolidation. Indeed, over the past 30 years, the banking industry has undergone dramatic consolidation.

Much of this consolidation occurred in three waves. The first major wave was in the late 1980s and early 1990s. During this time, the banking industry came under tremendous competitive pressure from a variety of external sources, such as non-bank financial institutions, as well as from internal sources, such as other banks seeking to expand (see **A Leader in Banking**, Chapter 10, p. 253). As a result, many poorly performing banks closed and were merged into healthier banks, and many healthy banks became aggressive in seeking opportunities to acquire former competitors for the sake of insuring their own survival. The second wave occurred around 1997, in response to the Riegle–Neal Act, which allowed direct interstate banking. This second wave, however, was somewhat different than the first in that it was marked by healthy banks acquiring other healthy banks. Moreover, while the number of mergers that occurred in this second wave was smaller, the size of the institutions merging was much larger. In 1998 alone there were 34 mergers where both partners had assets of over $1 billion. As a result of this consolidation there are fewer banks than there were 25 years ago, but those banks that remain are much larger and generally healthier. The third wave occurred, and is still occurring, as a result of the economic decline that began in late 2007.

Experts in the industry attribute the success of these mergers to three underlying economic causes. First, an increase in scale economies: as banks have grown larger their average cost per unit has declined. Doubling the size of a bank's loan portfolio, for instance, rarely necessitates doubling the size of the loan department staff. Thus, as revenues increase more rapidly than costs per unit, financial performance improves. Second, an increase in economies of scope: larger banks can often offer a wider range of products and services at lower marginal costs than smaller banks. Third, by merging with other banks, a bank is able to spread its portfolio of loans and deposits over a larger geographical area, thereby reducing its exposure to regional financial shocks. In so doing, the bank can lower its cost of capital and further leverage the sale and scope economies of size.

Where will this trend lead? How large can banks get before their size and complexity overwhelm the benefits of scale and scope economies? Certainly the turmoil that began in 2007 has caused banks to reconsider their strategies carefully. However, even that turmoil has led to further consolidation, as poor performers such as Washington Mutual and Wachovia faded out of existence and were absorbed into healthier rivals such as Wells Fargo and Bank of America. Thus, as long as the benefits of consolidation continue to outweigh the costs, we can expect the trend to continue.

Adapted from Federal Reserve Bank of San Francisco (2004) and
Federal Deposit Insurance Corporation: U.S. Commercial Banks Report (2004)

Box 4.3
Kroger Acquires 15 Harris Teeter Stores

On June 25, 2001, Kroger announced that they would be purchasing 15 Harris Teeter supermarkets, all of which were located in the region of north Georgia, in and around Atlanta. These stores were to be added to Kroger's 107 stores in the same region. Initially, the purchase was publicized by Kroger as a growth opportunity, and employees of the current Harris Teeter stores were assured that they would be afforded the chance to continue their service under the Kroger brand.

It was later announced, however, that Kroger would be closing six of the newly purchased stores, mostly because of their close proximity to existing Kroger stores. The remaining Harris Teeters from the purchase would either be remodeled and renamed as Kroger stores or sold for non-grocery use.

Prior to Kroger's action, the growing #2 supermarket in the Atlanta region, Publix, had been buying stores such as Harris Teeter in order to increase their market share. While some see the purchase as Kroger removing Harris Teeter from the Atlanta market, it also serves the defensive purpose of preventing Publix from acquiring these same locations. Kroger and Publix continue to remain the top two grocers in the metropolitan Atlanta region and continue to fight each other for competitive advantage.

Adapted from DeGross (2001)

With many options, a high degree of substitutability, low switching costs, and ample inducements for switching, customers have great power. Such conditions, however, are not sustainable over the long term, as they lead to persistent under-supply and, ultimately, to some sort of radical change in industry structure.

The lifecycle model suggests that beyond this point of maturity industries begin to decline. However, it is really more accurate to say that they change. Indeed, the processes of maturation, consolidation, and competitiveness create pressures on firms to find better ways to supply their customers. Those pressures will frequently lead to greater standardization in products and processes and greater homogenization of customer services and inducements. While focusing on standardization and homogenization increases efficiency and reduces cost, it also alienates those customers who value more personalized service and greater product customization. These customers are left with few good options. As a result, they become pools of unsatisfied demand, or what are sometimes called **niche markets**. These niches are small pockets of inelastic customers who want something different than what is valued by the majority of the market. Because of their inelasticity, they represent opportunities to new and innovative suppliers with new technologies and operating models. These new suppliers create new products and services that have the potential to become new "industries," and the cycle begins again.

ONGOING EVOLUTION IN THE ENVIRONMENT

Figure 4.4 is offered to depict the process by which markets evolve from startup, to growth, through maturity and decline, and into other new startups again. The figure is a model of **punctuated equilibrium**. Punctuated equilibrium is a concept advanced first in paleobiology (Eldredge & Gould, 1972) to explain the irregular but ongoing and continuous nature of biological evolution. However, it can also explain other types of evolutionary dynamics as well (Gersick, 1991).

For our purposes, it is helpful to think of the total evolutionary model as a series of sequential product lifecycles. Each grows and evolves according to the principles outlined earlier, following a recognized series of steps, with direct implication for the nature of the bargaining power and competitive forces affecting buyers, suppliers, and customers. However, over time, these very forces produce fundamental changes that trigger innovations and the emergence of new technologies, products, and processes. Those innovations in technologies, products, and services initiate again the cycle of industry emergence, development, and maturity. Thus, industries appear to evolve, changing form through iterative periods of predictable, regular, and incremental change, and brief, tumultuous, and radical change (Cheah, 1990; Nelson & Winter, 1973; Tushman & Anderson, 1986).

This process is often referred to as **creative destruction** (Abernathy & Clark, 1985), a term introduced by Joseph Schumpeter (1934) that is generally associated with entrepreneurship and technological innovation. However, its implications are much broader. Industries are constantly changing in response to stimuli that are themselves constantly changing. Customers are constantly "demanding" more for less. As they consider new and different options, so they create opportunities for new suppliers.

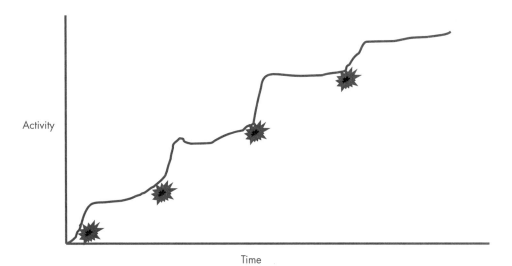

FIGURE 4.4 Environmental Evolution and Punctuated Equilibrium

At the same time, individuals, firms, and other entities like universities are constantly creating new products and technologies. Some of these find acceptance; others do not. But they all represent the potential to satisfy some customers somewhere. Personal computers, for example, were not created in response to customer demand but emerged through the work of inventors who were convinced that a new technology was possible. Radial tires, MP3 formatted music, microwave ovens—all emerged not in response to demand but from the research and development activities of suppliers who foresaw opportunities in the new technologies. As these technologies spawned new products and services, so too did the industry and the environment change, creating new opportunities, new options, and new competitive pressures.

Thus, there is a constant ferment of new products and services, fueled by the continuous opportunity for new profits, generated by the insatiable appetite of customer demand. These ongoing and continuous forces interact over the range of the product/industry lifecycle, favoring evolutionary and adaptive changes at some points and radical and revolutionary changes at others.

For example, consider a brief history of the airline industry. Though the Wright brothers made their historic flight in 1903, commercial air travel did not become a real option for nearly 30 years. Indeed, the early development of the industry was funded by the government, which saw military potential in the technology. In 1927, however, Charles Lindbergh captured the imagination of the American population with his flight across the Atlantic. Moreover, in 1925, the U.S. government began allowing mail to be carried by air. In the years that followed, several companies formed to capitalize on the new opportunity. Among these were the early ancestors of American Airlines—Pan American Airways (Pan Am), United Airlines, and Boeing. Initially, these carriers saw passengers merely as a source of supplemental revenue, on top of what they earned carrying mail.

As the number of carriers and the number of flights increased, so too did the quality of the service improve, the reputation for reliability and safety increase, and the overall demand grow. That growing demand represented an opportunity to both new entrants and established competitors. Thus, new capital flowed into the industry and revenues and profits grew. With increasing revenues and profits and expanding prospects for future opportunities, the investment in new technologies grew as well. Such investment was also fueled by World War II. All of this led to improvements in aircraft size, speed, and efficiency. The "stressed-skin" construction design, pressurized passenger cabins, the turboprop, and the jet engine were all a part of this ongoing technological escalation. Each new technology produced a revolution in competitive interaction and opportunity, offering customers more and longer routes, faster flying times, greater flying service and comfort, and lower prices.

Of course, while this all was transpiring within the U.S., a parallel cycle was developing in Europe. In Germany, France, and England, commercial air travel began in the 1920s. As it evolved and grew, so too did the investments in technology, equipment, and infrastructure, enabling the industry to expand and grow at a rate comparable to that in the U.S. Moreover, as the industry was expanding throughout the world, so too was the influence of government regulation. In the U.S., for instance, the creation of the Civil Aeronautics Authority, in 1938, and the Federal Aviation Administration, in 1958, led to standardized industry practices, enhanced public confidence, and slower but more uniform and controlled growth.

Finally, with deregulation in the U.S. in the 1970s and 1980s, the expansion of worldwide route systems, the growth of large international carriers, and the increased use of various partnering arrangements between carriers, the industry underwent another dramatic reorganization, with many carriers and service providers exiting the business through either failure or acquisition. Today, both in the U.S. and elsewhere, it is represented largely by two types of firms—either large, so-called major carriers, flying diverse fleets over complex "hub and spoke" transcontinental route systems, or smaller, regional, "discount" carriers, flying smaller fleets on "point-to-point" routes within limited regions.

What this history depicts is a cycle of ongoing evolution with periodic revolution. There have been several periods of initiation and startup, where new norms and practices have emerged in response to some radical change. There have been several periods of growth, where new investment flowed in and where revenues and profits rose. There have also been just as many periods of shakeout and consolidation, followed by periods of stabilization and maturity. Each sequence can be viewed in terms of a single lifecycle. However, together, they can all be seen as part of a larger punctuated evolutionary process. With each new revolution, the process of creative destruction removed the status quo and initiated a new period of emergence and growth, reinvigorating the lifecycle of the industry.

What Figure 4.4 depicts, then, is a series of connected and sequential lifecycles. It shows that industries are constantly changing. Sometimes those changes are incremental and evolutionary; sometimes they are radical and revolutionary. Sometimes the changes produce opportunities for new growth and new profits; at others they produce greater competition and reduced profitability. Thus, it is important for anyone who undertakes industry analysis to look past the immediate conditions and consider how those conditions came about and how they might portend changes for the future.

For example, competition in the airline industry has eroded virtually all of the profitability for the major carriers. Notice, however, that even in such an unattractive climate there are still new carriers emerging who are willing to try new operating models and to work in new areas. The low profitability of the industry has left large numbers of underutilized aircraft, offering further opportunity for innovative new entrants. Finally, the conditions of the industry have alienated some of its best customers. Those customers and their frustration over the current state of affairs provide the strongest incentive for new innovation. Indeed, numerous firms have sprung up offering shared leasing of private jets, private contract air transportation services, or pick-up and check-in services for travelers and their luggage. Ironically, it is the very state of the industry currently that is spawning the sorts of innovations that will one day produce a new cycle of creative destruction.

Cheah (1990) describes this cyclical and iterative effect in terms of yin and yang (see Figure 4.5). The two forces, the dark yin and the bright yang, are locked in an ongoing symmetry of motion, of continuous and ongoing evolution, where both are constantly evolving together in a symbiotic fashion. As one increases, the other decreases, until one or the other reaches its extreme. At that point, as represented by the dots in the figure, each carries the seed which spawns the other. And so the cycle begins and continues again.

This image, combined with the concepts presented in the other models, provides a solid foundation from which to view industry evolution and from which to conduct industry analysis. Environments and industries are constantly in motion. New products and services are constantly emerging, built on the newest technologies and designed to take advantage of current conditions and preferences. As they create superior value, the best providers derive competitive advantage and earn profits. But, like gravity, the forces of competition exert an inevitable and unavoidable pull on those profits. New technologies spring up and new competitors emerge. Customers look for better deals, demanding more for less, which provides opportunities for imitation and refinement of existing products and services. Opportunity and the potential for profit attracts new entrants and substitute products. The result is increased competition; marginal performers are shaken out and their assets and customers are consolidated into the remaining firms, which gain **economies of scale** and **economies of scope** with which to compete better.

Paradoxically, as those firms grow increasingly large, efficient, and standardized, as necessary, to meet growing demand, the most demanding customers are driven away. These customers are alienated by the emerging status quo and so begin to search for new and better options. When those buyers meet new and innovative suppliers, the seeds of creative destruction are sown and fresh industries begin to

FIGURE 4.5 The Symmetrical and Continuous Cycle of Yin and Yang

emerge. As industries emerge, the cycle begins again. In some cases these cycles are very long; in others they are very short. However, the process and the forces that drive them are always the same. Thus, by understanding these basic forces and the nature of how they interact and what they cause, students and analysts alike can begin truly to discern what an environment is like, how it evolved into its present state, and where it is likely heading.

CONCLUDING THOUGHTS AND CAVEATS

This material is meant as a general framework, a guide for interpreting and analyzing the environment. It would be a mistake to think that every industry evolves in exactly the same way or to think that competitors, customers, and suppliers are always going to be easy to identify and evaluate. Like the strategy process itself, environmental analysis can be messy and irregular. Information is often unclear and ambiguous; the various actors are hard to identify and the pace of events is hard to predict. Rather than making environmental analysis less important, though, this complexity and ambiguity make use of some accepted frameworks and principles all the more important. The concepts presented here provide some order to the otherwise complex and almost chaotic events of most environments. Thus, it is important that they be understood generally and are seen as a structure of common relationships, but also that they are applied individually to specific situations. Every environment is unique but all environments share some common features and follow some general rules. This framework and these models provide an outline for understanding those common attributes. These final points, then, are meant to highlight some special circumstances and illustrate some special issues related to the application of these models.

Hypercompetition

Hypercompetition is a term made popular by Richard D'Aveni in a book published in 1994. In it, D'Aveni describes how the evolutionary cycle in many industries, from emergence to maturity and again to reemergence, has accelerated to the point that the various stages are almost indistinguishable. Indeed, in the early 1990s, many speculated that hypercompetition was a fundamentally different sort of competitive dynamic than had been seen before. In this new dynamic, the old rules of competition and evolution no longer applied and concepts like lifecycles and bargaining power were outdated and obsolete. As a consequence, the process of strategy making was somehow fundamentally different as well. Strategy was less about competition than about creation and less about analysis than about innovation. Such thinking, however, proved to be an artifact of the time. As events soon showed, the basics of competitive dynamics and the economic realities of strategic competition had not changed in any fundamental way. Basic forces like supply, demand, and bargaining power continued to drive the evolution of the environment and the profitability of industries and firms.

D'Aveni's observations remain valid and important, though. The pace of evolution in many industries and in the environment overall is accelerating to a point that it appears "hyper" in relation to historical norms. What is important to remember, however, is that this acceleration is constant. In other words, the pace of change in the marketplace is always increasing. It is the idea that there are historical "norms" that is flawed. The speed of innovation, the pace with which competition reacts, and the intensity of market forces are all greater now than they were a decade ago. And they will be even greater still another decade into the future. One of the many challenges of doing environmental analysis is accepting that the pace of the overall process is constantly accelerating. There will always be new and exciting events emerging; there will always be a sense that the pace of change is increasing and that things were simpler and slower in the past. Thus, it is important not to fall into the trap of viewing the environment in terms of discrete categorical periods, like yesterday and today. Conceptualizing in simple categories of past, present, and future or thinking in terms of simple labels, like the industrial age and the information age, can be misleading and cause misunderstanding. While thinking in such terms is certainly easy and fine for casual conversation, it is important that we view the environment in terms of continuous and ongoing change.

Industry Definition

A key element of environmental analysis is industry definition. Yet the process of identifying and defining an industry is highly problematic. The North American Industry Classification System (NAICS) and its forerunner, the Standard Industrial Classification (SIC) system, both provide numerical indexing schemes for categorizing firms into industries. Yet, while both systems give the appearance of within-group similarity and between-group discrimination, neither delivers such precision practically.

The NAICS, the more recent of the two, was developed in 1997 through a cooperative effort of the U.S., Mexican, and Canadian governments. It uses a six-digit index to capture similarity on products and services as well as on the processes used to produce those products and services. For example, NAICS code 51 is for the business sector entitled "Information." That sector contains subsector code 513, which is "Broadcasting and Telecommunications." Subsector 513 contains industry group 5133, "telecommunications," which contains industry 51332, "wireless telecommunications (except satellite)." The system is reviewed every five years to maintain its relevance and to adapt as necessary to emerging business categories.

But even with a system like this there remains room for confusion. For example, NAICS industry number 722211, defined as "limited-service restaurants," includes pizza delivery shops, delicatessens, and carry-out and fast-food restaurants. While grouping these firms may seem logical when viewed in an abstract sense, it probably does not make much sense practically. Would the owner of a McDonald's franchise limit an analysis of his or her competitors to just these sorts of firms, or would he or she want also to include some full-service establishments as well? Many convenience stores, supermarkets, and gas stations offer prepared food for carry out. Should these firms be considered part of the same industry? How should location factor in? The NAICS takes in firms in Mexico, Canada, and the United States. Is a delicatessen in Brooklyn, New York, in the same industry as another delicatessen in Boca Raton, Florida? The problem is that the term "industry" has become clouded and confused by a number of overlapping and conflicting definitions.

For describing similar types of firms, engaged in similar types of business, and using similar technologies and operating models, the NAICS can be a useful tool. Also, for benchmarking performance levels, capital structures, or operating norms, it can be an efficient means for identifying appropriate referents. However, for doing actual strategic analysis on specific firms, a much more precise picture of the competitive landscape is needed. That is why it is important to start the analysis with a definition of the firm and its customers. Identifying the competition involves identifying those products and services which customers see as substitutes. For a McDonald's franchisee, this may encompass convenience stores near his or her locations. For a Brooklyn delicatessen, it may include full-service restaurants in the vicinity but probably not a deli in Florida. Doing the sort of good environmental analysis that can lay the groundwork for good strategy development requires understanding the competitive environment in a way that goes beyond broad and general categories. It means understanding those forces that actually affect the relationship between the firm and the customers it is trying to reach.

The Locus of Competition

The final comment then relates to the locus of competition. To understand this point, consider an old saying from politics. Thomas (Tip) O'Neill, Jr., a former congressman from the state of Massachusetts and long-time speaker of the U.S. House of Representatives, coined the phrase "all politics is local." This illustrates two important points. First, people vote on issues that are important to them personally and directly. Second, they vote only for those who are running in their particular districts or precincts. Thus, a Massachusetts congressman who is unpopular with voters in every other state could still be very successful if he was responsive to the needs of the voters in his or her district. O'Neill learned this lesson following the only electoral loss of his career, a race for a seat on the city council of

Cambridge, Massachusetts. He campaigned hard and gained considerable popularity across the various precincts of Cambridge, but he took for granted the voters in his own backyard and, as a result, lost the election (O'Neill and Hymel, 1994).

Business students and managers alike often make the same mistake when doing environmental analysis. They collect and analyze aggregated data representing broad categories of businesses, trends, and preferences. But in so doing they often overlook the specific nuances and details that affect their business directly. As Tip O'Neill reminds us, *all competition is local.* In this context, it means that competition occurs in the minds and hearts of individual customers. Customers cannot consider products and services that are beyond their reach or about which they have never heard. Even when using the internet, customers are concerned only with those products and services that fall within their field of vision and to which they have some access. Moreover, they are motivated only by those products and services that appeal to them directly.

Wal-Mart, for instance, competes in a global environment, but that environment is itself a collection of many different locations, each with its own unique set of competitive opportunities and threats. Delta is a worldwide carrier of airline passengers, but its competition occurs on each route, with whatever competitors are present to provide customers with alternative choices. Ford's success is a function of how many people find its products appealing, relative to the alternatives available, at the time of purchase.

The important thing to remember is that aggregate data are the result of many individual actions. However, individual actions are not the result of aggregate data. Thus, it is important not to focus just on data that are accessible, easy to gather, and easy to manage. So doing can lead to poor analysis. Microsoft looked just at other large software producers and so overlooked the threat posed by Linux and Red Hat. Coke looked just at Pepsi and the other soft-drink manufacturers and so overlooked the emergence of non-carbonated drinks such as Snapple and Sobe. Major recording labels focused just on one another and so overlooked the technological revolution that would spawn Napster, the iPod, and a whole new industry of music delivery systems. All competition is local and occurs around specific transactions between specific buyers and specific sellers. Understanding the environment means understanding the context in which these individual transactions take place.

KEY TERMS

Branding represents one of the primary mechanisms by which firms differentiate their products and services.

Contrived deterrence describes those investments made by incumbent firms that discourage new entrants from opting to compete. Incumbents' investments in excess capacity, altering cost structures, product differentiation, and vertical integration can all increase barriers to entry, and may also have an effect on smaller existing competitors.

Creative destruction, a term coined in 1942 by economist Joseph Schumpeter, describes the process whereby the economic structure of industries is revolutionized from within—old structures become replaced by new ones. For management, the concept suggests that only those firms that can respond to dynamic capital markets and relax their conventional notions of control and decision making can maintain superior, long-term returns.

Economies of scale describe a measure of economic growth wherein the average per unit costs associated with the production, marketing, or distribution of a product/service decreases as the number of units increases.

Economies of scope occur when the average total cost of production decreases as the number of different goods/services produced increases.

Elasticity is a measure of the rate of response of quantity demanded resulting from a change in price, with all other factors held constant. For products with high elasticity, a price increase will result in a decrease in revenue, since the revenue lost from decreasing quantity demanded outweighs revenue gains from the price increase.

Empty core markets exist when there is no sustainable, equilibrium, market-clearing price. That condition exists where capacity exceeds the quantity demanded at the price equal to minimum average cost.

Monopoly describes a market condition whereby only one firm produces (or provides an overwhelming majority of) a certain good. In such conditions, the demand curve for the firm is identical to the market demand curve. Monopoly firms will produce a quantity at the level where marginal costs equal marginal revenue. The ability to do this and the degree to which a seller has the ability to set the market price for a certain good is referred to as **monopoly power**.

A **niche market** is a focused, tangible segment of the general market that receives no or limited service from existing mainstream providers. Such narrow market segments, which tend to be either undetected or omitted by potential competitors, can be attractive targets for focused differentiators.

Punctuated equilibrium is a view describing organizations and industries as evolving through relatively long periods of stable and incremental change punctuated by relatively short periods of radical and fundamental change. These changes disrupt the established patterns of activity and provide the basis for new equilibrium periods.

Switching costs are the costs incurred when customers change from one supplier or market to another. These costs are a key factor in determining the bargaining power of suppliers/buyers. When switching costs are high/low, bargaining power of suppliers is high/low, and bargaining power of buyers is low/high.

QUESTIONS FOR REVIEW

1   Why is the definition of the business so important to environmental analysis? What are some key dimensions along which a business should be defined?

2   What is an open system and why is an understanding of open systems important to strategic management and success?

3   Describe the Five-forces model and its various dimensions. What do these forces point to collectively?

4   How can the lifecycle model be useful in environmental analysis? How might the various components of the Five-forces model change the range of an industry's lifecycle?

5   Explain the cycle by which industries grow, mature, decline, and then grow again. What are some evolutionary principles that aid in understanding this pattern?

6   What does it mean to say that all competition is local? What implication does this have for competitive advantage, strategic management, and firm performance?

7   Why is it important to define carefully the environment before conducting environmental analysis? To be most effective in the strategic process, how should the environment be defined?

8   Define elasticity. What forces impact elasticity and why is this economic force so important to strategic management?

Companion Website

For a chapter review outline with links to videos and other valuable web resources, please visit the *Strategic Management* website: www.routledge.com/textbooks/amason.

Chapter 5

Analyzing Capabilities and Resources

Assessing the Strengths and Weaknesses

HARLEY-DAVIDSON

Is there a more recognizable symbol of the American spirit of freedom and independence than the unmistakable brand of Harley-Davidson? Rarely has one brand elevated its relationship with consumers to that of a lifestyle in itself. Yet this motorcycle manufacturer managed to grow from a company that started in a small wooden shed to one that celebrated its 100th anniversary in 2003 with a nationwide ride that attracted huge corporate sponsors, well-known entertainment personalities, and people from all over the world.

Harley-Davidson began in 1903 as the dream of schoolyard pals William S. Harley and Arthur Davidson. A 10 by 15-foot wooden shed served as the first factory, and the only thing that distinguished this shack from any other tool shed was the name "Harley-Davidson Motor Company" scrawled across the door. Later that year the first dealer opened in Chicago, Illinois, and by 1908 Harley-Davidson had incorporated.

The world-famous bar and shield logo was used for the first time in 1910 and was registered as a trademark. In 1912 Harley-Davidson made company history when it sold its first exports in Japan, marking its first international sales. Its formal entry into motorcycle racing came in 1914, and on account of its dominance of the sport it earned the nickname "the Wrecking Crew."

Harley-Davidson became the world's largest motorcycle manufacturer in 1920, and the company's dominance continued into the next decade. By 1931 the only real competition came from Hendee Manufacturing, an India-based brand. Harley would later help to create its future competition by licensing blueprints, tools, and other equipment to the Sankyo Company in Japan. This would launch the Japanese motorcycle industry.

In 1969, Harley-Davidson merged with American Machine and Foundry (AMF). AMF was a sporting good and leisure product company that did not fit especially well the Harley-Davidson product and brand. Indeed, in 1981, 13 members of senior management orchestrated a leveraged buyout and took control of the company from AMF. By this time, however, the once proud organization had acquired a reputation for low quality and had fallen out of favor with consumers. Smaller, more reliable bikes now dominated the industry. Under the new management, however, quality became the theme and a complete turnaround was initiated. Over the next few years, many technological and production innovations helped to restore quality and the image of the company, which also realized that, when people bought a Harley, they were buying more than just a bike—they were buying an image and a lifestyle. This led to a greater effort in brand extension and a widening of the product line.

In 1986, for the first time since the merger with AMF, the company returned to the public stock market. The same year, it expanded its portfolio with the acquisition of Holiday Rambler Corporation, a producer of motor homes. The next major acquisition came in 1992 with the purchase of a minority interest in Buell Motorcycle Company. Buell provided a smaller racing-style complement to the company's now traditional large cruiser. A 90th anniversary party took place in 1993 and attracted over 100,000 riders to celebrate in a parade of the legendary machines.

Since the year 2000, Harley-Davidson has held roughly 27% of the North American motorcycle market and its share in the heavyweight bike segment has been even larger, and it has been making money beyond just market share. In the years 2000 to 2009, it reported an average profit of $655 million on sales that averaged $4.475 billion. While the recession has hurt motorcycle sales worldwide, impacting Harley-Davidson along with the rest of the industry, no one can argue that the brand is now a symbol of resurgence and strength and that the company is well positioned for a successful ride into the future.

INTRODUCTION TO ORGANIZATIONAL ANALYSIS

Strategic management is about creating and sustaining competitive advantage. Competitive advantage emerges when a firm creates value for its customers, some of which it captures and extracts in the form of profits. What this means is that, for competitive advantage to be realized, there must be a seller, a buyer, and an exchange that both find valuable. To appreciate this better, it is important to understand three related concepts: **use value**, **exchange value**, and consumer surplus (Bowman & Ambrosini, 2000; Priem, 2007). Use value is the subjective valuation of a product or service by a particular customer—in essence, what the product or service is actually "worth" to a particular buyer. Exchange value, on the other hand, is the actual price at which an exchange takes place. The difference between these two values is called consumer surplus. Consumer surplus was introduced in Chapter 1 and is the net value the customer derives from the purchase, over and above the price and other costs paid. The relationship among these values was illustrated in Figure 1.1 (see p. 12).

It is important to remember that consumers spend their money where they believe they can derive the greatest satisfaction (Bach, Flanagan, Howell, Levy, & Lima, 1987; Bowman & Ambrosini, 2000). Customers choose to purchase from Firm A, rather than from Firm B, because there is some reason for them to so do. Firm A, then, is in a competitively advantageous position, and that advantage translates into profitable transactions and, ultimately, earnings. As discussed in previous chapters, a portion of that advantage is attributable to characteristics of the demand and to the options that the customer has available. Thus, a portion of the advantage is attributable to the nature of the environment. But there is also a part of the advantage that is attributable to the firm itself and the value offered by its products and services. For instance, why would customers buy from Firm A at all? What is it that makes Firm A a more attractive option than Firm B or some other alternative supplier? Customers buy from Firm A because they derive greater consumer surplus from the purchase than they would from some other action. Thus, based upon Figure 1.1, Firm A provides the buyer with greater use value, a more favorable exchange value, or the best combination of both.

But how is Firm A able to do this? How does it create better use value or how is it able to provide a more favorable exchange value? What is it about Firm A that makes it more attractive than any of the various alternatives? These questions relate to the organizational side of strategic analysis and to what is commonly called the resource-based view (RBV) of the firm (Barney, 1991; Peteraf, 1993; Wernerfelt, 1984).

As explained in Chapter 1, strategy and strategic success are best understood as resulting from an interaction between the firm and its environment. Recall that the SWOT analysis, one of the basic tools of the strategic manager's trade, is simply a framework for assessing the external forces of the environment and the internal capabilities of the firm. On the external side, industry structure, competitive dynamics, bargaining power, and the evolving nature of supply and demand are the major parts of the story. However, they do not explain it all. To understand competitive advantage completely, we must also understand the internal side, how the firm creates value in the eyes of the customer and how it emerges from the ferment of environmental options to appear uniquely attractive to customers. Understanding these issues requires knowing something about the firm's capabilities and resources, hence the resource-based view of the firm.

The story of Harley-Davidson illustrates the value of the resource-based view very well. Harley-Davidson is known best for motorcycles, and most of its various products in some way or another capitalize on the image created by its motorcycles. However, the motorcycle industry is very competitive. Indeed, some of the historically best-known makers of motorcycles—firms such as Triumph and BMW—have found it difficult if not impossible to compete effectively in the face of competition from Honda, Suzuki, and Yamaha. Indeed, an analysis of the motorcycle industry, using the tools presented in the previous chapter, might well lead one to conclude that, because of the high bargaining power of the buyers and the substantial availability of high-quality substitute products, profitability would be all but impossible to achieve and sustain. Yet Harley-Davidson has managed not only to compete in this highly competitive environment, but to thrive. How has it managed this?

In short, Harley-Davidson has managed to develop and leverage a set of exclusive and valuable resources, which make its products uniquely and especially attractive even in relation to other high-quality competitors. For example, Harley-Davidson has an unparalleled history. It is one of the oldest and largest motorcycle makers in the world. Yet it is distinctly American, having been founded in Milwaukee, Wisconsin, and having supported the U.S. war efforts through two world wars. Following the 1969 film *Easy Rider*, Harley-Davidson became inextricably linked with the tumultuous period of cultural upheaval that was the 1960s and 1970s. Finally, the company itself became a symbol of the American entrepreneurial spirit during the management-led buy-back from AMF in 1981. Indeed, in the early 1980s, following the recapitalization, the company's slogan was "The Eagle Soars Alone." By illustrating its story of success with an eagle, Harley-Davidson further linked its reputation to this symbol of American culture.

But there is more to this story than mere symbolism. Harley-Davidson also works diligently to foster the belief that its motorcycles are more than simply modes of transportation. Rather, its products are branded as symbols of freedom and independence. To ride a Harley-Davidson is to enter a lifestyle of genuine expression and nonconformity. Harley owners are members of an exclusive group. To promote this shared identity, in 1983 the company developed the Harley Owners Group. The website for the group states that it is "more than 900,000 people around the world united by a common passion: making the Harley-Davidson dream a way of life." By connecting with its customers at a level beyond their simple need for transportation, Harley-Davidson is able to enrich and add value to the ownership experience. Beyond even this cultural heritage and name recognition, however, Harley-Davidson builds high-quality motorcycles that look stylish and perform well. Indeed, following the recapitalization, its products are considered among the highest quality and most innovative in the industry. Moreover, the company makes and sells a range of well-designed and appealing accessories that feature the Harley-Davidson brand name and logo.

These various strengths, capabilities, and resources combine to give Harley-Davidson extraordinarily high use value among customers. With such high use value, it is able to charge prices or exchange values that are not only higher than its costs but also higher than those of most other motorcycle manufacturers. As a result, Harley-Davidson is able to generate substantial surplus for its customers as well as substantial profits and returns for its shareholders. In essence, then, because of the way Harley-Davidson combines and utilizes its resources, in this particular environment, it is able to generate competitive advantage.

THE RESOURCE-BASED VIEW

The example above illustrates the importance of organizational resources to strategic management. Firms are constantly seeking to gain advantage and to translate that advantage into profits. In a practical sense, that means appearing more attractive than any of the other options in the eyes of their customers and thereby getting customers to spend money for their products and services. This basic contest—between rival firms for individual transactions—lies at the very heart of strategy. It is the ability to win these basic contests, over and over again, which drives a firm's performance and ultimately determines its success. To win these basic contests, a firm must make deliberate decisions about the procurement, development, and deployment of its resources. Those firms, like Harley-Davidson, that marshal and use their resources wisely will generate greater use value, provide a more favorable exchange value, or offer greater consumer surplus by providing customers better combinations of both. Those firms will then earn a measure of competitive advantage and the opportunity for profit that goes along with it.

But what sorts of resources can provide that advantage? What sorts of resources make a firm more attractive than its rivals to a prospective customer? The RBV holds that competitive advantage accrues to specific types of resources—those that meet four criteria: (1) value, (2) rarity, (3) inimitability, and (4) non-substitutability. As firms control resources that meet these four criteria, they are able to provide greater consumer surplus through either creating better use value or providing better exchange value, or both. As a result, they are able to generate more and more profitable transactions, which lead to better performance.

Value

What are valuable resources? Valuable resources are resources that consumers desire or that give a firm an ability to produce products and services that consumers want. For instance, a good location for a hotel could be a valuable resource, as it provides customers with convenience or allows them to be near some desirable destination. A good credit rating is a resource that a firm could draw upon in building efficient facilities or acquiring choice locations. A key technology could be a valuable resource in that it enables the delivery of customer service in a more efficient or more satisfying manner. The ability to provide online service, for example, is a valuable resource for many banks that results in a substantial amount of business.

It is important to understand that valuable resources are those that lead to profit-rendering transactions. As such, they can be **tangible resources**, as in the fleet of tractors and trailers used by a trucking company, or **intangible resources**, as in the reputation for reliability and expertise held by a surgical care center. In both cases, the resources are valuable because they enable the creation and delivery of products and services that customers find desirable and worthwhile. Analyzing these resources, then, involves looking beyond just the visible attributes and characteristics of a firm in an effort to discern the underlying drivers of the value that customers see. Wal-Mart, for example, is valued because of the huge selection it offers at low costs. However, underlying the low-priced products and convenient locations is a vast network of infrastructure dedicated to the efficient procurement of goods and movement of inventory. Coca-Cola also has a powerful competitive advantage, attributable to its reputation, brand recognition, and place in the memory of so many of its customers. As with Wal-Mart, though, these sorts of valuable resources are intangible and embedded in the structures, systems, and histories of the firms.

Rarity

By itself, the value of a resource is insufficient to assure competitive advantage. If every firm had the buying power and logistical capabilities of Wal-Mart, consumers would not find Wal-Mart uniquely attractive. Rather it would be only one of many identical options. If every soft drink enjoyed the same name recognition and brand loyalty as Coca-Cola, then the value of those resources would quickly diminish and Coca-Cola would have to find some other way to stand apart from the competition. Consider the fact that there are many other motorcycle makers who produce models that mimic the style and look of Harley-Davidson. Yet these motorcycles are not Harleys and so do not hold the same degree of attractiveness for consumers. The desirability or value of a resource, then, is only one of the criteria which must be met for competitive advantage to emerge and to be sustained. In addition, resources must be rare. Value and rarity together provide great opportunity for competitive advantage and profit, as they give the seller a unique ability to supply some desired product or service.

Like value, however, the antecedents of rarity are not always obvious. Take, for example, the Starbucks coffee shop in downtown Athens, Georgia. In the middle of a bustling college town, one would expect to find any number of similar such shops. Indeed, within walking distance of this Starbucks are no fewer than three other gourmet coffee shops, offering coffee, lattes, pastries, and a host of other related products, around the clock. How could this Starbucks location or any of the other competitors hope to gain an advantage? The answer lies in understanding that, their various similarities notwithstanding, these stores are not exactly the same. Each offers a slightly different location, a slightly different set of surroundings and features; each has different personnel, different histories, different reputations, and a historically different clientele. At different times and for different segments of the market, each may appear to offer a uniquely different combination of products and services, a uniquely rare bundle of resources.

What specifically are these rare resources? The answer to that question lies in the eyes of any customer who values one of these stores over the others. Some may prefer Starbucks, owing to its national presence, familiarity, and reputation. Others may prefer a locally owned shop for the very opposite reason, because it is not a large national chain. Still others may see subtle differences in the locations, depending upon which for them is the most convenient. Thus, even in the face of apparent similarity, there are still nuances of dissimilarity that can make one or another store appear rare and unique. In assessing rareness, then, it is again important to look beyond the surface, to the many attributes on which firms' resources can and do differ. Indeed, it is often in these subtle differences that the greatest opportunity lies.

Inimitability

Any resource that is valuable and rare can provide opportunities for competitive advantage and profit. Such advantages and profits will dissipate quickly, however, if those resources are effectively imitated. IBM once held a commanding competitive advantage in the personal computer business. Its name recognition and reputation, combined with its ability to make reliable PCs, represented a rare and valuable combination of resources that IBM leveraged into substantial profits. However, as those profits attracted competitors and as those competitors sought to imitate IBM's designs and reliability, the uniqueness of the IBM machines began to decline. With its uniqueness effectively imitated and the value of its product diffused among a host of imitators, IBM's competitive advantage began to erode and its profits began to fall. Ultimately, it exited the computer hardware business altogether, selling out to Lenovo of China (see Box 5.1). Thus, as computer hardware became increasingly homogeneous, the ability to appear unique declined and the opportunities for competitive advantage and profitability declined as well.

Interestingly, one of the precipitating factors of this homogeneity was the use of common components in the computers themselves. The central processors were almost all made by the same two manufacturers, Intel and AMD. The disk drives were typically made by a handful of firms such as Maxtor, Seagate Technology, and Western Digital, and memory was typically supplied by firms such as Kingston Technology or Samsung Electronics. In an effort to be efficient and to reduce their costs, many computer manufacturers became little more than assemblers of these common components. As a result, the unique and rare value of their resources and products declined. Thus, even though the production and product costs of these firms declined, the common availability of such easily substitutable products enabled buyers to bid down the price, increasing their own surplus but reducing dramatically the profits to the firm.

One lesson, then, that students and business leaders alike should bear in mind, given this example, is that **diffusion** of a core capability can undermine competitive advantage. Many firms, in the interests of lowering costs, are all too willing to outsource key elements of their processes or products. However, while the cost savings from such outsourcing can be appealing, it is important to think about the long-term implications and the potential for imitation of the firm's basic competitive advantage-generating resources.

As was the case with value and rareness, the determination of inimitability is subtle and obscured by a range of overlapping issues. For example, Sam's Cola, the

---

Box 5.1
IBM and Lenovo

A Giant Exits the Personal Computer Business

In December 2004, Hong Kong technology giant Lenovo (Lenovo Group, Ltd.) announced that it would acquire a majority stake in IBM's PC business for $1.75 billion. The deal made Lenovo the #3 manufacturer of computers in the world, behind Dell and HP. At the time of the agreement, Dell was the single largest player in the market, with a 16% share in worldwide PC sales. HP was close behind at 14%, while IBM had 5%. Before the purchase, Lenovo held 2% of the market, ninth overall, but was the dominant player in China. HP and Compaq completed a similar merger in 2002 in which HP purchased control of the struggling line of Compaq PCs, so as to compete better against Dell.

The IBM–Lenovo deal was structured with Lenovo paying IBM $650 million in cash and up to $600 million in common stock, subject to staggered, three-year lockups. The deal also made IBM the second-largest shareholder in Lenovo, with an 18.9% stake in the company, and Lenovo assumed $500 million of IBM debt.

Industry experts speculated that Lenovo's purchase of IBM was an attempt to go after Dell and its market share, although trade publications suggested that HP was in a better position to do so in America. Other experts believed that Lenovo's expertise in and dominance of the Asian market would make it a better competitor against Dell than HP, which may be forced down a path similar to that of IBM of focusing more on consulting than PC production. Indeed, many trade articles praised IBM for managing to "unload" its PC business while keeping its more profitable business units intact and in-house.

The IBM–Lenovo deal passed a national security and trade review in March 2005 and became official. After agreeing to buy IBM's PC business, Lenovo received a $350 million investment from a group of private equity firms, which it used in May 2005 to buy back 435.7 million shares that it had issued to IBM in the deal. By December 2005, Lenovo appointed former Dell and IBM executive William J. Amelio as chief executive officer and president.

---

private-label soda of Wal-Mart's Sam's Club, is an imitation of Coca-Cola. But is it an effective imitation? Well, that depends upon who you ask and how you measure effectiveness. Surely it is very similar in terms of composition, packaging, and taste. Yet there is more to Coca-Cola than merely the taste or the packaging. Thus, the attempted imitation has had limited success among those consumers who see high use value in Coca-Cola. However, among consumers who see little difference in the use value of different sodas, Sam's Cola has been an effective imitation. Blockbuster rents and sells movies and games and has seen substantial imitation of its services by numerous competitors bent on taking some of its market share and profits. Because the use value offered by providing access to movies and games was easily imitated, Blockbuster has struggled to maintain its competitive advantage and its profitability.

Understanding what is or is not likely to be effectively imitated means understanding the nature of the value that the product or service provides. In the case of Coca-Cola, that value comes largely from the brand, its reputation and familiarity. Those sorts of resources are hard to imitate. Blockbuster, on the other hand, generates value by making available movies and games in convenient locations. Imitating those resources simply requires having access to the same movies and games and having equally attractive locations or a more convenient means of delivery, such as offered by Netflix. Thus, as firms are able to develop, control, and sustain their hold on resources that are both valuable and rare, they are able to sustain their competitive advantage.

Non-Substitutability

Imitating a valuable and rare resource can be difficult. Thus, it can make sense sometimes simply to substitute it with some equivalent resource or product. The ease of substitutability, then, is the final criterion on which competitive advantage depends. Resources that are easily substituted cannot provide sustained competitive advantage because, once substituted, they lose some of their value.

Apple Computers was an early pioneer in the business of personal computers and personal computer software. Indeed, most customers considered Apple's products to be superior to the competition. Thus, those products and the resources which created them were valuable and rare. They were also difficult to imitate, as Apple kept the source code of its operating system as well as many of the engineering details of its hardware proprietary. From the perspective of Apple's management, maintaining control over the company's rare and valuable resources was a wise move, designed to prolong its competitive advantage. However, it provided an opportunity for competitors to produce products which, while different from Apple's, performed many of the same functions and so became effective substitutes. As those substitutes grew in popularity, Apple's competitive advantage declined to the point that it was almost eliminated from the industry.

The same effect can be observed in the long-distance telephone business, where newer technologies like cellular and voice-over-internet have reduced the demand for traditional services. The same is true in the steel business, where the use of electric-arc furnace recycling mills and the development of new composite materials have cut into the market share of integrated mills that produce steel from raw ore. The ability to substitute the value-generating function of a resource reduces its value along with the competitive advantage associated with it.

The resource-based view of strategy, then, views competitive advantage as arising from the differing capabilities that firms have as a result of their differing resources (see Box 5.2). As a result of those differing resources and capabilities, some firms are simply known for and identified by specific capabilities—Dell, with its online ordering and customization system, or Honda, with its reputation for high-quality engineering and reliability. Because of their resource endowments and capabilities, some firms are simply able to offer things that few competitors can match, for example Bank of America with its network of over 17,000 ATMs and branch locations, or Halliburton, with its worldwide logistics capabilities. These capabilities, and the resources which underlie them, provide firms with **distinctive competencies**. The ability of those competencies to generate value for customers, while remaining distinct to the firms that possess them, is a key to competitive advantage and profit.

Box 5.2
Resources, Capabilities, and Competitive Advantage

Sustainable competitive advantage emerges from resources that are ...

Valuable	Valuable resources are used by firms to create products and services that customers find desirable. They allow firms to exploit opportunities and to respond to threats.
Rare	Resources that are rare are held by just a very few. As such, when valuable resources are also rare, they are likely to be in great demand.
Inimitable	Inimitability simply means difficult, costly, or impossible to imitate or develop. Resources that are inimitable are not likely to lose their value through diffusion.
Non-substitutable	Resources that have no obvious or direct equivalents are difficult or costly to substitute.

Valuable, rare, inimitable, and non-substitutable resources give rise to competencies that are valuable to customers and distinct to particular organizations. These distinctive competencies form the basis of an organization's competitive advantage.

THE VALUE CHAIN

A tool for further understanding and decomposing the value-generating activities and resources of an organization is the **value chain**, devised by Porter (1985) as a means of illustrating the various categories of value-adding activities that organizations perform. Each category represents a potential source of competitive advantage. Like many of the other models in the field of strategic management, the value chain is based on a simple but powerful and broadly applicable idea—specifically, that the value that customers see, and the value that leads to profits, results from a series of distinct but interconnected activities. Consider, for example, this textbook and think about what went into getting it into the hands of the customers. First, there had to be an author—someone who actually wrote the content. But content, in and of itself, is insufficient to constitute a book. There had to also be a publisher, who would provide editorial services and who would convert the raw content into the printed and bound volume that would be sold. But, to sell the book, there also had to be a sales force, combined with a marketing effort, to promote the book and to make the users aware of its existence and attributes. Even with the book selected and ordered, there was still need for logistical support, to move the books in the proper numbers from publication, to warehouse, to booksellers, and ultimately into the hands of the consumers. Thus, even in this simple example, we can see a chain of value-adding events that begins with the collection of inbound materials, moves, through some process of refinement and operations, into sales and marketing, and ultimately to those who actually buy the product itself, the customers. These various types of activities (see Figure 5.1) are called the primary value-generating activities of the value chain.

Primary activities are those that contribute directly to the creation, manufacture, marketing, sales, and service of products and services. In this regard, the primary activities of a firm's value chain are related to the accounting term of **direct costs**. Direct costs are defined as that portion of total cost that is directly expended in providing a product or service for sale. They can be traced directly to units of the product or service and include such things as raw materials, labor, and inventory. In the textbook example above, the costs of the content, the editorial

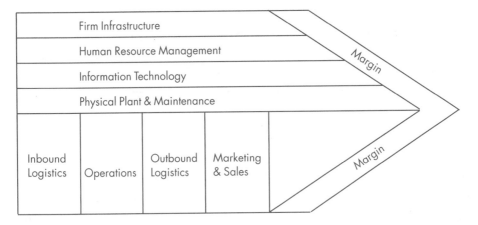

FIGURE 5.1 The Value Chain

services, the materials, the binding, packaging, and shipping, and the sales and marketing are all costs directly attributable to the total cost of each individual textbook. Thus, one way to think about the primary activities in a value chain is as those activities through which the firm incurs direct costs.

Of course, thinking about it this way makes it clear to see that it takes more than just the primary activities to run a firm and to produce and sell a product. Thus, the value chain also illustrates the **support activities**, as they are called, which maintain the firm and provide the necessary infrastructure. Just as the primary activities are related to direct costs, so are the support activities related to **indirect costs**, which are that portion of total cost indirectly expended in providing a product or service for sale. Often referred to as overhead, indirect costs cannot be traced to a given unit in any simple or transparent way and involve things like utilities, physical plant and maintenance expenses, human resource administration, and IT infrastructure. These sorts of costs and the activities that they support are essential to a firm's operation and may often be at the very heart of its competitive advantage.

Returning again to the textbook example, consider the publisher in this case. Routledge has made substantial investments in technology over the years. That technology enables many of the processes required to edit and print a textbook. However, few of those costs relate exclusively to this or any other specific product. There are also substantial costs associated with the selection, training, and compensation of the Routledge employees. These costs include administration of the retirement and health insurance plans, as well as the recruitment and retention of talent. There are costs associated with the firm's infrastructure, its buildings, the maintenance of its equipment and grounds, and the taxes on its property. All of these various costs must be paid for the firm to continue to operate. However, none of these activities or costs is immediately obvious in terms of the textbook's competitive advantage. Yet all of them are essential to putting the book on the market and delivering it at a profitable price.

The value chain, then, can serve two important functions in analyzing the capabilities and competitive advantage of an organization. First, it can serve as a valuable reminder of the various categories of value-adding functions in which firms engage. Where customers see superior use value and where firms are able to capture a profitable exchange value, the sources of that value can be traced to some combination of activities depicted in the value chain. Second, the value chain can facilitate an important analytical process, designed to identify the key success factors for competitive advantage within a particular industry and for finding areas of strength and weakness within the firm. As identified in the previous chapter, key success factors are simply those parts of the value chain that are essential for profitable competition within a given industry. By benchmarking its strengths and weaknesses against these key factors of success, a firm can assess its resources and capabilities, its strengths and weaknesses, in a way that is specifically suited to its competitive situation.

COMPETITIVE PROFILE ANALYSIS

Competitive profile analysis combines the information and insights gained in the environmental analysis with the information and insight in the analysis of the firm. While it is grounded in economic theory, the application of competitive profile analysis is really just an exercise in logic. The idea is simple: to identify, develop, and leverage those resources and competencies essential for success, given the conditions of a specific industry and environment. The result should be a firm whose resources and capabilities are configured and deployed in a way that is appropriate to the emerging competitive conditions of its environment. Wayne Gretzky, perhaps the greatest professional hockey player of all time, nicknamed "The Great One" by his fans and peers, once said that "a good hockey player plays to where the puck is; a great hockey player plays to where the puck is going to be." Christensen, Raynor, and Verlinden (2001) describe how firms can leverage this principle and "skate to where the money will be" by positioning themselves to take advantage of evolving trends and conditions. Competitive profile analysis is a tool for identifying this position and configuring the resources and capabilities of the firm to take advantage of it.

Practically, it starts with a thorough environmental analysis, as described in Chapter 4. Based on that analysis, the strategist then develops an ideal profile of the capabilities and resources needed to succeed in that particular industry. The strategist will use the value chain to map out that profile by "assigning" values to each of the various activities. So, staying with the textbook example, we could assess the competitive nature of the textbook industry and the emerging trends within the textbook publishing environment. Based on that information, we could assess the contribution and importance of each of the primary and support activities within the value chain, in an effort to discern which are likely to drive value creation and yield the most competitive advantage, both presently and in the future.

As the example illustrates, the inbound logistics function is very important. Indeed, without the right content—content that will be attractive to and valued by the market—competitive advantage will be difficult to achieve. Moreover, in addition to being valuable, content providers are rare and hard to imitate in that, once signed to a particular publisher, they are committed to that publisher exclusively and so are unable to provide content for others. Thus, the inbound logistics function is a key success factor in this industry and a key source of competitive advantage.

The next function is operations, which in this industry involves graphics, typesetting, printing, binding, and a host of other production-related functions. However, it also includes such things as online distribution, indexing, and editorial value added. These functions are an important contribution to the final product. However, they cannot make up for deficiencies in other areas, nor are they likely to be unique to any one firm, as they are often based on broadly available technologies and on know-how that can be acquired in the market. Thus, although important, their importance to competitive advantage is somewhat lower.

Box 5.3
Resource-Based/Value-Chain Analysis in the Textbook Industry

This is an example of how the two concepts illustrated in this chapter, the resource-based framework and the value chain, can be used to analyze an industry's key success factors and an organization's strengths and weaknesses.

The analysis should begin with an assessment of the environment and industry, as was described in Chapter 4. That process starts with the identification of the competitive environment. Once identified, the competitive environment can be assessed in terms of its growth stage (Figure 4.3, p. 91) and the forces which affect bargaining power (Figure 4.2, p. 85). The next step is then to assess the various general macro-environmental trends affecting the industry. These sorts of trends include such things as changes in technology and their effect on publishing, changes in demographics and their effect on demand, and changes in copyright law, nationally and internationally, and the effect of those changes on supply and demand.

The point of the environmental analysis is twofold. First, it is important to understand the opportunities and threats, the supply and demand, the growth, the competition, and the profitability prospects for the industry. Second, the environmental analysis is a key input to the next step in the strategy process, the analysis of the organization's resources and competencies, its strengths and weaknesses. The reason that the environmental analysis must precede the organizational analysis is because resources and capabilities are neither important nor unimportant, intrinsically. Their value comes from their use within a specific context. Thus, it is essential to understand that context fully before undertaking an assessment of the firm's resources.

With the environmental analysis completed, the organizational analysis begins with the primary activities of the value chain. Each activity is evaluated and given a score. In this example, the scores range from 10, which means the activity is supremely important and a key factor of success, to 1, which means that the activity is a relatively unimportant factor. The scores for each activity are subjective and based upon the judgments of the person doing the analysis, in relation to two key issues—first, the environmental analysis and the industry's key success factors and, second, their rating in terms of the four criteria from the resource-based framework. Capabilities and resources that are valuable and also rare, difficult to imitate, and hard to substitute are especially important. For the industry in this example, an assessment of the primary value-chain activities might look like that in Table 5.1.

THE PRIMARY FUNCTIONS

Inbound Logistics

The score of 9 is based on the fact that content, organization, and author reputation are among the principal selling points of a text. Moreover, because the author is contractually bound to the publisher, the relationship is both rare and difficult to imitate. Of course

TABLE 5.1 Assessing Key Resources and Value-Added Functions

Functions/ Resources	Value	Rareness	Inimitability	Substitutability	Rating
Inbound Logistics	High	Very high	Very high	Modest	9
Operations	Modest	Low	Modest	Modest	5
Outbound Logistics	Modest	Low	Low	Modest	4
Sales & Marketing	Modest	High	Modest	Low	8
Service	Modest	Modest	Modest	Low	6
Firm Infrastructure	High	Low	Modest	Low	5
HR Management	High	Modest	Modest	Low	8
Technology	Very high	Low	Low	Modest	5
Physical Plant	Low	Low	Low	High	3

substitutability is somewhat lower because a publishing company can sign only a limited number of authors, leaving others available to sign elsewhere. Nevertheless, this function is a key point of value creation in this value chain and is likely to be based upon some persistently valuable resources. As such, it receives a high score in terms of its importance to overall competitive advantage.

Operations

The score of 5 for this set of functions is lower for two reasons. First, most of these activities are invisible to the customers and have little impact on their purchase criteria. Things like graphics quality, appearance, and even cost may matter to some final users. But final users typically are not the ones who make the purchase decisions. To the instructors who do, those sorts of issues are generally secondary. More importantly, even if those issues were key to the adoption and purchase decision, it is not clear that a firm could gain competitive advantage based upon them. The reason is because the technologies and talents that contribute to operations are not especially rare. Many firms have access to the same publishing technologies, and, where they do not have access, they may be able to find comparable technologies or people who could provide substitute functions. Thus, this set of value-adding functions receives a relatively low score in terms of contribution to competitive advantage.

Outbound Logistics

The score of 4 for outbound logistics follows much the same thought process of the operations functions. While all of the various activities that go into outbound logistics—things like shipping, warehousing, inventory, and order management—are important, few really contribute in an affirmative way to the buying decision or to the margin on the product. We might say that the outbound logistics are necessary but not sufficient for the product to achieve competitive advantage. Moreover, many of the sorts of capabilities needed for high-quality outbound logistics are widely accessible through specialist vendors. While it is difficult to substitute outbound logistics, there are numerous paths and providers who offer a range of options from which to choose in getting goods and services to the customer. Thus, this set of value-adding functions receives a relatively low score in terms of its importance to competitive advantage.

Sales and Marketing

Perhaps as important as the content is the sales and marketing effort that promotes it. Here again, the contribution of this function to the competitive advantage of the text is substantial. Given the nature of the customer, the product must be promoted to get it into the hands of the instructors who are in a position to select it. Without such an effort, even good content may go unnoticed (the better mousetrap fallacy). Moreover, the resources necessary for good sales and marketing take time to develop and are difficult to substitute. They may be imitated, though, as sales personnel and marketing expertise can be acquired. Still, on balance, this value-added function contributes substantially to competitive advantage and is built upon resources that can make that advantage sustainable. Thus, this set of functions receives a relatively high score of 8.

Service

While not an obvious source of competitive advantage, service after the sale is important because of the high potential for repeat business. Instructors who use and become comfortable with a text are likely to continue using it. Thus, it falls to the service function to gather their feedback, to incorporate it into future editions, and to adjust as necessary to shifts in demand. While most firms endeavor to provide the same sorts of services, there are few ways to substitute this basic function. Thus, substitutability is low but inimitability and rareness are no more than modest. On balance, then, this set of functions receives a score of 6, somewhere near the midpoint of the range.

THE SUPPORT FUNCTIONS

Just as the assessment of the primary functions depends upon the environmental analysis, so does the assessment of the support functions depend upon the analysis of the primary functions. Having assessed the primary functions, managers and analysts can assess the support functions, looking again for the key factors that will determine competitive advantage in this particular industry.

Firm Infrastructure

In an industry with low margins and relatively high fixed costs, firm infrastructure—the IT network, the managerial decision processes, and the organizational structure—could be the difference between profitability and loss. Thus, an efficient organization, with few layers between the inbound logistics and the sales, marketing, and service functions, could be a key to competitive advantage and profitability. Of course, given the consolidation in this industry and the familiarity of the competitors, the chances are good that such efficient practices are imitated whenever they are observed. As such, they are not likely to be rare. Thus, this group of support functions rates a score of 5, in the middle of the range.

Human Resource Management

Recall that the key sources of competitive advantage in this industry are inbound logistics, sales and marketing, and service. In some way or another, then, competitive advantage rests on the ability of the people in the field to form and maintain relationships with potential authors and customers. From the perspective of the authors and customers, those relationships are with the people from the firm more so than with the firm itself. That means that HR management is very valuable, as it is this function which selects, socializes, and trains the individuals. Perhaps even more importantly, it is this function which retains them and so preserves the rareness and inimitability of the resource. Thus, it is seen as a key source of potential advantage, with a score of 8.

Technology Development

The publishing industry has seen a dramatic revolution in technology over the past decade. From simple printing and binding, the technological requirements have advanced to electronic distribution, custom publishing, and integration of online materials. Thus, the value of this function in support of the primary functions is undeniable. Unfortunately, though, the majority of the technological tools that are used are available on the open market. Moreover, even when firms do innovate, they often must make their innovations public, on their website or as a part of their marketing, and so accessible to their competitors. Thus, as important as this function is, its rareness, inimitability, and substitutability make it an unlikely source of sustained competitive advantage. Thus, it receives a modest score of 5.

Physical Plant and Maintenance

This final item is a classic example of an essential function that will likely provide little if any direct and affirmative contribution to competitive advantage. Moreover, the resources here are highly substitutable and accessible. Thus, this set of support functions receives a low score of 3.

ASSESSING THE GAPS

For each of these categories, the firm could now be assessed in relation to industry leaders or other "state of the art" benchmarks. Using the same scoring system, a manager or an analyst might ask: How strong is this firm's human resource function? Given that this function was rated an "8" in the first step of the analysis, it would be important that the firm rate highly on it. If it does, then there would be a match between a particular strength of the firm and an opportunity within the environment. If there is a gap, such that the firm is well below where it needs to be, then the analysis would have identified a weakness in the firm's resource and competency profile. Alternatively, where there are gaps in the other direction—for instance, if the firm had a score of 8 on physical plant or on operations—then the analysis would have identified an opportunity for costs savings or for the redirection of some resources.

This analysis can also be used to identify activities that should, or at least can be, effectively outsourced. Clearly, operations, outbound logistics, and infrastructure functions could be outsourced with no great loss to competitive advantage. However, other key functions, such as inbound logistics, sales and marketing, or human resources management, that lie very near the source of the firm's competitive advantage, should not be outsourced.

Outbound logistics are similar in that they are an essential function, but not a function that contributes tremendously and uniquely to competitive advantage. Naturally, while books have to be shipped on time and must be inventoried and tracked appropriately, such logistical functions rarely add much value to the text. Moreover, these sorts of abilities and functions are also generally characteristic of many firms. Granted, a publisher that is frequently late with shipments, makes mistakes in order quantities, or fails to bill for its shipments accurately will not generate much competitive advantage. However, among all the publishers that do all these things at least somewhat well and reliably, the key determinants of competitive advantage will not relate to these functions. Thus, again, while important, outbound logistics are not a key to competitive advantage.

But sales and marketing are tremendously important. The instructors who select textbooks and the students who read them are busy and distracted, with very little time to peruse the market's various offerings and select the one that suits them best. They therefore rely heavily on the sales force, on the pre-publication marketing, and on the reputation of the publisher and author. Indeed, there have been many good textbooks, authored by outstanding experts in their fields, which have failed to gain acceptance in the marketplace because of poor sales and marketing. Not only is this function valuable, it is also rare and unique. An established relationship and a good reputation are key elements of an effective sales and marketing effort. Building a strong reputation and developing those trusted relationships takes great time and effort but, once established, they represent competencies that are difficult to imitate. Thus, a competency in sales and marketing can be a key source of competitive advantage.

Finally, service after the sale is modestly important. Upon using a text, customers may want to feed back information, to see some changes in the content, to see the content arranged differently, or to have some additional supplemental material. They may ask for the ability to customize the content or to have some different delivery media. The ability to gather this input and to respond effectively to it is part of the service function and is potentially important to the ongoing competitive advantage of the text. However, it would probably not be as important as the inbound logistics or the original sales and marketing functions.

As illustrated in the example, the same analysis could be performed on the support functions, based upon the values assigned to the key primary functions. Some of the support functions will represent essential activities that must be emphasized, so as to maintain the working of the key primary activities. Others are perhaps less central to drivers of competitive advantage and so can be de-emphasized, to enable reallocation elsewhere. It is important, though, to remember that all of these assessments and values are based upon the environmental analysis. A thorough and insightful analysis of the industry and its competitive structure, including the pace of technological change and changing demographics, incorporating the diffusion of innovation and the imitation of successful practices, is what drives the assessment of the key competencies and resources that a firm must possess.

The final step in the analysis is to evaluate the firm in relation to an ideal profile of key competencies. That involves asking: How well does your firm stack up? On each of the value-chain activities, what is the real and current position of the firm? A comparison can then be made of the ideal and current scores. A gap between an ideal score of "8" and a current score of "5" would suggest the need to invest more heavily in the development of that activity. At the same time, an ideal score of "3" against a current score of "8" might suggest the prospect for some cost savings through the elimination of some resources, an opportunity to reallocate some resources from a less important function to a more important one, or an opportunity for new business through the provision of this activity for other firms.

CONCLUDING THOUGHTS AND CAVEATS

The Fallacy of the Better Mousetrap

Customers can only value that which they can see and appraise. In other words, the only products or services that can compete for a customer's business are those to which he or she has access. This is an important caveat, as many have fallen victim to the "better mousetrap" fallacy. The better mousetrap fallacy had its origins in something Ralph Waldo Emerson was reported to have said in 1871: "If a man can write a better book, preach a better sermon, or make a better mousetrap than his neighbor, though he builds his house in the woods, the world will make a beaten path to his door." While there is an appealing and equitable logic to this suggestion, research in the field of entrepreneurship underscores the reality that a better mousetrap, a better invention, a better technology, a better product, or a better service will not necessarily make a better and more profitable business. Indeed, Timmons (1999) explains that profits reflect timely interactions between the products and services that customers find attractive and a host of other contextual circumstances that make those products and services valuable and difficult for other firms to imitate. Thus, even a truly better mousetrap might be ignored if it is never noticed by the market or if it is improperly marketed to consumers who do not have mouse problems! Going a step further, it is important to remember that resources themselves are not valuable intrinsically. Their value derives from their use and the contextual conditions in which they are employed.

Consider Lincoln Electric, a company based in Cleveland, Ohio, with a long history of success. For much of the twentieth century, Lincoln Electric dominated the welding business in the U.S., becoming one of the most profitable and frequently imitated firms in the entire country. The key resource on which it built its success was its unique piece-rate compensation system, which allowed it to achieve productivity rates double or better those of its competitors but still link product quality directly to the efforts of specific employees. As a result, Lincoln's welders were often less expensive while still being more reliable than its competitors. For Lincoln, the result was a powerful competitive advantage that yielded higher sales volume and higher profit margins. Moreover, because the system involved a variety of interconnected elements, including employee selection and retention, job design, bonus pay, and guaranteed employment, it was very difficult to imitate. For so long as the manufacture of welders remained a labor-intensive business, there were few if any alternatives that competitors could substitute for the productivity advantages that Lincoln enjoyed.

In the 1980s, however, Lincoln Electric undertook a new strategy of aggressive international expansion. In so doing, it sought to replicate its valuable and rare compensation system in its new overseas plants. Unfortunately, many of its human resource practices were ill-suited to the countries in which it sought to grow. As a result, the expansion was a disaster and the company lost hundreds of millions of dollars.

As this example illustrates, resources do not exist in a vacuum, nor are they valuable in and of themselves. Rather, they are valuable in specific contexts, under specific conditions, and in specific combinations. Resource-based analysis, then, should never be undertaken in a general and abstract way. Doing so reduces the whole process to a quest for the "holy grail." Indeed, many managers, students, and academics alike have misunderstood this very point and so have reduced organizational analysis to a futile search for resources that are intrinsically valuable, without comparable alternatives, and completely inimitable and non-substitutable. Such resources are largely illusory. Thus, analyses of that sort are doomed to frustrate and fail.

Real and specific resources should be assessed in relation to real and specific contextual conditions, just as competitive advantage should be assessed at the moment of the transaction. What is it that customers find valuable and why do they see greater value in transacting with one particular firm than with another?

From there, work backwards to the resources that enable the transaction to take place, in the context that customers are able to consider. Doing this will make the assessments of strengths and weaknesses, and of resources and value chains, much more practical and relevant to the process of strategic management.

The Ongoing Nature of Sustainability

Just as context and conditions are important, so too do those things change. As a result, resources that are valuable and rare today may be less so tomorrow, and resources that seem to have no value today might be very valuable in the future. This is an especially important caveat as it relates to the sustainability of competitive advantage. Sustained competitive advantage is built upon resources that are valuable, rare, inimitable, and non-substitutable. However, over the long term, few resources retain their value and few will remain extremely rare if they are highly valued. Moreover, most resources can be imitated or substituted, given sufficient time and motivation on the part of competitors. Indeed, economics teaches us that the presence and use of highly valued resources creates a strong incentive for imitation and substitution. Indeed, even Coca-Cola, the venerable leader of the carbonated soft-drink industry, has seen its competitive advantage erode as consumers have increasingly embraced non-cola substitutes such as bottled water, sports drinks, and fruit juices.

What, then, becomes of the pursuit of sustainable competitive advantage? Is any competitive advantage truly sustainable? The answer is that it is all a matter of perspective. Sustaining an advantage, even for a short time, is still an important achievement as it allows the firm to reap greater profits and to realize greater returns. At the same time, no competitive advantage is sustainable indefinitely. History teaches that even the Roman Empire collapsed eventually, despite its unrivaled hegemony in military, political, and economic power. Indeed, a study of more recent industrial history would show that many firms, such as Xerox, K-Mart, McDonald's, and Compaq, have enjoyed tremendous competitive advantage at one time or another. Yet they all have seen some or all of that competitive advantage erode as technology and demographic patterns changed, as consumer tastes evolved, and as competition adapted.

Similarly, some resources have retained their value for many generations. Diamonds, for example, have been considered a precious stone for centuries. The ability to control that resource has thus afforded a few firms the opportunity for substantial competitive advantage. The De Beers Group, for example, has been in operation since 1888 and, in its early years, controlled nearly 90% of the diamond market. However, even De Beers has seen some of its market power and hegemony erode. As noted on its website, the emergence of competition has led to a decline in market share, to the point that De Beers has chosen to shift its strategy, away from a "supply-driven" approach to one focused more on customer service and retail distribution.

Sustainability, then, is a fluid and continuously moving target. Firms pursue it daily, yet they never achieve it fully, as each day the challenge is renewed. By way of analogy, if the pursuit of sustained competitive advantage can be compared to a race, then it is a race that is run on a treadmill. While we can generally see those firms that are in the lead, their ability to sustain that lead depends upon their ability to continue working harder than the firms behind them. As a firm's competitive advantage persists, so is it sustained. The longer a competitive advantage can be sustained, the more profit the firm can realize from it. However, for the same reasons that there are no perpetual motion machines, there is no competitive advantage that is sustainable absolutely. With time, the friction of the market, the drag of competitive rivalry, and the burden of constantly changing tastes and technology will undermine any competitive advantage, offering opportunity to new rivals and prompting in market leaders an incentive for adaptation and change.

Causal Ambiguity and Social Complexity

As Barney (1991) notes, "firms cannot purchase sustained competitive advantage on open markets." Indeed, the relationship between competitive advantage and the resources that underlie it is quite often complex and difficult to discern, embedded in human interactions, historical endowments, and networks of tacit knowledge. Thus, achieving competitive advantage is not as simple as many would make it out to be. Rather, the link between any particular resource and competitive advantage is said to be causally ambiguous and socially complex. The process of gathering resources and creating from them competitive advantage is an imperfect one, which cannot be reduced to a simple and common formula.

Causal ambiguity exists when the connections between a firm's resources and its competitive advantage are not well understood. Under such conditions, it is difficult to know which resources produce which outcomes. As a result, the process of resource acquisition and development becomes much more imprecise, uncertain, and expensive. For example, consider a situation where comparable firms, located in close proximity to one another and offering similar products and services, do not perform equally well. As with the coffee shop example earlier in this chapter, there are a number of small variations among the firms that could account for the performance differences. But which differences in particular are the most important? The locations are not exactly the same. The employees are different and the products and services have some modest variations. The management of the firms is individual and so the personality of the stores themselves may also be somewhat dissimilar. However, even though these differences are observable, it is difficult to know just how each impacts performance or even whether any of them contributes to the performance differences. Thus, the link between the various resources of these shops and competitive advantage is ambiguous.

Causal ambiguity also makes it difficult for one firm simply to imitate the success of another. As illustrated in the example of Harley-Davidson, there is more to competitive advantage than just the ability to build high-quality and stylistically attractive motorcycles. There is also more to the competitive advantage of Harley-Davidson than just the image, the history, or the Harley Owners Group. While all of these various attributes contribute to the overall advantage, it is hard to know just which is the most important and which contributes most to competitive advantage. As a result, it is difficult to imitate the competitive advantage by simply imitating the resources.

The same sorts of principles and effects apply also to social complexity. Social complexity simply means beyond the ability of most to understand or influence. Competitive advantage is generally embedded in bundles of resources that connect to one another and to the people and operations of a firm in complex ways. As a result, competitive advantage is rarely attributable to any single, solitary resource or ability. The best example of this is that of a sports team with the best and highest-paid athletes. Such teams do not always win championships. Indeed, it is very often the case that such teams perform below expectations. Producing a championship team involves more than simply hiring the best players or paying the highest salaries. There is also chemistry, the cohesiveness and coordination of the team, the attitudes and atmosphere in the clubhouse, and the willingness to play within the system. None of these alone is sufficient to assure a winning team; yet all of them are necessary.

In the same way competitive advantage depends upon a complex interaction of resources and conditions. Southwest Airlines, for example, is a very successful passenger airline in an industry where many firms are struggling to survive. What is the key to its competitive advantage? There are certainly a number of contributory factors. Southwest has a unique and attractive culture that creates a pleasant environment for employees and customers. It has limited variety in its inventory of aircraft, which saves on maintenance costs. The route structure at Southwest is designed to serve popular cities but to avoid direct competition with the major carriers and the expensive gate fees of the major airports. This route system has very few interconnecting flights, so passengers and their luggage travel "point-to-point," meaning fewer lost bags, fewer missed flights, and fewer system-wide delays. Finally, the employees at Southwest are encouraged to have fun and are given considerable discretion in making each flight an enjoyable experience for their customers. All of these things together interact to create the competitive advantage that the airline enjoys. While any single part of its resource configuration might be enviable—and even valuable—by itself, the competitive advantage is the result of all of them working in conjunction with one another in a complex web of interacting forces.

Thus, as Barney (1991) points out, competitive advantage is not a commodity that can be bought and sold. Rather, it must be crafted, cultivated, and maintained. It must be developed with forethought, insight, and patience, as the relationships between causes and effects will often be ambiguous and the benefits and capabilities of resources will often be embedded within networks of social interactions. In short, the resource-based view—indeed, the organizational side of strategic analysis—is more than a simple recipe for gaining competitive advantage. Rather, it is a tool for understanding how competitive advantage works, where it comes from, and under what conditions it can be sustained.

SUMMARY

This chapter, on organizational capability and resource-based analysis, follows the previous one on environmental and industrial analysis because that is the flow of the logic in the strategic process. Competitive advantage emerges as organizations fit themselves into their environments. Recall that the concept of fit was introduced in Chapter 3 and was defined as the alignment of the organization's resources, its strengths and weaknesses, with the nature of the opportunities and threats within its environment. Assessing fit, then, requires first understanding the nature of the environment, both as it exists presently and as it is likely to exist in the future. With that understanding, the next step is to evaluate the organization in terms of its capabilities and resources. The object of that analysis is to determine how the organization's profile of strengths and weaknesses fit what is or what will be required for the particular competitive environment.

To facilitate and guide that analysis, strategic management offers two simple yet powerful concepts. The first is the resource-based view of the firm; the second is the value chain. Both were explained, and an example of how they should be integrated within a single analysis, called competitive profile analysis, was offered. From the perspective of the resource-based view, competitive advantage and profitability rest upon the development and use of resources that are valuable, rare, inimitable, and non-substitutable. From the perspective of the value chain, competitive advantage is attributable to a sequence of value-generating activities that can be decomposed and assessed in their constituent parts. By combining the two models, and through competitive profile analysis, we can get a sense of which capabilities contribute the most to competitive advantage and what sorts of resources underlie those capabilities. More importantly, we can get a sense of how the firm should be structured and how its resources should be cultivated and deployed to capture competitive advantage in the future.

It is important to keep in mind, though, that resources and the competencies that they enable are valuable only when applied in the appropriate context. Indeed, some of the earliest strategy literature emphasized the importance of strengths and weaknesses that were appropriate in relation to the extant opportunities and threats in the environment (Andrews, 1971). It was from this early theorizing that we derived the SWOT analysis. That framework and analysis are the basis for this chapter and the one before it. In analyzing the environment, as described in Chapter 4, we get a systematic and sophisticated understanding of the opportunities and threats, both presently and in the future. In analyzing the firm, in terms of its resources and value chain, we get a sense of the key strengths and weaknesses within the context in which the firm operates. Combining the two perspectives, the external and the internal, through competitive profile analysis provides a powerful lens through which to see and assess the firm, its strategy, its competitive advantage, and its prospects going forward.

KEY TERMS

Diffusion describes the process by which innovations are adopted and spread by firms and individuals other than the original innovator. The process was formally identified in 1962 by Everett Rodgers, who noted that diffusion occurs at different rates over the course of the introduction of a new product.

Direct costs are the costs incurred by a firm's primary activities—in other words, the activities that contribute directly to its revenue-generating activities.

Distinctive competencies are the specific capabilities of a firm that exceed the capabilities of its competitors. A unique location, a strong reputation, or a key technology are all examples of competencies that would be distinctive to a particular firm.

Exchange value is the price paid by the customer and realized by the producer. It is the value at which the purchase or the exchange takes place.

Indirect costs are costs that relate to the support functions—in other words, the activities that contribute indirectly to the revenue-generating functions of a firm.

Intangible resources are those that cannot be seen and measured in an objective fashion. Reputation, culture, or visionary leadership are all intangible resources, neither immediately obvious nor easily measured or replicated, but still very important to organizational performance.

Primary activities are those activities in the value chain that contribute directly to the products and services that customers see and buy. In the most common depiction of the value chain, the primary activities are inbound logistics, operations, outbound logistics, sales, and service.

Support activities are those activities in the value chain that do not contribute directly to revenue but rather support those functions, such as operations, sales, or service, that do contribute directly.

Tangible resources are those that can be seen and measured in an objective fashion. Locations, facilities, technologies, and finances are all examples of tangible, measurable resources.

Use value relates to the qualities of a product or service as perceived by the customers and in relation to their needs. These customer judgments about value, attractiveness, and desirability are subjective and bound to the context in which they occur.

The **value chain**, which was made popular by Michael Porter (1985), is a framework for illustrating the sequential activities in which firms engage to create value for the customers. However, it is a common and highly generalizable framework that applies in a multitude of settings.

QUESTIONS FOR REVIEW

1 What is the key to Harley-Davidson's competitive advantage? Can the success of this firm be attributed to any one resource, capability, or attribute?
2 How is organizational analysis different from environmental analysis (discussed in Chapter 4)? What do the differences in these two important analyses imply about strategy and competitive advantage?
3 What is the resource-based view of strategy and competitive advantage? What are its principal tenets and contributions?
4 Describe the value chain in general and then in terms of a specific firm. Can you articulate the functions in a practical way and explain how each contributes to competitive advantage and strategic success?
5 Describe the steps in the competitive profile analysis. How does this analysis reflect the same basic principles as the SWOT framework discussed in Chapter 3?
6 Fit, between the environment, the strategy, and the firm, is a major driver of strategic success and has been an important concept throughout this text. How does competitive profile analysis use the concept of fit to produce better strategy?

7 What is the fallacy of the better mousetrap, mentioned earlier in this chapter, and why is it such a pervasive and vexing problem?

8 Define the terms causal ambiguity and social complexity, as they relate to the resource-based view and competitive advantage. Why are these theoretical concepts of substantial importance to practicing managers?

Companion Website

For a chapter review outline with links to videos and other valuable web resources, please visit the *Strategic Management* website: www.routledge.com/textbooks/amason.

Chapter 6

Strategies for Competitive Advantage

Value, Customers, and Transactions

HOME DEPOT AND LOWE'S

Home Depot opened its first store in Atlanta in 1978 before expanding from Georgia into Florida and then into the rest of the United States. Framed around the concept of the "built from scratch" warehouse, it was quickly embraced by professional contractors as well as by the rapidly expanding "do-it-yourself" market. So successful was the Home Depot concept that traditional hardware and building supply stores were quickly eliminated from the markets in which the firm opened its outlets. The smaller regional and local home improvement stores were simply unable to compete with this superstore concept and the low prices and massive selection that it offered. As Home Depot developed its many do-it-yourself learning programs and cultivated its brand identity, smaller chains such as Ace Hardware, True Value, and Hechinger's began to disappear.

North Carolina-based Lowe's, a chain founded in 1946, began changing its strategy in an effort to respond to Home Depot in the early 1990s, converting the majority of its retail centers into a similar warehouse format. Lowe's, however, decided to refine the Home Depot model by moving away from the rugged contractor look, choosing instead to target the female segment of the home improvement market. As a result, it developed nicer looking stores, with higher-end products, while still managing to maintain similarly low prices and high levels of inventory and selection.

Lowe's chose this approach following market research, which showed that the majority of home improvement decisions were made by women. It therefore designed its stores with less clutter, more spacious aisles, and redecoration centers that focused on kitchen and bathroom design. In essence, Lowe's devised a strategy that was a refinement of Home Depot's approach, similar in some ways and yet slightly different in others. As a result, it was a strategy with broad appeal to both women and men who wanted the large selection and low price but who also found Home Depot unappealing and unfriendly.

Now, many years later, after the market for these home improvement superstores has begun to mature, it is interesting to note that both firms have performed very well. Home Depot continues to be the market leader, with over 2,250 stores in the U.S., Mexico, Canada, and China. Moreover, for the three-year period prior to the start of 2010, Home Depot had revenues averaging just over $73 billion, with earnings that averaged $3.8 billion, an average return of $.052 on every dollar of sales. During the same period, Lowe's operated approximately 1,700 stores, with earnings of just over $2.5 billion on revenues of approximately $48 billion, again for an average return of $.052 on every dollar of sales. At the start of 2010, Home Depot had a market capitalization of nearly $57 billion, compared with $37 billion for Lowe's. While both firms suffered setbacks in volume, profits, and value in 2008–9 as a result of the general economic decline, both continue to be strong competitors, with considerable resources to invest in future strategies and growth.

THE NATURE OF COMPETITIVE ADVANTAGE

The previous chapters discussed competitive advantage in terms of its antecedents and effects. Competitive advantage is the object of strategy and of strategic effort. It arises amid environmental conditions where the bargaining power of customers and suppliers is limited and where options for product substitution are rare. It emerges from resources that are valuable, rare, inimitable, and non-substitutable, and it can be sustained only for so long as those resources can be maintained and protected. It relates to customer satisfaction and perceptions of value, as, among all the various and available alternatives, firms with a competitive advantage are seen as the most attractive option by their customers. Finally, competitive advantage leads directly to performance, in terms of sales, profits, and, ultimately, firm value. But what exactly is competitive advantage? That is the topic that this chapter will address.

To understand competitive advantage, we need to recall some basics. First, it is important to understand that competitive advantage emerges in the transactions between buyers and sellers. Firms can hold rare and potentially valuable resources; they can also occupy valuable and protected market space. However, none of that matters in any tangible way until customers act and transactions take place. Thus, while it is necessary to understand the environment and the firm's resources as the sources of competitive advantage, it is just as important to remember that these things are not competitive advantage itself. Instead, the competitive advantage is the reason that a purchase is actually made. At the most basic level, competitive advantage is the answer to the question: Why does a customer choose the products or services of Firm A over those of Firm B? Competitive advantage is really evidenced only when there are profitable transactions, because it is in those transactions that customers reveal their judgments about the relative value of the various products and services competing for their attention and preference. So, when a customer buys a Honda CRV rather than a Toyota RAV-4, it is because the Honda offered some superior value to that particular customer. When a firm contracts with Dell rather than with Lenovo as its computer vendor, it is because that firm, as the buyer, perceives an advantage in dealing with Dell. When a client chooses to retain a particular law firm rather than one of that firm's competitors, it is because that client perceives superior value in transacting with that vendor as opposed to another. Competitive advantage, then, is the reason why a firm succeeds over its rivals in a particular competitive episode.

Competitive Advantage as an Interaction

Competitive advantage occurs because a particular firm has some specific value-generating capability that other competing firms do not possess or cannot immediately replicate or substitute. While this statement is a brief summary of the resource-based view, as discussed in Chapter 5, it also carries implications that go beyond the relationships to a firm's resources. For example, what makes a capability or a resource valuable? The most immediate and tangible demonstration of value is the price a buyer is willing and able to pay. Thus, to say that a firm has some value-generating capability implies that it can produce goods or services that someone is willing to buy. As described previously, then, assessments of a firm's value-generating capacity must take into simultaneous account the resources and capabilities of that firm and the valuation of those resources and capabilities by the buyers.

Buyers, however, do not exist in a vacuum; buyers have alternatives, either to purchase elsewhere or not to purchase at all. Moreover, buyers' valuations of any firm's products and services will reflect, at least in some measure, the attractiveness of the alternatives available. Where there are few attractive alternatives, customers may value a given firm's products more. Where there are numerous attractive alternatives, customers will value a firm's products less. This focus on the context in which buyers make determinations of value is the focus of the **industrial economic view** of competitive advantage, which was discussed in Chapter 4. As explained in that chapter, competitive advantage arises from conditions where the options and the bargaining power of buyers are limited by the desirability of the product or service and by the absence of suitable alternatives.

Competitive advantage, then, reflects the intersection of two sets of interdependent forces or conditions. On one side are the contextual forces and conditions of the competitive landscape. These include such things as the bargaining power of the sellers and buyers, the availability and attractiveness of the various alternatives, the willingness of competitors to offer inducements, and the ability of customers to search for alternatives. On the other side are the resources and capabilities of the firm: these must be sufficient to generate value in the eyes of the customers, and to generate that value in a unique and special fashion, if the products and services are to be desired over the alternatives. So understanding competitive advantage requires understanding that all transactions occur at the intersection of these two sets of forces, and that it is through these transactions that competitive advantage emerges.

Focusing on Transactions

Viewing competitive advantage at the intersection of the conditions in the environment and the capabilities of the firm focuses attention on the transactions through which competitive advantage actually emerges. Of course, transactions are the building blocks of strategic success and firm performance. At one point or another, all of the effects of strategic management are manifested in the stream of transactions between a firm, its customers, and its suppliers. As such, transactions represent key linking pins between goals and objectives, the competitive environment, a firm's resources and capabilities, and a firm's performance (Hofer & Schendel, 1978).

Understanding that competitive advantage emerges in this key linking event can provide a number of benefits to the practice of strategic management. Foremost among those is focusing the attention of management in the proper place. Whereas every firm needs profits to survive, profits are still a reflection of other more basic realities, such as favorable competitive conditions or the presence of valuable and rare capabilities. Thus, focusing on profits, rather than on the things that lead to profits, can be a mistake. Sales growth is another common goal among many firms. Yet sales growth too is a reflection of other things, like the stage of environmental development, a superior resource position, or a temporary imbalance between demand and supply. Thus, sales growth is also the result of other more basic forces on which managers can and should focus. As discussed in Chapter 2, a variety of different financial measures can be used to assess a firm's success. However, all of those measures reflect the basic underlying cause of performance—competitive advantage. Thus, strategic managers would do well to focus on competitive advantage, its development and its maintenance. If they are able to do that and do it well, then the chances are good that financial performance will follow.

Viewing and understanding competitive advantage at the transaction level can also serve to keep management hungry and vibrant. Competitive advantage is not a designation of superiority. As the case at the beginning of this chapter illustrates, two competing firms, with overlapping markets and strategies, can both achieve some measure of competitive advantage. And that advantage can shift, ebb, and flow through the actions of competitors, through the changing tastes of customers, and through the simple evolution of the environment. Even in those instances where one firm seems to be better positioned, or simply better managed, than another, its advantage is still a temporal achievement, earned one transaction and one customer at a time. Because the tangible benefits of competitive advantage are realized one transaction at a time, viewing competitive advantage as an ongoing and continuous pursuit can serve to keep management focused and motivated. To return to an analogy used earlier in the book, pursuing competitive advantage is like running a race on a treadmill; no position is ever fully assured and, as strong an advantage may be, there are always potential threats and always opportunities to build more.

Viewed at the transaction level, competitive advantage is less about the firm and its attributes than it is a reflection of many interacting factors. To really understand this, it might be helpful to think in terms of a sports metaphor. As discussed in Chapter 1, such metaphors can be misleading and should be used with caution. In this instance, however, the metaphor actually illustrates well the true nature of competitive advantage. As mentioned, success in business is often related to one team besting another on the field of competition. Thus, competitive advantage is often equated with winning. Yet it is important to note that one win does not make a winning season; a team can win one game and still lose the next. But because no team can win a championship without winning multiple individual games, each individual game is a stepping stone to a winning season. In the same way, no firm can perform well without earning multiple profitable transactions. And, by winning multiple competitive contests, over and over again, a firm ultimately outperforms its rivals. Winning, then, is an episodic event that occurs one transaction at a time. Performance, on the other hand, is measured both in terms of single competitive episodes and as the aggregate result of many such episodes.

It is also true in sports that games can be won by underdogs—teams with less talent, or with some apparent disadvantage in terms of setting or competitive position. As the old saying goes, that is why they play the games, because the team that is thought to be the best does not always win. In business, the same is true; competitive advantage is decided in the marketplace, in the midst of the competitive interaction among firms, as customers evaluate their options and make their decisions. And, as in sports, the underdogs can and often do win. Consider that Lowe's was the second mover in the implementation of the superstore concept. Yet its strategy was still successful, producing growth and substantial earnings. When Lowe's adopted this new approach, Home Depot was much larger, with more stores, more extensive financial resources, and greater name recognition. Interestingly, Wal-Mart was once an underdog to K-Mart, with little name recognition, little purchasing power, fewer locations, and few resources to throw into market research and development. Fortunately for underdogs, customers' decisions are not based on analysts' assessments or on measures of aggregate market strength but reflect their own individual values and judgments, along with the variety of options available to them. As a result, what appears to be an advantage on paper can often fail to translate into an advantage in the marketplace. Indeed, as illustrated by the story on AMD and Intel (see Box 6.1), firms can be substantial underdogs and yet still be effective competitors in specific episodes and circumstances.

So it is both important and helpful to understand competitive advantage as it is manifested at the transaction level. Adopting this perspective allows us to see clearly three fundamental attributes of competitive advantage. The first is that it is a reflection of value and that value is determined by the customer. Firms cannot determine for themselves the value of their own resources and capabilities, products, and services; those determinations must come from the market and from the collective actions of consumers. The second is that determinations of value are context specific, and so competitive advantage must also be a reflection of the context. Customers do not exist in a vacuum and their determinations of value involve more than just the attributes of the products and services in question. Past experience, competitive options, economic conditions, and momentary fads and fashions can all affect the context in which a customer assesses the options and

Box 6.1
Competing with Intel

AMD's Strategy to Break a Monopoly

The single most important component in a PC is the central processor, and for nearly three decades Intel has been the leader in PC processors. Intel began making these processing chips for personal computers over 35 years ago. At that time, no one foresaw the computer industry that exists today. Moreover, since the end users of computers never saw Intel's products, no one foresaw the company's evolution into the market juggernaut it has become. However, through relentless effort in the area of product innovation, and through some innovative marketing practices, Intel has become a dominant force in the PC business and one of the most recognized brands in the industry.

Intel's closest rival is Advanced Micro Devices, or AMD. Although AMD entered the industry at about the same time as Intel, it is only about one-tenth as large. Indeed, so strong was Intel's market presence and competitive advantage that it had a partnership with virtually every PC manufacturer and retail outlet, and in effect every end user knew the names of its processors. In trying to compete, AMD was often left to work around the margins, taking what business it could when Intel was unable to fill the demand. Nevertheless, there have been instances where this balance of power has shifted to favor AMD.

For example, AMD launched its "War in the Store" initiative and managed to compete successfully with Intel. Rather than concentrating on marketing and brand recognition, AMD focused on features and variety, offering more products, greater accessibility, and better functionality. Initially, some executives and market analysts were skeptical of the new approach. But the results showed that the plan could work, as AMD's worldwide share of mainstream microprocessors rose from 5.7% in 2004 to 15.3% in 2005.

For many years, speed was the only basis on which processors were evaluated, and for most of that time Intel was a step ahead of the competition. However, part of AMD's new initiative was developing chips that outperformed Intel on other measures. For example, AMD processors used less energy and were smaller in size, which was significant to customers with large banks of servers packed into relatively small spaces. AMD's high-end, multi-core processors were also engineered to run existing software, lowering the costs of installation. By comparison, Intel's server processors were larger, ran hotter, and required software adjustments to take full advantage of their speed. As a result, AMD was able to capture more of the U.S. server-chip and multi-core processor markets.

AMD channeled millions of dollars from these businesses into the retail market, in the form of rebates, in-store promotions, employee training, and advertising. And, when Intel faced a shortage of components and kept aside key components for its closest partners, AMD was quick to respond by sending its top sales people to those competitors irked by Intel's actions. As a result, AMD-based desktops gained considerable ground.

Adapted from Edwards (2006)

makes the decision to buy. Finally, because value is a reflection of context, competitive advantage must be episodic. In other words, competitive advantage occurs in specific competitive episodes, where the specific desires and tastes of buyers and the particular capabilities and resources of sellers meet, amid the ferment of contextual forces described earlier in the text. As any of these conditions, whether for the buyer, the seller, or the context, change, so too is the nature of the competitive advantage likely to change.

Determined by the Customer

As discussed in the previous chapter, the resource-based view holds that competitive advantage emerges from resources that are valuable, rare, inimitable, and difficult to substitute. However, value is a function of **scarcity**. Scarcity simply means an insufficient supply to meet the existing demand. When something is scarce, there is not enough of it to go around. What is important to note about scarcity, then, is that it reflects information about both supply and demand. Valuable resources must be scarce resources. Thus, valuable resources must also be resources that are demanded and demanded in meaningful amounts. So resources cannot be intrinsically valuable; rather, their value is defined by a combination of their desirability and their availability. The same is also true for products and services; their value is reflected by the willingness of customers to pay for them.

If there is a weakness in the resource-based view, it is this apparent **tautology** (Priem & Butler, 2001). Specifically, competitive advantage is thought to be a reflection of resource value. However, it is the ability of any resource to produce profitable transactions that makes it valuable in the first place. Thus, while the value of a resource is what leads to competitive advantage, it is also the ability of that resource to generate competitive advantage that makes it valuable. As a result, it is impossible to identify reliably valuable resources *a priori* because value is manifested only through the resource's use. As a practical matter, then, value is determined by the customer, as it is customers who decide what is valuable to them and so what they will use and buy.

While fine-grained definitional issues like this are of more interest to researchers than to managers or students, the point is important nevertheless. Specifically, the pursuit of competitive advantage is about generating value for customers, not about the pursuit of special and uniquely valuable resources, products, or services. Resources are merely a means to an end; value to the customer is the end itself. Practically speaking, then, the challenge is to acquire and utilize resources that will create products and services which customers will value and for which they will pay.

What makes this so especially challenging is that customers' tastes vary and change. So creating products and services that customers will find valuable can seem like trying to hit a moving target. Creating value is challenging as well because a host of other competitors are all seeking to do the same thing and are often seeking to do it in the same way. On top of that, selling products or services inevitably involves making at least some part of those products and services available for observation, inspection, and refinement. In creating competitive advantage for themselves, firms often must provide for their competitors the very example by which those competitors can later challenge them. Creating value is a challenge because much of the money and effort associated with product and service development must be invested prior to the introduction to the market. The pursuit of competitive advantage is therefore an ongoing effort of trial and error, learning and adaptation, where customers are ultimately the arbiters of success, choosing which products, which services, and which resources are, in fact, the most valuable and which firms will have the greatest competitive advantage as a result.

A Reflection of Context

It is the reality of these shifting conditions that makes this second tenet so important. Customers reveal their determinations of value and their judgments about competitive advantage in their purchases. However, those purchases are influenced by more than just characteristics of the products or services. They are also influenced by the conditions in which those purchasing decisions take place. Economists note that **demand curves**, the mathematical functions that are used to illustrate the relationship between consumption and price, often shift in response to such things as changes in customer tastes, changes in overall economic conditions, and the availability of substitutes. Shifts in the demand curve reflect a fundamental alteration in the value that customers see in a particular product or service.

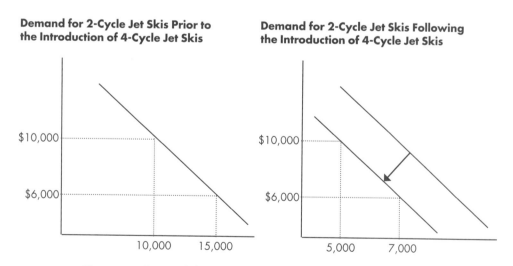

FIGURE 6.1 Changes in Context/Changes in Demand

For example, Figure 6.1 provides an illustration of a demand curve, showing the relationship between the price and quantity of jet skis, with 2-cycle engines, purchased in a particular region of the country during a given season. In the first instance, the prices range from $10,000 and $6,000 and the level of consumption varies between 10,000 and 15,000 units. Of course, the price and consumption levels reflect other sorts of differences as well. The more expensive units may be the ones with the larger engines, more advanced instrumentation, or a better brand name. Similarly, the less expensive units may be the "starter" models, with fewer features, smaller engines, or shorter warranties. The aggregate of these differences, though, is the demand curve illustrated. Given the income level of the consumers, the costs of the suppliers, and the relative supply and demand, this curve illustrates the collective valuation of the products by the market and prices that customers are willing to pay.

Consider, though, how that function changed shape with the introduction of 4-cycle jet skis. These newer machines were, in the eyes of most users, technologically superior to the older ones. They were quieter, with lower emissions, better gas mileage, and more power. As a result, many of those buyers and potential buyers who had formerly purchased, or formerly wanted to purchase, the 2-cycle machines no longer valued them at the same level. Thus, the new demand function shows lower overall demand, ranging between 5,000 and 7,000 units, even though the prices across all the various models remained essentially the same. In essence, a technological change had shifted the demand curve, altering the nature of the relationship between the buyers and the sellers of the 2-cycle machines. What is important to notice, though, is that this shift was completely **exogenous** to the relationship between the buyers and the sellers. In other words, it had nothing to do with the buyers or with the products; instead, this change was caused by forces outside of the relationship between the buyers and the sellers and thus was simply a part of the context.

This sort of contextual force influences the nature of competitive advantage by influencing the value that customers place on particular products or services. Consider the most obvious case from the previous example: those firms that introduced the 4-cycle machines would find their competitive advantage strengthened, while those firms that were late in introducing 4-cycle machines would see their competitive advantage eroded. However, it is possible to take this example one step further and to imagine the reaction of the firms whose advantage was eroded. Having seen the demand for their products decline and the value of their products reduced in the eyes of the customers, these firms would want naturally to invest their own efforts in imitating the innovations of their competitors by introducing their own 4-cycle machines. This sort of ebb and flow, between buyers and sellers and across competitors, reflects the ongoing ferment of the environment, discussed in Chapter 4. New technologies, new competitors, new products and services, changes in consumer tastes and in societal fashions, shifts in demographic patterns, and changes in the economy all affect the context within which customers judge and value various products and services. As a result, all of these sorts of changes affect competitive advantage.

Underscoring further the points in Chapter 4, that is why it is so important to approach environmental analysis from a dynamic perspective. Indeed, if there is a weakness in the way that environmental analysis is typically understood, it is the failure to take into account the dynamic and ongoing nature of change. Context matters to competitive advantage, and context is always evolving and changing. The bargaining power of the buyers and sellers, which is driven by how badly either group needs or wants a specific transaction, affects the value that customers place on a given product or service. Thus, shifts in any of the conditions that affect bargaining power will affect competitive advantage. The level of rivalry among competitors, which is driven by the relative level of supply and demand and the willingness of competitors to target one another's customers, will affect the value that customers place on a given product or service and so will affect competitive advantage. Even the ease with which new firms can enter the industry affects competitive advantage by imposing a time limit on the exclusivity of a firm's offerings.

Episodic

Because competitive advantage occurs at the intersection of dynamic forces and conditions within the environment and the firm, each occurrence is episodically specific. In other words, it is possible that competitive advantage can occur in a particular instance where a firm produces a valued and rare product or service which has no immediate substitute and which attracts the value and demand of customers, but which does not occur again. So in each competitive episode the battle for competitive advantage is renewed. In each instance, customers are presented with potentially new and different sets of options from which they must choose. And, in each instance, firms are revising their offerings, developing and acquiring new resources and new capabilities, imitating one another's successes, and learning from the successes and failures of previous episodes. As a consequence, every competitive episode is essentially unique because, with each iteration, some of the variables on either side of the transaction change, even if only modestly.

What this means is that no competitive advantage is safe. Moreover, no disadvantage is insurmountable. Nokia and Ericsson came from positions of relative obscurity to take much of the cell phone market from Motorola. Yet neither firm has been able to prevent the rapid growth and success of LG, Samsung, and Apple. Even Microsoft, with its enormous cache of talent, money, and motivation, could not prevent the rise of Linux as a competing and often favored product. The reason is because each competitive episode occurs as specific customers, with specific needs, go into the marketplace in search of the best value. As they do, they encounter unique and finite sets of options, products, and services with specific attributes and features, at specific prices and terms, offering a particular level of value to particular customers. Customers choose the option that, to them, appears to offer the greatest value, the greatest surplus, and the greatest advantage. That chosen supplier, then, in the mind of that customer and in economic fact, was competitively advantageous. However, the advantage exists only for so long as that set of conditions continues to exist. Any change, on the part of the customer, on the part of the firm, or on the part of the exogenous context, can affect that advantage and so can have real and tangible effects on the performance of the competing firms.

Understanding and learning to manage the episodic nature of competitive advantage is at the heart of what is called the **dynamic capabilities** perspective. More will be said about this later in this chapter. For now, though, it is enough simply to know that competitive advantage emerges through the interaction of two dynamic conditions or forces—the conditions or forces in the environment and those within the firm. As a consequence, competitive advantage itself is highly dynamic and subject to change. The pursuit of competitive advantage, therefore, is an ever changing, ever adapting, and continuously ongoing challenge.

TYPES OF COMPETITIVE ADVANTAGE

Traditionally, scholars in the field of strategic management have distinguished between different types of competitive advantage. For example, Porter (1980) outlined three fundamental approaches to competitive advantage: focus, low cost, and differentiation. Inasmuch as every firm sought competitive advantage, and because competitive advantage was achieved through one of these basic means, these three approaches were labeled and are still referred to as **generic strategies**. Viewing these three generic strategies at the transaction level can help us to understand how and why they actually function and what each means for buyers, sellers, and the ongoing pursuit of competitive advantage.

Focus

To begin, it is important to remember that, in every purchase, customers, acting rationally as best they can and in their own best interests, seek the best value. As defined earlier in the text, the best value simply means the greatest level of consumer surplus. Where the use value of a product or service is sufficiently high, even a high price can yield high consumer surplus. At the same time, even if the use value is low, a sufficiently low price can still yield high consumer surplus. Thus, value to the customer should not be perceived as meaning any particular level of quality or any particular level of price. Instead, value to the customer is the difference between overall use value and the total cost of the transaction. Total value to the customer, then, is synonymous with consumer surplus, and consumer surplus is a reflection of both the level of use value and the cost of the transaction. Given this, we can categorize competitive advantage by the way in which a firm seeks to increase consumer surplus: either by targeting use value or by targeting the cost of the transaction. Where the use value for a firm's products and services is sufficiently high, firms can make profitable transactions even when their costs are high. Alternatively, firms can work to reduce their costs and, by so doing, can gain the ability to make profitable transactions even when the use value of their products or services is not especially high.

More will be said about each of these conditions in a moment. For now, though, what is important to notice is that both sets of conditions are specific to a particular group of customers or to some subset of the overall market. Creating high use value can mean targeting and segmenting a particular set of preferences, specific to a particular set of customers. Returning to the jet ski example, not everyone has need or desire for a jet ski. Moreover, even among those who do, different buyers will be attracted to different things. Some will value speed while others will value reliability and the assurance of a warranty. Some may want styling or the ability to carry more passengers. The point, though, is that creating high use value for any of these groups requires *focusing* on the preferences they value. In the same way, firms that seek competitive advantage by endeavoring to reduce their costs must still be the most attractive option relative to the available alternatives. Thus, such firms must provide value to these customers, not by focusing on specific tastes and preferences but by becoming the best choice, within the context of the options available. In every case, then, the pursuit of competitive advantage requires an element of focus. Focus is less a generic strategy and less a source of competitive advantage than a characteristic of every strategy that leads to competitive advantage.

Every successful strategy has some measure of focus. That focus will be either on the unique preferences of a specific group of customers or on a specific space within a market where a firm believes its products and services appear as the best option among many alternatives. Thus, as illustrated in Figure 6.2, focus transcends the other generic strategies, as every strategy and every competitive advantage,

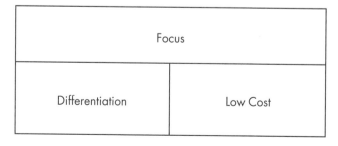

FIGURE 6.2 Porter's Three Generic Strategies and Types of Competitive Advantage

whether cost based or differentiation based, will have some degree of focus. The challenge is to match the degree of focus appropriately to the segment of the market and to the type of competitive advantage that is being pursued.

Differentiation

One path to competitive advantage is through increasing use value. By focusing on use value, a firm can increase the desirability of its products and services, even when the prices of those products or services are high. Consider the example of Breitling watches. Breitlings are designed to appeal to a particular group of customers—those with some affinity for or connection to aviation. They are styled in a particular way so as to appeal to such customers. They are marketed in a particular fashion, again to catch the eye of those particular customers. And they are advertised through their affiliation to prominent individuals and organizations connected to flying. Thus, they are watches that are made for and sold to a particular group of individuals who value this particular styling and this particular appeal.

At the same time, this relatively small, relatively homogeneous, and relatively wealthy group of individuals has few options for this type of watch. There are few other watchmakers who have the same sort of styling and offerings. More importantly, there are few other watchmakers who have invested the necessary time and effort to cultivate a reputation as the preferred maker of aviation watches. Thus, there are few if any other makers who can offer the level of use value to customers who value this sort of watch as Breitling. Indeed, as Breitling stimulates interest with its advertising, and as customers become attracted to this type of watch and so begin considering their options for buying one, they will often find that Breitling is one of only a very few alternatives. As a result, those buyers are likely to be highly **inelastic**.

Understanding differentiation-based competitive advantage requires understanding **elasticity**. As it was described in Chapter 4, elasticity is simply the sensitivity of demand to the cost of acquisition. Inelastic customers have very little bargaining power, see very few substitutes, and are not likely to be swayed by new or alternative products. For these customers, there is one preferred option and one preferred supplier. That supplier, then, can be thought of as having **monopoly power** over those particular buyers. For example, consider that different people have different soft-drink preferences. Some prefer Coke strongly, some prefer Pepsi strongly, still others prefer different sorts of drinks altogether. However, for those who prefer Coke strongly, small differences in price or in packaging, advertising, or placement will make little difference. Indeed, these customers are not likely to care about taste-test results or about which drink is winning the battle for market share. They simply know that they prefer Coke. So, for them, there is no real competition between the two major suppliers. Coke is the monopoly provider, *de facto*, for this group of buyers. As a result, these buyers are inelastic, unwilling to consider other options, unwilling to substitute any other product for their favorite, and unwilling to entertain competition for their purchases.

As illustrated in Figure 6.3, this sort of inelasticity enables those firms that supply such preferred products and services to charge premium prices. Breitling watches are much more expensive than the average watch and Coke is more expensive than any number of other no-name brand sodas. Yet, because of their inelasticity, customers are willing to pay premium prices for these products or are willing to expend more time and energy in the search for them. The higher cost notwithstanding, if the use value is sufficiently high, customers will still derive greater surplus from purchases that satisfy their preferences. The strategy of differentiation, then, is one that seeks to create competitive advantage through the cultivation of high use value, inelasticity, and monopoly power for the specific provider.

As with all things, however, this is easier said than done. Developing that sense of preference requires finding and focusing on a particular segment of the market. It requires understanding the preferences and desires of that group of buyers sufficiently well to create for them the sort of products and services that they will value highly. It requires creating a sense of exclusivity, where those customers will see the particular firm as the one best option for this type of purchase, to the exclusion of other alternatives and potential substitutes, even when those other alternatives and substitutes are less expensive. It requires the creation and delivery of products and services that are in fact of sufficient quality to make good on the appeal of the image and the advertising. Finally, it requires being able to price these products at a point that is sufficiently high to provide a good return, despite the costs of

Premium Price
Consumers are
Willing to Pay

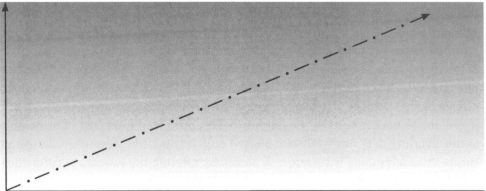

Consumers are
Completely
Indifferent

Consumers
Will Accept
Only One

FIGURE 6.3 Elasticity and Price

development, marketing, and placement, but that is not so high that it creates a disincentive for customers. Differentiation, then, is a strategy that necessitates higher costs but that yields high margins, by creating higher use value for the customer.

Low Cost

The explanation of differentiation-based competitive advantage reflecting customer inelasticity begs the question: What sort of competitive advantage reflects customer elasticity? Not surprisingly, the answer is low-cost-based competitive advantage. Understanding this type of competitive advantage requires imagining those instances where customers see no discernible difference in and have no particular preference among the various suppliers of the desired product or service. In essence, they are indifferent among the alternatives. This indifference gives such customers great bargaining power. They can play one provider against another; they can also simply walk away and purchase some substitute product or service instead. Because customers are indifferent, the product or service in question becomes a **commodity**. When customers see very few differences in the use value derived from any particular provider, they maximize their consumer surplus by purchasing at the lowest overall cost.

It is important to note, however, that the lowest overall cost means more than simply the lowest purchase price. This oversimplification has led to great misunderstanding of low-cost competitive advantage and the sort of strategic actions that a company can take to achieve it. For example, consider that most consumers view gasoline as a commodity; most see few if any real differences in the use value derived from various providers of gasoline. As such, most consumers buy based upon the lowest price. No one, however, would drive across the country to save a dollar a gallon, nor would many be willing to drive across town to save 20 cents per gallon. Rather, customers place some value on their time and on the energy and effort required to make the purchase. The total cost of the acquisition, then, involves the price, the search time, and a number of other factors. In purchasing a new piece of machinery or in buying a new computer system, a procurement officer might consider the reliability and the cost of the repairs, along with the initial out-of-pocket costs of the hardware. This perceived **total cost of ownership** is the figure that is most relevant to low-cost competitive advantage. Low-cost competitive advantage is therefore achieved by offering the lowest cost of ownership to customers who see identical or nearly identical use values across the range of comparable products or services.

As with differentiation, achieving competitive advantage in this fashion is easier said than done. Indeed, achieving low-cost competitive advantage is a challenge because, by its very nature, it involves creating value for customers who are largely indifferent and **elastic**, and so have substantial bargaining power. The challenge is to be the best option to those customers, despite their willingness to consider other options. Wal-Mart, for instance, is recognized for its strong low-cost competitive advantage. Everything that the firm does is designed around the elasticity of its buyers. Wal-Mart's prices are very low. If it is not the absolute lowest on all the items it carries, it is certainly very near the lowest. Wal-Mart also carries an enormous inventory. While most if not all of the things that it sells are available elsewhere and from other providers, few if any of those providers carry the full variety of things that Wal-Mart carries. Finally, Wal-Mart stores are virtually everywhere. With over 3,000 locations, a Wal-Mart is within easy reach for the vast majority of consumers throughout the U.S. Thus, because its inventory is so vast, because its prices are so low, and because its locations are typically so convenient and accessible, Wal-Mart is the lowest-cost option for most consumers. Indeed, rather than drive around, searching for and comparing prices on a wide range of different items, most consumers simply choose to buy from Wal-Mart. They do so because of the convenience of knowing that the store will have what they want and will have it at or near the lowest available lowest transaction cost.

A number of things about this example are worth noting, however. First, it is important to note that none of this happens by accident. Wal-Mart has deliberately set out to be the best choice for elastic consumers. Thus, it has invested enormous amounts of resources in the development of systems for managing its vast stocks of inventory. It has matched that system to a network of stores that serve as both customer outlets and market research centers, gathering data on what customers do and do not value. It has deliberately sought to position its stores in the path of customers and in such a way as to facilitate convenience and ease. Wal-Mart, then, has aggressively cultivated the message that it is, at once, the best one-stop shop, with the easiest access, the widest array of options, and the lowest prices. Thus, it has deliberately set out to become the best option to customers who are highly elastic and so willing to consider options.

The second observation from this example is an extension of the first: specifically, because Wal-Mart knows that its customers are elastic, it also appreciates that those customers are willing to seek out and consider other options. Indeed, Wal-Mart's customers were once customers of K-Mart, Walgreens, Sears, and others. Yet it was their elasticity that brought them to Wal-Mart. Because it offered them a better deal, in the form of a lower overall cost of acquisition and ownership, these customers left the other suppliers and came to Wal-Mart. By their very nature, then, these customers could just as easily move away from Wal-Mart if and when a better lower-cost option becomes available. So, sustaining its advantage requires that Wal-Mart be relentless. It must understand that customers come to Wal-Mart not because of high use value but because the store provides a common level of use value at the lowest possible cost. Thus, Wal-Mart can provide the most consumer surplus only for so long as it remains the lowest cost alternative.

The low-cost strategy, then, seeks competitive advantage by being the lowest total cost option to elastic customers. Even where the use value associated with a particular seller is no greater than the use value associated with any other seller, a firm can still gain competitive advantage by offering the lowest cost of ownership, thereby maximizing consumer surplus to the buyer. Such a strategy will necessarily involve very low margins and so necessitate that the firm has very low costs. Moreover, achieving and sustaining this sort of competitive advantage is a relentless challenge. Success with a low-cost strategy involves becoming the best option for customers who are elastic and largely indifferent across the range of sellers. These customers have little if any true loyalty and will be willing to move around in search of the best options. Thus, keeping them satisfied requires persistence and ongoing effort.

DIFFERENTIATION, LOW COST, AND PERFORMANCE

It should go without saying that, in the right context, both differentiation and low-cost-based strategies can lead to competitive advantage and financial success. Of course, which of these two basic strategies is most effective depends upon the nature of the environment and the resources and capabilities of the firm. Moreover, because of the various and fundamental differences in these two strategies and these two types of competitive advantage, each will produce different sets of operational imperatives and different patterns of financial success.

To appreciate this, compare two firms such as Target and Nordstrom. Both are performing well, with growing revenues and profits. However, these firms are pursuing somewhat different strategies and different types of competitive advantage. Nordstrom's competitive advantage is built largely on differentiation, with high-quality, designer merchandise, upscale locations, and top-notch service. Nordstrom seeks to cultivate bargaining power over its buyers by being a destination of choice that is valued despite the presence of alternative providers offering lower prices. Target, on the other hand, has a competitive advantage oriented more towards low cost. With a much larger inventory and much greater variety in that inventory, it seeks to appeal more broadly to elastic customers as the best choice for a range of staple items. It is important to note that, while Nordstrom is not the most highly differentiated provider in its industry, and while Target is not the lowest cost of all providers, the distance between them and the implications of their different strategies is still evident in a comparison of some financial and operational data (see Table 6.1).

Target is clearly much larger than Nordstrom, reflecting its broader focus and appeal. At the same time, sales and earnings per square foot for Target are both substantially lower than they are for Nordstrom. Coupled with the fact that Target's inventory turns over more quickly, these differences reflect the fact that Nordstrom

Table 6.1

Nordstrom and Target: Comparing Low-Cost and Differentiation Strategies
(based on year end data, 2009)

Nordstrom	Target
$8.258 billion/187 stores = $44,160,248 (sales per store)	$65.357 billion/1,698 stores = $38,490,577 (sales per store)
Net income $441 million/ROS 5.1%	Net income $2.49 billion/ROS 3.8%
Store sales/profit per square foot = $368/$19.50	Store sales/profit per square foot = $289/$10.60
SGA % of sales = 29.8%	SGA % of sales = 20.5%
Inventory turnover = 5.76	Inventory turnover = 6.54
Average sq. ft. per store 120,000	Average sq. ft. per store 132,786

charges substantially higher prices and likely carries substantially more customized and expensive inventory. It is also interesting to compare the two companies on selling, general, and administrative (SG&A) expenses as a percentage of sales. For Target, SG&A expenses are 20.5% of sales; for Nordstrom they are 29.8% of sales. Thus, Target is able to leverage greater sales volume off of its overhead than Nordstrom. Yet, in terms of profitability, as a percentage of sales, Nordstrom produces a return on sales of 5.1%, which is higher than Target's 3.8%.

This simple comparison illustrates how both strategies, differentiation and low cost, can be successful but for different reasons. Low cost necessitates a relentless focus on efficiency, standardization, high volume, and low average costs. It is no accident, then, that Target has high inventory turns. Target strives to increase the efficiency in its supply chain, to move items into and out of the system quickly, so as not to incur unnecessary costs. It is no accident that it has enormous square footage, with nearly 1,700 locations averaging over 132,000 square feet. With the purchasing power of its enormous scale, the variety of products in its inventory, and the ability to move those products quickly and efficiently through its supply chain and stores, Target is able to appeal to a vast market of elastic customers. As a result, it has sales of over $65 billion and profits of over $2 billion.

Nordstrom, on the other hand, employs a different strategy, reflecting its pursuit of a different sort of competitive advantage. Its products are much more specialized and its services are much more personal. As a result, its customers are less elastic. However, Nordstrom also recognizes that its more customized and expensive offerings will appeal to fewer people. Thus, it has fewer locations—187 stores averaging 120,000 square feet—and a lower overall sales volume of just over $8 billion. However, because of its higher prices, Nordstrom has higher sales per location, higher sales per square foot, and a higher overall profit margin. But premium prices and higher margins reflect operational realities that cost money. As is necessary to provide top-level service, Nordstrom devotes a higher percentage of its revenues to administration and overhead. It also devotes greater energy and resources to acquiring and carrying the right types of inventory, to appeal to the preferences and tastes of its customers. Thus, Nordstrom's inventory moves somewhat slower than the inventory at Target.

Competitive advantage, then, can be thought of in terms of differentiation and low cost, centered on a specific space within the market. Low cost is generally focused broadly but need not always be so, provided customers are considering options only within a limited range. The important thing to remember about low-cost-based competitive advantage, though, is that it seeks to capitalize on customer elasticity. Because elastic customers have high bargaining power, this strategy must offer a low cost of ownership. That entails operational efficiency and the ability to reduce prices while offering convenience and ease. Differentiation, on the other hand, is often associated with a narrower scope. However, the breadth of the market is less the issue than the ability to make that market inelastic. To reduce elasticity, and so reduce customer bargaining power, it is necessary to appeal to customer preferences in a way that cannot be easily imitated. That will often require higher costs and a willingness to sacrifice some volume. However, this strategy will generally produce higher prices and higher margins.

CONCLUDING THOUGHTS AND CAVEATS

Simple Supply and Demand?

It is important to note that strategic management and the pursuit of competitive advantage are practical and tangible efforts. While much of this chapter has focused on economic principles, strategic management is more than simple supply and demand. Rather, it is about managing the firm over the landscape described by economic theory. The distinction, between simply allowing the invisible hand of economic logic to determine performance and purposefully exercising strategic choice and control over the firm, is the issue of determinism and voluntarism, discussed in Chapter 4. As mentioned there, it is a distinction that often means more to theorists and researchers than it does to practicing managers. It would be a mistake, however, to overlook the issue altogether, because strategic success requires managing the interplay between these two sets of forces.

Certainly the deterministic, economic realities of the firm's environment are key factors. Understanding bargaining power, substitutability, barriers to entry, and elasticity is essential to formulating and implementing good strategy. But just as important is understanding that none of these conditions is fully fixed. Through purposeful strategic actions firms can create inelasticity, despite the availability of substitute products. Coffee, for example, is a commodity, available in any number of places. Yet Starbucks has been successful differentiating itself and earning good margin in a market that many would have labeled commoditized and unattractive. Through purposeful strategic action firms can find attractive spaces even in markets that are competitive and where bargaining power of the customer is extremely high. Southwest Airlines, for example, has been very successful in an industry with high customer bargaining power and high elasticity. It has done this by serving markets that were underserved by the major carriers and by flying direct routes to these less crowded destinations. Interestingly, Wal-Mart employed a similar strategy for many of its early years, choosing to avoid direct competition with K-Mart and Sears by locating in small, rural markets considered too small and out of the way to be served by these larger retailers. Moreover, even where there is great substitutability, such that customers are elastic and sellers have little bargaining power, there is still room for growth and profit. By catering to the motivations of elastic customers and capitalizing on the substitutability of their products and services, firms such as Wal-Mart, BP, Cemex, and Georgia Pacific have enjoyed great success.

The opportunity and the challenge of strategic management, then, is that there are always possibilities. But those possibilities emerge from the economic landscape. Thus, the pursuit of competitive advantage involves the development and implementation of strategies that leverage a firm's resources in unique and creative ways, so as to create value for customers who live in and are influenced by the constellation of forces in the environment.

Monopoly, Limits to Competition, and Competitive Advantage

In many ways, strategic management can be seen as a process of cultivating small, pseudo-monopolies. Recall that a monopoly is simply a situation where there is only one supplier. Where there is only one supplier, there is no competition and so few limits on profitability. Of course, even monopoly profits are limited by the resource constraints of the buyers. Still, where there is no competition, profits are certainly easier to achieve and sustain. Thus, strategic management can be viewed as a process where firms seek to attract customers and to limit competition, in effect creating for themselves monopoly-like conditions. Indeed, the different types of competitive advantage discussed earlier can be seen as different paths to monopoly power. With monopoly power, firms can charge prices over their costs because of the inelasticity of their buyers. Firms do this by positioning their products and services so that they represent the highest available level of consumer surplus to their customers.

For example, consider that there are only five rental car companies with locations on-site in the airport of McAllen, Texas. While any number of other companies may be available outside the airport, this small handful of suppliers has monopoly power over arriving travelers. Indeed, this is true even for customers who are highly elastic and inclined to consider only the cost of renting the car. Such an elastic customer would rather pay an additional $20 in rental fees than have to pay $30 in taxi fares to travel to and from an off-site vendor. Thus, by being on-site these five companies gain monopoly power and reduce the competition for their customers.

There are also instances, though, where monopoly power is less a function of limitation than it is a function of choice. Consider tennis rackets, which are very important to people who play tennis seriously. There are literally dozens of makers of rackets, each with their own models and designs. Yet most serious tennis players have their favorites. Some prefer Donnay, while others prefer Prince, Gamma, Volkl, or Head. And all of these brands, along with others as well, have been used by top-ranked professionals in winning grand slam events. So, while it would be difficult to argue that any one make or model is truly superior to the others, many tennis players choose to purchase and use only their favorites, thus maximizing their own consumer surplus by buying the brand of racket that gives them the greatest use value, price notwithstanding. Note, however, that in so doing they are themselves limiting competition and ceding monopoly power to their preferred supplier.

These two cases illustrate competitive advantages resulting first from a low-cost-based and second from a differentiation-based strategy. In the first case, the intent is to gain a measure of power over elastic consumers by limiting the range of competitors available for consumers to take into account. That monopoly power then yields above market prices and margins because the monopoly providers are the ones that offer the lowest overall cost. In the second case, the intent is to gain a measure of power by rendering the consumers less elastic and thereby limiting the range of options that they will consider. This monopoly power yields above market prices and margins because customers see higher use value in the particular brand of the specific providers.

Stuck in the Middle

In articulating the generic strategies outlined above, it was Porter's contention that no firm could succeed for long in a position that was in between the most differentiated provider and the lowest-cost provider. Such firms were said to be "stuck in the middle" and so at a persistent disadvantage to those competitors who offered greater use value as well as to those who offered lower transaction costs. While subsequent research has provided more insight into this issue (Hill, 1988), and while many scholars, Porter (1980) included, would now agree that this is an over-simplification of a complex issue, there remains considerable confusion about what it means to be stuck in the middle and whether or not firms can be successful when so positioned.

To help understand the issue, it is important to remember two key principles. First, all competition is local. This principle was explained in Chapter 4 but bears repeating now. It is relevant because determining whether a firm is stuck in the middle requires understanding the nature of the competition. To be stuck in the middle, in the way described above, a firm must be "stuck" between other real competitors, operating within the same space and competing for the same customers. Otherwise, the designation has no real meaning and no real impact on competitive advantage. Herein lies part of the confusion: simply because a firm is not the lowest-cost provider anywhere does not mean that it cannot be the lowest-cost provider for some group of customers and for some subset of the market. In the same way, just because a firm is not the most differentiated among all providers does not mean that it is not the most differentiated for some group of customers or some subset of the market. Thus, firms that are neither the most differentiated nor the lowest-cost providers in general may still hold strong competitive advantages by being the most differentiated or the lowest-cost providers within specific markets. For example, the car rental companies at the McAllen airport need not have the lowest costs or the highest degree of differentiation among all car rental companies. Indeed, they need not even be the lowest cost or the most differentiated in the city of McAllen. They simply must be either the lowest cost or the most differentiated within the McAllen airport, to that subset of customers who are able and likely to consider them. Thus, in the eyes of different groups of customers and at different times, all of these five firms will likely be attractive. It is possible that all five can have some measure of competitive advantage by being somewhat more differentiated or offering a somewhat lower-cost option, to some group of customers, at some point in time.

The second principle to remember is that all purchases reflect the desire by consumers to increase their surplus, which is a function of both use value and total cost. Thus, every purchase reflects a trade-off of sorts between high use value and the higher costs often associated with it and low use value and lower costs often associated with it. Every strategy, then, reflects some combination of differentiation and low cost. Indeed, there are no purely low-cost strategies. Even among low-cost providers, there is typically some effort made at adding value, to provide some qualitative differentiation to the product and to reduce elasticity of the buyers. Similarly, there are no purely differentiation strategies. Even the most differentiated provider must acknowledge that customer resources are finite and so, at some point, must make some effort to acknowledge the importance of cost.

It can be helpful to think of these two strategies as combinations of two basic types of effort. Such a combination is best represented by the concept of a **production possibilities frontier** (see Figure 6.4). A firm can choose to focus either exclusively on differentiation or exclusively on low cost. Position A on the curve could represent a firm such as Neiman Marcus—a high-end, luxury retailer, smaller (41 stores) and even more specialized than Nordstrom—with high levels of customization and service, and subsequently high prices. Such a firm serves highly inelastic customers with strong preferences and little sensitivity to cost. On the other hand, a firm at position X on the curve would focus most heavily on costs. A firm such as Wal-Mart serves highly elastic customers, with products and services that are substitutable and easily imitated and that offer few if any opportunities for premium pricing.

Yet it is important to note that this curve represents a continuum, where firms can choose to concentrate almost entirely on differentiation or almost entirely on low cost, or to trade off the pursuit of one for the other. Thus, a firm might decide to compete mostly on differentiation but also to make some effort to reduce costs. Because resources are finite and typically suited for particular uses, it is not possible to focus fully on differentiation while focusing fully on costs. Thus, emphasizing low

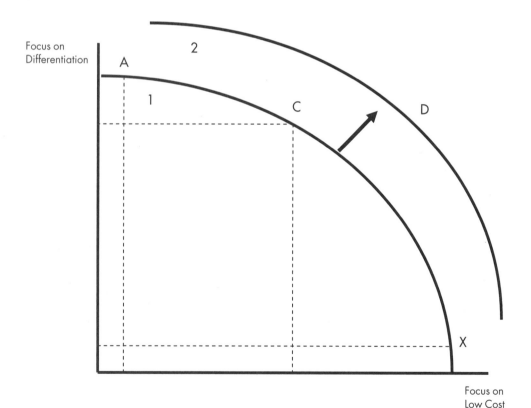

FIGURE 6.4 Combination Strategies Illustrated by the Production Possibilities Frontier

cost means moving to the right along the curve. The amount of movement reflects the amount of emphasis. Nevertheless, to one degree or another, differentiated producers do this all the time, offering incentives or discounts for their products and services or by providing special financing, extended warranties, or additional services at no extra cost. Efforts such as these exemplify attempts to mitigate the full cost of the product or service's premium price. As a result, they represent combinations of differentiation and low-cost strategies (Parnell & Wright, 1993).

In the same way, a firm that is focused almost exclusively on low cost may choose to add some features to its product or some additional services to its delivery. For example, gas stations along interstate highways serve highly elastic customers and so must be focused intently on costs. However, by also offering attractive facilities, clean restrooms, and a brighter, more accessible atmosphere, they may entice customers into shopping on more than just cost—in effect, making those customers less elastic. Such a strategy would represent movement along the curve away from and somewhat to the left of the "X" position. Such a strategy would also be a combination of low-cost and differentiation elements.

Of course, these two examples are somewhat limited, in that they do not recognize the possibilities for strategies that combine increasing amounts of differentiation and low-cost elements. These sorts of strategies are more than mere movements along the curve and rather represent shifts onto another curve altogether. Shifts in the production possibilities frontier reflect the impact of new technologies, new inputs, new models, and new methodologies. Dell, for instance, assembles PCs, using many of the same components as other manufacturers, such as HP or Lenovo. However, Dell introduced a different production model, incorporating online order taking, inventory and parts delivery, manufacturing, and shipping. The result was a process that produced machines of equal or superior quality, with a higher degree of customization, at greater speeds and lower costs. In essence, Dell's innovation shifted the production possibilities curve, leaving the firm, represented at position D on curve 2, at a persistent advantage to any firm still on curve 1. Because of its superior technology, Dell was therefore able to offer more differentiation and lower costs. Rather than being stuck in the middle, it could provide more differentiation at the same level of costs and lower costs at the same level of differentiation. Shifts such as this occur frequently. Indeed, the example at the beginning of the chapter illustrates how Home Depot developed a new and innovative model that shifted the frontier of possibilities. As a result, it was able to offer greater selection and variety, but at lower costs than its competitors, driving many of those competitors out of the market.

Viewing strategies as combinations of low cost and differentiation allows us to see a near infinite number of positions along the continuum between the two and to position firms, in relation to one another, along this continuum. Nordstrom, for instance, is focused more on differentiation than is Target, and that difference showed up in the financial comparisons made earlier. Nordstrom, however, is probably still focused somewhat less on differentiation than Neiman Marcus or other high-end retailers such as Burberry or Saks Fifth Avenue. At the same time, just because Target is focused more on low cost than it is on differentiation, it is probably still focused more on differentiation than a firm such as Wal-Mart and certainly more than a firm such as Dollar General. Thus, every firm's strategy can be seen as a combination of some low-cost and some differentiation elements. Which combination ultimately yields competitive advantage, though, is a function of how that strategy fits within the specific contours of the environment in which the firm is competing.

Dynamic Capabilities

It is crucial to understand that competitive advantage is not a characteristic of the firm, nor is it a commodity that can simply be bought or sold. Firms do not acquire competitive advantage and then never lose it, nor do attractive positions in an industry remain attractive indefinitely. Rather, competitive advantage is the result of a dynamic and ongoing process. Demand is constantly shifting and adapting as competitors move into and out of various markets. Firms innovate and competitors imitate, thereby creating new and refined alternatives from which customers can choose. Thus, there is an ongoing ferment of activity, some purposeful and some accidental, some driven by forces in the environment and some driven by the actions of the firm. It is in the midst of this ferment that the firm must position itself, its products, and its services, so as continually to offer value to the customers.

So, when Home Depot introduced the superstore concept to the building supply business, it did more than simply create advantage for itself. It also demonstrated to competitors such as Lowe's a concept that they could replicate. It created in the mind of customers the expectation that building supply products could be inexpensive and accessible, and it created for investors the expectation that sustained returns of 15% and 20% were possible in an industry that heretofore had been considered mature and stagnant. As a result of this innovation, the landscape of that particular environment changed forever. Whole new categories of customers were drawn into the market and competition was initiated on a new and higher plane. Models of store location, store design, and store operation changed dramatically, necessitating innovations in managing supplies and suppliers. Human resource practices changed as needed to provide better service and better education. And all of these things contributed to earnings that attracted investors and competitors alike.

Thus, as Home Depot was innovating in an effort to build its competitive advantage, so too was it contributing to a set of evolutionary forces that would make that competitive advantage increasingly difficult to sustain. Indeed, you could say that, by developing its competitive advantage and in cultivating its successful strategy, Home Depot was sowing the seeds of its future competitive challenges. The apparent paradox in this will be discussed later in the book. For now, it should serve to illustrate the importance of the dynamic capabilities perspective in envisioning, developing, and sustaining competitive advantage. No asset is valuable intrinsically and no resource or competitive position will retain its value indefinitely. The pursuit of sustained competitive advantage, then, is really a process of ongoing development, learning, and change. And the resources that are the most valuable over the long term are those that are the most flexible, offer the most opportunity for adaptation, and can change along with the conditions in the environment.

The case at the beginning of this chapter illustrates how even strong advantages can erode, through the actions of competitors and with the changing tastes of the market. All of the market share and margin that Lowe's now enjoys came at the expense of Home Depot. However, it was in response to Home Depot's dramatic success that Lowe's launched its new strategy. For both firms, the question now is, What will come next? Will either of the two introduce some new business model or technological innovation that will shift the curve again? Or will new competition come from the outside? By now both understand that there are no resources, assets, or positions that the other cannot replicate in some measure. Thus, the only means of gaining advantage must come from the ability to move faster, to experiment and implement more efficiently and effectively, and to respond quicker to changes in the market.

SUMMARY

This chapter discussed the nature of competitive advantage and the strategies that can lead to it. The most important point is that competitive advantage emerges and is best understood at the level of the individual transaction. Indeed, transactions are the key linking pin between strategy and performance. Strategy leads to action and actions lead to the transactions from which revenues and earnings flow. Transactions, then, are the focal point of strategy and the fulcrum of strategic success. As such, they provide a logical and powerful lens through which to view and understand competitive advantage.

In viewing competitive advantage at the transaction level, three things become clear. First, competitive advantage is a reflection of value, which is determined by the market and by the judgments of customers. Second, the drivers of value are context specific, and so competitive advantage is also a reflection of context. And, third, judgments about value are episodic, which means that competitive advantage occurs in discrete episodes. These three principles are key to understanding competitive advantage, along with the two principal theories that have been used to explain it. Those theories, the externally focused industrial economic view and the internally focused resource-based view, are in fact different sides of the same coin. One concentrates on the environmental conditions in which customers evaluate their alternatives and make their choices. The other is fixed on the firm and the resources and capabilities it leverages to make products and services attractive to potential buyers. At the meeting of these interacting sets of forces and conditions are the individual transactions, where customers determine what products and services provide the greatest consumer surplus and value. Where there is superior value there is also competitive advantage and transactions that render value to the buyers and revenues and to the sellers.

For customers, that value will always reflect some combination of two generic motivations—to satisfy either a preference for something in particular, with less regard to cost, or a preference for something common, at the lowest possible cost. These motivations give rise to two generic forms of competitive advantage, either differentiation based or low-cost based. More than anything else, these strategies reflect the elasticity of the buyers. So, a differentiation-based approach is appropriate when the demand is inelastic and a low-cost-based approach is appropriate when the demand is elastic. Consistent with the earlier discussions, these generic strategies and generic forms of competitive advantage are best understood at the transaction level. So a differentiation-based strategy is one that seeks to increase and capitalize upon inelasticity, either by restricting options or by increasing the use value of a particular product, service, or brand. Conversely, a low-cost-based strategy is one that endeavors to reduce transaction costs for the buyer, so as to leverage and capitalize on the elasticity of the demand. In both instances, though, success is determined by the customers' perceptions of value in the context of all the other alternatives and options. And, with each successful transaction, the firm creates value for its customer, solidifying its competitive advantage and enhancing its own success.

Strategy, then, which is often thought of as a high-level activity, involving long-term thinking and planning and broad organizational commitments and actions, can also be seen as an effort to win a series of many miniature competitive episodes. Indeed, just as no team wins a championship without winning many individual games, so too is strategic success actually a function of many individual successes in multiple and distinct competitive episodes, which are ultimately won or lost at the transaction level.

KEY TERMS

Commodities are goods of uniform value and quality that are produced by multiple suppliers, such that buyers see them as being interchangeable.

A demand curve is a graphical representation of a mathematical function, describing the relationship between the price of a commodity and the quantity demanded at that price.

The **dynamic capabilities** perspective, as articulated by Teece, Pisano, and Shuen (1997), is the ability to develop and sustain competitive advantage through renewing competences so as to achieve congruence with a rapidly changing environment.

Elasticity is a condition whereby a certain percentage change in the cost of a good results in a more than equal percentage change in the demand for that same good.

An **exogenous** (from the Greek *exo*, meaning "outside," and *genes*, meaning "production") change is a change in the state of system from factors external to the model and not explained by the model.

Generic strategies is a term coined by Michael Porter (1980) to describe three basic approaches to achieving competitive advantage: "Cost leadership," "Differentiation," and "Focus."

The **industrial economic view** is the explanation of competitive advantage provided by the field of industrial organization economics. I.O. economics, often referred to as the economics of imperfect competition, studies the strategic behavior of firms and the structure of competitive markets.

Inelasticity is a condition whereby a certain percentage change in the cost of a good results in a less than equal percentage change in the demand for that same good.

Monopoly power is the ability to charge above marginal costs, even in the presence of competition. Suppliers with monopoly power can behave as if they were monopolies because of the inelasticity of the demand for their products and services.

Production possibilities frontier is the term used to describe a graphical depiction of the different combinations of goods that a rational producer can make with certain fixed amounts of resources.

Scarcity in economic terms is defined as not having sufficient resources, goods, or services to fulfill the extant demand. By implication, then, scarcity implies that wants and needs cannot be satisfied simultaneously, which means that trade-offs must be made.

A **tautology** is a self-evident true statement with multiple parts that is true regardless of the truth of the parts. For example, the statement "either all sheep are white or not all of them are" is a self-evident truth.

Total cost of ownership is a term originally developed by the Gartner group and reflects all the various direct and indirect costs related to purchasing an asset.

TCOO includes not only its purchase price but all other aspects of its further use, such as installation, training, and maintenance.

QUESTIONS FOR REVIEW

1 How would you describe the competitive nature of the home improvement industry? Does either Home Depot or Lowe's have a discernible competitive advantage? If not, does that mean that neither firm has an advantage?
2 What does it mean to say that competitive advantage occurs at the intersection of the industrial economic and resource-based views? Are these theoretical perspectives at odds with one another or are they complementary?
3 If resources, products, and services are not valuable intrinsically, what gives them value?
4 How is scarcity distinct from value and why is scarcity so important to competitive advantage?
5 How can competitive advantage ever be sustained if it occurs only in specific episodes?
6 Explain the relationship between low-cost and differentiation-based strategies and the economic concept of elasticity.
7 What does it mean to be "stuck in the middle"? Why is that position so disadvantaged and when might combinations of low cost and differentiation be indications of a superior strategy?
8 What are dynamic capabilities, and does this view of strategy and competitive advantage differ from the industrial economic and resource-based views?

Companion Website

For a chapter review outline with links to videos and other valuable web resources, please visit the *Strategic Management* website: www.routledge.com/textbooks/amason.

Chapter 7

Corporate and Multi-Business Unit Strategy

PEPSICO AND THE RESTAURANT BUSINESS

In late 1996, PepsiCo CEO Roger Enrico made a bold proposal to his board of directors to change the company's direction. Enrico advised spinning off PepsiCo's major restaurant division, which included global giants Pizza Hut, Taco Bell, and KFC. Would the board go for Enrico's proposal after PepsiCo had invested so much in its restaurant business?

History

In 1971 Andrall Pearson took over as CEO of the newly formed PepsiCo Inc., following Pepsi Cola's 1965 merger with Frito-Lay. Pearson sought to diversify into the quick-service restaurant business, a line he felt would offer PepsiCo a "captive market" for the company to push its fountain drinks while positioning itself in a very high-growth potential industry. PepsiCo made its first move in 1977 with its acquisition of Pizza Hut, in a deal that was valued at over $317 million. At the time, Pizza Hut was the nation's largest pizza chain, with nearly 1,500 company-owned stores and another 1,300 franchised units. PepsiCo, however, believed there was additional opportunity and that the world market for Pizza Hut could support over 5,000 stores.

A year later, PepsiCo expanded further by acquiring the little-known Mexican food chain Taco Bell, in a deal valued at $148 million. Taco Bell then had fewer than 1,000 stores, half of which were company owned and half of which were franchised. This purchase would prove to be PepsiCo's best investment, as over the next 20 years it would grow Taco Bell North America (TBNA) into a chain of over 7,000 company-owned and franchised stores.

In 1985, the company further strengthened its position in the fast-food industry by acquiring Kentucky Fried Chicken: on October 1, 1986, it completed the acquisition from RJR Nabisco for $841 million in cash. Over the next ten years PepsiCo expanded both the KFC brand and its own soft-drink line by converting over to Pepsi the fountain-drink sales of 5,500 stores previously served by Coca-Cola. Commenting on the purchase, CEO Wayne Calloway remarked, "We're acquiring a highly successful company that has established itself as a leader in a very large and rapidly growing market."

To facilitate international growth of its restaurant businesses, PepsiCo created PepsiCo Restaurants International (PRI). PRI expanded the three restaurant brands through company-owned stores, franchisee agreements, and international affiliate stores. Table 7.1 displays its widespread expansion of each restaurant brand into international markets by early 1997.

By year-end 1995, PepsiCo had established itself as the world's largest restaurant conglomerate. The Pizza Hut, Taco Bell, and KFC chains accounted for nearly $20

Table 7.1
PepsiCo Restaurants International in 1997

Restaurant Brand	Company Owned	Franchise Agreements	Unconsolidated Affiliates	# of Countries Present
Pizza Hut Int'l	940	1,550	575	84
KFC Int'l	990	2,500	430	74
Taco Bell Int'l	20	75	–	17

billion in sales worldwide, with close to 30,000 different locations. Pizza Hut was the world leader in pizza and held over 50% share in the $16 billion U.S. pizza industry. Despite its modest global presence, Taco Bell was the runaway leader in U.S. fast Mexican food sales. TBNA held nearly a 70% market share and accounted for $5 billion in PepsiCo sales. Lastly, KFC added another $7 billion in sales and held a remarkable 70% share of its market. Amazingly, all three ranked among the top five restaurant chains in the country.

The Tricon Spin-Off

As it had hoped to do, PepsiCo capitalized on the rapidly expanding U.S. fast-food industry. However, this market began to show signs of maturity in the mid-1990s, and same-store sales either flattened or declined at all three chains. Thus the board agreed in January 1997 to the spin-off of Pizza Hut, Taco Bell, and KFC into an independent publicly traded company.

The board's approval of the spin-off paved the way for PepsiCo to trim its holdings and restructure to focus on its primary business portfolio—soft drinks and snack foods. Its stock skyrocketed close to 11% on the day reports of the spin-off began to surface, and the deal was completed on October 6, 1997. PepsiCo shareholders received one share of the new company, Tricon Global Restaurants, for every ten shares of PepsiCo they owned (about $5 billion in new shares). PepsiCo also received $4.5 billion cash from the new company. When it was all over, PepsiCo profited well over $7 billion from its inflation-adjusted purchases of the three chains, then known collectively as Tricon restaurants. By the end of 1999, PepsiCo's revenues had declined by one-third, but its earnings had risen by over $100 million. Tricon's name was officially changed to YUM! Brands on May 17, 2002, and the company remains a global leader in the fast-food industry.

INTRODUCTION

To this point in the text, the discussion of strategic management has focused on what is called **business-level strategy**—the pursuit of competitive advantage by a single business within a specific competitive environment. Business-level strategy is associated with firms operating in single industries and serving single market segments and can be thought of as the answer to the question: How will a firm compete against its rivals in a given industry or a particular market? Competitive advantage, as discussed in the previous chapters, emerges from this sort of single business competition.

However, as illustrated in the PepsiCo example, some businesses compete in more than one product market, with multiple and different business units, each of which operates within its own industry, with its own customers, competitors, and market dynamics. Honda, for example, manufactures automobiles, and so competes with firms like Toyota, Ford, and Hyundai. But Honda also produces lawn mowers, and so competes with firms like Murray, Toro, and John Deere, and jet skis, and so competes with firms like Bombardier and Yamaha. And, of course, Honda began by making motorcycles, and so competes with firms like Kawasaki, BMW, and Harley-Davidson. Honda thus competes in a variety of different industries, in a variety of different markets, and with a range of different competitors.

Moreover, each of the different **strategic business units**, as they are frequently called, in firms like Honda or PepsiCo may operate somewhat independently of the others. Indeed, it is possible that a firm could hold a strong competitive advantage in one or more business units, while having little or no competitive advantage in some others. For example, consider Microsoft and its effort to enter the cable television business. For years, Microsoft has sought to carve out a space for itself in the cable industry, investing $1 billion in Comcast in 1997, $5 billion with AT&T in 1999, and $2.6 billion in the U.K. cable operator Telewest in 2000 (Peterson, 2004). The overall strategy is to connect the full range of home entertainment conduits—television, movies, music, and the internet—through Microsoft software, run on the converter boxes of these cable providers. To date, however, none of these various initiatives has been successful, but, despite the poor performance of this business unit, Microsoft's software business continues to operate very well.

Like Microsoft, Toyota is well known for its primary business, automobiles. As one of the largest car makers in the world, and with 2005 earnings of over $12 billion, Toyota is often seen as just a car maker. However, through its various subsidiary business units it is also involved in prefabricated houses, in rooftop gardens, in consulting, and in advertising (Rowley, 2006). Of course, even with some recent and well-publicized problems in quality and safety, Toyota's competitive advantage is much stronger in automobiles than in any of these other businesses. Presumably, though, its management would not be in these other businesses if it did not think that, at some point and in some way, they would benefit the company as a whole.

Similarly, Microsoft's management seems to believe that the cable television business could one day be a key to the next generation of Microsoft software, leaving the company better off despite the struggles of these diversified initiatives.

CORPORATE-LEVEL STRATEGY

Corporate-level strategy is about the different businesses a firm chooses to enter and its intentions in entering those businesses. Thus, while business-level strategy answered the question, How does a firm compete in its business?, corporate-level strategy answers the question, In what businesses will the firm compete? The distinction is an important one for a number of reasons. First, each business and each business environment is unique. Microsoft's knowledge and brand, which it uses to great advantage in the software business, does not necessarily translate into competitive advantage in the cable business. Similarly, Toyota's reputation and position in the automobile industry may not be of significance in the advertising world. At the same time, PepsiCo's marketing and financial strength were clearly beneficial to its restaurant unit. Moreover, by investing in the restaurant business, especially in the Taco Bell chain, PepsiCo achieved substantial growth and profits that, at the time, were unavailable in the traditional drinks business.

The distinction is also important because competition in some industries will occasionally involve investments in others. More will be said about this later. For now, though, consider that Sara Lee produces a host of different food and non-food items, such as Bryan and Hillshire Farm meats, Sara Lee and Bimbo baked goods, Hanes and Bali undergarments, Champion sportswear, and Kiwi shoe polish. Sara Lee's products are sold primarily through large grocery store chains like Kroger and Publix as well as the "big box" retailers like Wal-Mart and Target. Because of their size and reach, these large retailers enjoy tremendous bargaining power, which they use to extract favorable prices, delivery, and payment terms from their vendors. Indeed, given their market presence and scale, such retailers can often name their price, extracting substantial margin and leaving their vendors little recourse. A firm like Sara Lee, however, will have substantial bargaining power of its own. With the large number of products and brands it controls, it can use this bargaining power to resist pressure, to improve the placement of its own brands on the store shelves, and to leverage acceptance of its new products. Sara Lee, then, gains a benefit from its **diversification** over and above the performance of its individual products and brands. In other words, it gains market power through its diversification, and it can use that power to strengthen its competitive advantage and financial performance, even if some of its individual products and brands are not themselves profitable.

Corporate-level strategy involves choosing and managing all of the various business units in which a firm competes in such a way that the strength of the whole firm is maximized. This may involve entering markets and industries that are substantially different from its core business or entering businesses that have yet to show their full potential or that might seem unattractive on their own. It may involve exiting businesses or redirecting investments as necessary to move the firm away from stagnant industries into newer growth opportunities. It may involve any number of such decisions in combination. However, it will always involve viewing the firm as a whole and regarding its different business units as investments that add value both directly and indirectly.

Corporate-Level Strategy and Portfolio Management

In many ways, managing corporate strategy is like managing an investment portfolio. Indeed, one of the earliest and most influential models of corporate strategy, the BCG matrix, suggested just that. As illustrated in Figure 7.1, the BCG matrix is a simple four-quadrant framework, with two dimensions on which business units are evaluated. These two dimensions are the growth rate of the business itself and the relative position of the business within its market or industry. Each business unit is evaluated on these two dimensions and positioned in one of the quadrants on the 2 × 2 matrix. Its position then determines its strategic purpose and direction.

Business units that were slow growing were considered to be either "dogs," to be liquidated, or "cash cows," to be used as sources of investment capital. Neither of these conditions warranted additional investment, however, because of their poor growth expectations. At the same time, businesses that were growing rapidly were considered to be either "stars" or "question marks." Owing to their high growth rate, both of these types of business required substantial investment. However, stars also had sound market positions and offered relatively certain and strong returns. On the other hand, question marks were much more speculative and risky, while still being quite expensive. Without significant improvements in their market position, question marks could not be sustained for long; with improvements, however, they became stars.

This simple model was both powerful and important in that it integrated the underlying principles of business strategy into a framework that could be used to assess multi-business unit firms. The performance of each unit was a reflection of both the attractiveness of its market and its performance in that market. At the same time, there was more to the performance of a whole corporation than just the strength of its units. A firm could not have just stars in its portfolio because stars required investment and so consumed capital. Stars needed to be supported by cash cows, which also played a key role in the overall portfolio by generating the money for further investment. Moreover, because the growth rate of stars would inevitably decline, firms would constantly be seeking new stars through their investments in question marks. Of course, as the new stars emerged, and as the

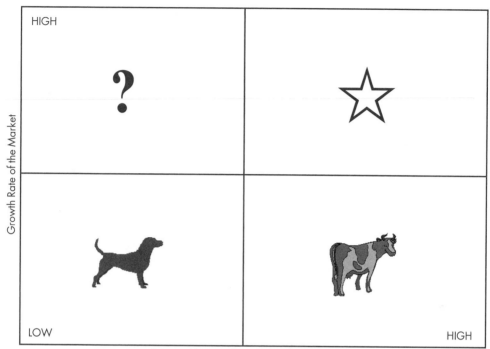

FIGURE 7.1 The BCG Matrix

growth rate of older stars declined, those older stars became cash cows. Ultimately, as the cash cows became less attractive, they were liquidated and their resources plowed back into the development of new markets and businesses. This framework, then, offered a picture of how multiple business units could work together to maximize the long-term performance of the firm. In so doing, it illustrated how the value of the corporate whole could be enhanced through specific combinations of very different types of businesses.

As mentioned, the BCG framework has been around for quite some time. And, while our understanding of corporate strategy, along with the sophistication of how it is analyzed, has evolved substantially, the underlying principle for application remains unchanged. Corporate strategy is about maximizing the value of an entire firm by managing which businesses it will be in and how those different business units will work in combination. Much like the management of an investment portfolio, corporate strategy focuses on the value of the whole, as a result of the performance and interaction of the various pieces. Business units, like individual investments, can be especially strong performers or they can perform not so strongly. In either case, though, the performance of each unit is secondary to its contribution to the overall portfolio. Corporate strategy, then, seeks to produce a more valuable corporation, where the value of the whole is greater than the summed value of the individual parts.

The Challenge of Corporate Strategy

To illustrate the fundamental challenge of corporate strategy, the challenge of making the value of the whole worth more than the summed value of the individual parts, consider figures 7.2 and 7.3. Figure 7.2 illustrates three businesses, A, B, and C, each of which pursues its competitive advantage, in its own competitive environment, and through its own strategy. As such, each business is successful or not based upon the success of its strategy and the strength of its competitive advantage. As a result of that success, each business has some quantifiable value.

As discussed in Chapter 2, a common way to estimate that value is with a **net present value** (NPV). Recall that the NPV of a business is a function of four factors. The first is the future cash flow that the business is expected to produce. Whether the business is a going concern or a new startup, there is an expectation that it will produce tangible and real earnings at some point. That stream of earnings or cash inflows can be reduced to a present value based upon their **time value**. Thus, assessing the NPV requires knowing the time horizon over which any cash flows will be realized. The third factor is the risks and opportunity costs associated with those cash flows; cash flows that are uncertain have a lower present value than those that are more certain. With those variables—the amount of future cash flows, the time horizon over which the cash flows are realized, and the risk level—the present value of the future earnings can be calculated.

Each of these businesses, then, represents a stream of future earnings and so has some quantifiable present value. That present value is the minimum amount the owners would be willing to accept in selling the businesses. Similarly, a buyer would not want to pay more than the present value unless he or she saw some opportunity to increase future earnings. For example, suppose that Business A has a present value of $1 million. If that fact was well known and generally accepted, then no buyer would pay more than $1 million for the business unless he or she had some expectation that future earnings would increase. At the same time, if the seller also

Value = (npvBA + npvBB + npvBC)

FIGURE 7.2 Valuing Multiple Business Units

anticipated that future earnings would increase, then he or she would be unlikely to sell at a price below the present value based upon the expectation of the increased future earnings. So the final factor in calculating the net present value is the amount invested. Investing too much, even in a good business with strong and secure future earnings, can still yield a poor net present value. Similarly, if the purchase price is sufficiently low or if the future cash flows can somehow be increased, investing in a business with poor earnings and poor prospects might still yield a good return.

Viewing an acquisition as an investment opportunity, it is easy to see that positive NPV investments are those where the present value acquired is greater than the value invested. The challenge, then, is either to find firms that are undervalued or to increase the earnings of an acquired firm above the value on which the acquisition value was based; and therein lies both the challenge and the opportunity of corporate strategy.

To illustrate, consider that each business in Figure 7.2 has a present value based upon its expected future earnings. Acquiring these businesses would require paying an amount equal to or greater than their present value. The summed value of the three businesses, then, would be $\Sigma(PVB_A + PVB_B + PVB_C)$. Of course, making the acquisition would itself involve some additional costs for things like due diligence, processing fees, and legal and investment banking services. Moreover, in publicly traded firms there is often a premium of as much as 30% associated with the acquisition itself (Jensen & Ruback, 1983). Some of that premium simply reflects a natural market dynamic, where the actions of the acquiring firm bid up the price of the target. However, there is an additional explanation for this purchasing premium, involving the information asymmetry between the buyer and the seller. Essentially, sellers typically know more about their own firms than do buyers. Thus, it is far more likely that a buyer will overpay than underpay. In addition, acquiring firms often feel pressured to complete an acquisition once it is announced and initiated. Thus, as the price of the target escalates, many acquiring firms will continue with the deal and overpay for the acquisition.

For all of these various reasons, though, acquisitions generally involve the buyer paying at least a price equal to the target firm's present value, along with an additional premium over and above that value (Nielsen & Melicher, 1973; Rosen, 2006). Moreover, once a new business is acquired, there are the additional ongoing costs associated with their management. Those ongoing administrative costs will vary, depending upon the degree to which the acquired businesses are integrated into the corporate whole. However, even in cases where there is little or no operational integration, some new administrative costs must result. There will be costs associated with reconciling and reporting the financial activity of the firms and with any corporate-level management, salary, benefits, real estate, etc. Even where there is very little corporate staff or infrastructure, there will still be some new administrative costs associated with the common ownership of the businesses.

Box 7.1
Mergers and Acquisitions

Do Most Big Deals Pay Off?

Despite the attention and buzz they often receive in the media, most big acquisitions fail to deliver all the value that is anticipated when the deals are conceived and negotiated. That is the conclusion of a fascinating study of large mergers and acquisitions undertaken during the years 1995 to 2001. The study, sponsored by *Business Week*, reported that a majority of the firms involved in these major deals failed to create new value. What does that really mean in practical terms? It means that the vast majority of those firms would have been better off had these deals never taken place. The finding is especially remarkable when you consider the sorts of deals that were studied.

For example, during the period considered, Travelers Group completed a $70 billion merger with the banking giant Citicorp. Insurer Concesco spent $7.1 billion to acquire subprime lender Green Tree Financial. Daimler Benz, the German automobile giant, spent $38.6 billion to acquire Chrysler, one of Detroit's famous big three automobile makers. And America Online invested $166 billion to acquire Time Warner. In all, the study considered 302 mergers and acquisitions, totaling trillions of dollars and affecting millions of employees and investors. Given the scope of the study, the findings are all the more impressive and sobering.

Why were the results so abysmal? Why would smart executives, with all sorts of access to the data and analytics necessary to make good decisions, make so many and such large blunders? The answer is simple: the acquiring firms simply paid too much. In other words, the deals were not necessarily bad deals. Rather, they were bad deals at the price at which they were executed. This is what the article and many economists refer to as the "winner's curse." More often than not, the acquiring firms are so eager to complete the deal, so intent on appearing to win the battle for control of the target firm, that they pay too much, and in many cases way too much. As a result, even a good deal can never produce enough in marginal return to offset the enormous premium paid by the buyer. Of course, that premium goes directly to the sellers. And, as the study points out, sellers realized an average gain of 19% on their shares.

While paying premium prices on the acquisitions, the buyers frequently also overestimated the likelihood and value of the expected synergies. Consolidations often proved to be logistical nightmares that were more complicated and much more expensive than anticipated. The merged firms were often unable to retain key employees or to keep key customers satisfied. Expected costs savings from streamlined back-room operations never materialized, and unexpected problems delayed the benefits of integration. So, not only did the acquirers quite often spend too much on their acquisitions, they also typically failed to realize all of the benefits that they had expected when the deal was contemplated.

To actually judge the quality of the acquisition, the study focused on stock market values one year after the deals had been executed. While a year may seem too short a time to judge acquisitions of this magnitude, it is important to remember that stock market values are forward-looking measures. Thus, the study really measured whether the deals were assessed as successful by the market. Were investors buying or selling the stock, and was the stock price moving up or down as a result? On that measure, 61% of the acquiring firms fell in value. Even when combining the winners with the losers, the results were still negative, as the average return, for all the acquiring firms, was 9.2% below the return for the S&P 500 over the same period of time. Thus, one year later, the preponderance of the market assessed these deals as failures.

What this all means, then, is that the acquiring firms transferred wealth from their own stockholders to the stockholders of the firms they acquired. At levels that are truly startling, those firms that acquired others during the period beginning in 1995 and ending in 2001, and in deals valued at over $500 million, were worse off because of their efforts. These data should serve as a powerful reminder that success in mergers and acquisitions, indeed in corporate strategy in general, is illusive and difficult to achieve. As such, managers would do well to be cautious and deliberate in considering any corporate-level strategic move.

Adapted from Henry (2002)

What is especially important to note is that all of these additional costs must be paid out of the earning streams of the combined businesses. In other words, earnings will still come into the firm through only one source—the activities of the individual businesses—which means that the present value of the combined whole can be represented by the expression $\Sigma(PVBA + PVBB + PVBC) - (AQC + ADC)$, where AQC is the total of the acquisition costs and ADC is the total of the new administrative costs (see Figure 7.3).

In comparing figures 7.2 and 7.3, it is easy to see and understand why the value of the whole corporation will almost always be lower than the summed value of the individual business units. That value must be lower because the earnings from

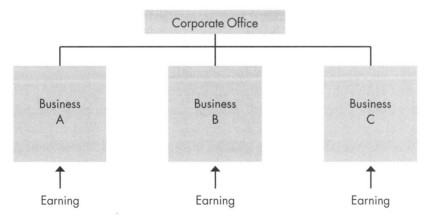

Value = (npvBA + npvBB + npvBC) − (aqc + adc)

FIGURE 7.3 Valuing the Corporate Whole

the business units remain the same, while the costs are increased as a result of the acquisition and administrative expenses. The only way that the value of the whole could be greater than the sum of the individual units, then, is if the combination of those units somehow increased the net of their present values. Consequently, for corporate strategy to be successful, the value of the whole has to be worth more than the sum of the individual parts. The earnings and net value of the business units must somehow be increased as a result of their involvement in the larger corporation.

That is the fundamental challenge of corporate strategy: to enter and manage businesses that are made more valuable through their inclusion in the corporation. Simply entering new businesses, whether successful or not, will not create new value. Simply doing business in new industries, whether attractive or not, will not create new value. Rather, entering a new business or industry will most often consume value by imposing new costs. Returning to the example of PepsiCo, it was successful not because of the attractiveness of the restaurant industry or even because of the strength of the businesses it purchased. It was successful because of the value that was added to those businesses after they were acquired. That sort of success—indeed, success in corporate strategy generally—is very elusive, and research has shown that many more efforts at diversification fail than succeed (Porter, 1987).

It is important to note as well that the challenge of corporate strategy transcends the **mode of entry** into the new business or businesses. In the preceding example, the corporate parent diversified into businesses A, B, and C by acquiring them. Suppose, however, that the parent started these companies from scratch and grew them organically. Would the calculation and causes of success have been any different? The answer is, probably not. The parent company would still have to invest an amount near or equal to the present value of the new businesses' resources and assets. In addition, the parent company would still likely have a variety of new costs associated with corporate overhead that would have to be paid out of the earnings of the business units. Thus, the corporate whole would still be faced with the challenge of adding value over and above the expected value of the business units individually. Otherwise, the value of the corporate whole would still be lower than the summed values of the individual business units.

Because the parent or diversifying firm will generally pay the full present value of any business or asset that it acquires, and because that parent will most always impose some new costs on that business or asset, the only way it can be successful is by adding value that was not reflected in the original price. The challenge of corporate strategy, then, is to take a business or asset with some known value and to strengthen its earning ability, so as to make it more valuable as a part of the corporate whole than it was when operating independently. The result is a corporate whole that is worth more than the sum of its individual parts, an effect known as **synergy**.

Synergy is simply the additive effect whereby two things, with some known value, become more valuable through their combination than they were independently. Honda, for example, likely derives synergy from being in both the motorcycle and the automobile business. Certainly the reputations of the two business units affect each other. Moreover, it is likely that some of the technologies of the two units inform the others. The business units may also coordinate the sourcing of raw materials and so gain bargaining leverage over the vendors. The corporation as a whole definitely represents a stronger, safer bet to the investment community, which enables a lower cost of capital at the corporate level than could be obtained at the level of the individual business units. Synergy, then, may come from any number of different interrelationships among the value chains of a firm's business units. But what will always be true is that synergy will provide those businesses some ability to do things that they simply could not do if they were stand-alone businesses and not a part of the larger corporation.

Corporate Strategy and Competitive Advantage

While competitive advantage is generally considered a business-level phenomenon, it is important to note the connection between synergy, competitive advantage, and corporate-level strategy. A successful corporate strategy increases the net value of its business units. As a practical matter, this means increasing the net earnings of the business units over time. As discussed in previous chapters, earnings relate directly to competitive advantage. So, successful corporate strategy really strengthens the net competitive advantage of the business units. In other words, corporate strategy employs all the resources of the organization in such a way that the net competitive advantage of the whole is maximized. To explain it in another way, the synergy that is produced by an effective strategy can be thought of as a unique and valuable resource that is very difficult to imitate and very difficult to substitute. As such, a successful corporate strategy can yield strong and sustainable competitive advantage.

As if to underscore this point, Porter (1987) describes the true test of corporate strategy as being whether it produces an organization that is better off than it would have been otherwise. As illustrated in the previous example, being better off simply means that the business units are worth more together than they are independently. But how does corporate strategy make a diverse set of business units better off than they would have been otherwise? How does a firm use corporate strategy to strengthen the competitive advantage of its business units? Porter describes four general approaches: portfolio management, restructuring, transferring skills, and sharing activities.

Portfolio Management

The portfolio approach to corporate strategy is often associated with the **conglomerate** organizational model. Rumelt (1974) defined conglomerate firms as companies that diversified into multiple, unrelated businesses through the acquisition of large numbers of business units. The conglomerate approach was to acquire solid and well-run companies, in attractive industries, and then to allow those businesses to continue operating autonomously. Because the units were independent, there was little need for corporate-level management beyond shared services like legal, finance, and executive-level planning. Strategic and operational management was handled at the business level, by the individual managers, who were evaluated based upon unit success. In this respect, each business unit was its own **profit center**, responsible for its own revenues, costs, and profits. And the corporate whole prospered as the business units prospered. The key to this strategy, then, was the identification and acquisition of strong and well-managed business units and the provision of basic services that would allow them to operate more efficiently. What synergy there was in this model resulted from the sharing of corporate overhead, the access to lower-cost capital, and the superior knowledge of the corporate management.

The BCG matrix, described earlier in the chapter, grew out of this concept of corporate strategy. The corporation viewed the group of business units as a portfolio of varied investments. Corporate management then allocated capital across the investments based upon their various growth and performance expectations. This created an internal capital market where management had access to better information than other private investors about the companies in its investment portfolio. Similarly, the business unit managers had better communication with and participation from their investors. The result was a more efficient capital market, with lower transaction costs and better information. Because of the greater information symmetry and because of the opportunity for the investors to be more involved in their investments, conglomerates were thought to be better at allocating capital than the public market. Moreover, because the corporation represented a market unto itself, with multiple and diverse sources of cash flow, it was seen as being less risky than any single business organization.

In addition to the lower cost of capital, corporate management provided oversight and counsel to the business unit managers, along with administrative support in the areas of human resource management, accounting, and infrastructure. Across these various functions and areas, the conglomerate model sought to build synergy by offering the business units the freedom to focus only on their key, value-adding operations. Being able to off-load a measure of their administrative overhead onto the corporation, and gaining the freedom to focus just on their own products, services, customers, and competitors, helped to make these individual businesses more profitable. Thus, the portfolio concept was and still is a basis for a successful corporate strategy. Indeed, GE and Berkshire Hathaway could both be described as successful conglomerates, operating in a range of dramatically different industries, with largely autonomous business units and synergy that comes only through subtle interventions by corporate headquarters.

For most other firms, though, the portfolio approach has proven problematic more often than not. The reason is that, while they seem logical and reasonable in concept, the various benefits are actually quite difficult to achieve in practice. For example, while administrative aspects like human resources and accounting may seem reasonable areas in which to consolidate, these functions often work very differently in different types of industries and firms. Thus, conglomerates that became too diverse or were involved in too many dissimilar industries often found that the expected cost savings failed to materialize. Corporations can end up adding costs at the corporate level without reducing them adequately at the business level. Being involved in too many dissimilar businesses can also reduce the value of the counsel and advice that corporate management provides. Corporate-level managers often find that they simply lack sufficient expertise to add value in the broad variety of businesses in which they are diversified. Even in the area of financial synergy, the expected benefits often fail to materialize. The lower risk associated with having multiple sources of cash flow, for example, offers little to stockholders that they cannot achieve by simply diversifying their own investment portfolios. Moreover, while an internal capital market may provide for better information, it is also subject to greater bias. Corporate managers can be slow to recognize their own mistakes and biased in their assessment of their own portfolios. As such, they may be slow to sell underperforming businesses or be influenced by considerations other than just the economic performance of their units. Thus, the efficient flow of capital across the business units can be hindered by a host of different human biases, conflicting motivations, and political interests.

Despite some apparent advantages, then, the portfolio concept of corporate strategy has been shown to be workable only in rare instances. Indeed, the stock market is so skeptical of the conglomerate approach to corporate strategy that the stock value of an acquiring firm frequently declines upon the announcement of an unrelated acquisition (Berger & Ofek, 1995; Servaes, 1996). So the challenge for the portfolio manager is actually to achieve the expected financial and administrative synergies that were foreseen at the time of the decision to diversify. Without those synergies, the corporation will inevitably impose new costs and impediments without necessarily creating new revenues or savings—the result of which will be a corporation that is worth less than the sum of its parts.

Restructuring

The second approach described by Porter is restructuring. In some ways, this model is the antithesis of the traditional approach to corporate strategy. Whereas corporate strategy determines what businesses a firm should be in, the restructuring approach looks ahead to the firm getting out of its businesses. Perhaps the single biggest key to success in the restructuring approach is the spread between the cost of the acquisition and the price of the sale, along with the earnings that can be achieved in the interim. To facilitate those earnings, and so to increase the value of the acquired business, the corporation restructures the business in an effort to make it worth more than it was worth before the acquisition. The synergy in this approach comes from combining the undervalued assets of the business unit with the managerial expertise and resources of the acquiring corporation.

There are three key requirements for making this strategy work: the ability to spot undervalued opportunities, the expertise to reorganize the business unit's assets and activities as necessary to unlock that unrecognized potential, and the discipline to see each investment as a means to an end and so to sell it and extract its newly increased value. Of course, developing these skills is easier said than done. After all, what company would not want to find that proverbial diamond in the rough? Almost any manager would like to buy an undervalued company at a discounted price, make some changes in that company's operating model and management, and then sell the investment at a premium. However, recognizing those opportunities in time to capitalize on them before their value becomes public knowledge, and so apparent to everyone, is difficult.

Take the example of PepsiCo, discussed earlier. The investment in Taco Bell came early in the development of that firm and its industry. While everyone recognizes the value of Taco Bell in hindsight, the potential for that value was apparent to a relative few at the time of the acquisition. Thus, PepsiCo saw in Taco Bell an opportunity that few had recognized and so was able to "buy low and sell high." Like PepsiCo, any firm that hopes to follow this corporate strategy must have a well-developed sensitivity to market opportunity. It must be able to discern environmental change and to envision the impact of that change on the affected industries and companies. This sort of opportunity recognition, though, is an inexact science. Still, restructuring is a corporate strategy that has proven viable for some firms over the years.

Another of the keys to success seems to be timing. As industries go through their typical evolutionary cycles, there are certain points in time where the opportunity for restructuring is greater than others. As industries advance in their maturity, for instance, some of the firms that were formerly successful will inevitably face decline. Firms and industries in this condition can seem to be ripe for restructuring. K-Mart, for example, was acquired following its bankruptcy by Edward Lampert's ESL Investments, a firm that specializes in the restructuring of underperforming assets. By all accounts, the investment was a good one, as the value of the K-Mart business is much greater than the price ESL paid. The restructuring will mean that K-Mart, in all likelihood, will one day exit its traditional business. But that is just fine with K-Mart's stockholders, as the firm had long since lost most of its competitive advantage to Wal-Mart and Target. By reorganizing K-Mart's operations to reduce inefficiency, and by not reinvesting in the discount retailing business, ESL is able to extract and redirect large amounts of cash away from K-Mart's traditional assets and business model and into other new investments. Over time, the result will be a company that is very different and very much more valuable than the one that was originally acquired. This approach to corporate strategy, then, can be successful for those with the right skills and resources.

Transferring Skills

Whereas the previous approaches focused on the relationship between the corporation and the business units, the final two concentrate more on the relationships among the business units themselves. To understand these two approaches, it is helpful to reflect back on the discussion in Chapter 5 and recall that the value chain provides a graphical depiction of the various activities in which a firm engages to earn a profit. Each of these activities should be viewed as a potential source of competitive advantage. Wal-Mart, for example, has unique and substantial capabilities in the area of inbound logistics. Those capabilities enable it to manage more inventory at a lower cost than any of its competitors. A significant measure of Wal-Mart's competitive advantage, then, can be traced back to its strength in inbound logistics. Transferring skills is an approach to corporate strategy where different business units leverage a single area of strength. That single area of strength becomes the source of synergy to the corporation, enhancing the competitive advantage of the individual business units and making them more formidable competitors in their respective industries and markets.

For example, Honda competes in the automobile business, in the motorcycle business, and in the personal watercraft business, among others. What is common across these business units, though, is Honda's competency in the area of engineering and internal combustion engine design. It is able to transfer this skill effectively across all of the businesses, making them all stronger competitors. Disney competes in a host of different businesses and industries, from theme parks to movies, television, and retail merchandise. But almost all of these businesses draw value in some way from Disney's creativity and strength in character and story development. Even among business units that seem unrelated, there is an opportunity for synergy and the sharing of valuable resources and skills. GE, for example, competes in a wide range of businesses both related and unrelated, from light bulbs to jet engines to hydroelectric power generation. Although these businesses are all very different, GE is able to leverage its competencies in human capital management, capital budgeting, and strategy across them all, to the benefit of the corporate whole.

In terms of the hypothetical firms depicted in figures 7.2 and 7.3, the sharing of skills can be seen as enhancing the competitive advantage of the individual units, enabling them to compete more effectively in their own industries. As a result of this resource sharing, the combined value of the corporate whole is greater than the summed value of the business units, had they continued to operate independently. Corporate strategy, then, may add value by capitalizing on the lateral connections across the units. These connections may reflect the relatedness of the products and services—as in the case of Honda—or they may not—as in the case of GE. In every case, though, the objective is to increase the competitive advantage and earnings of the entire corporation by sharing the skills of some units with the others.

Sharing Activities

The final approach to corporate strategy builds on the same concept as the previous one but takes the idea an additional step. Rather than simply transferring competencies from one business unit to the others, sharing activities involves two or more business units actually linking their value chains together and sharing a common set of resources. The advantage of this is that it provides scale economies in the shared activity. For example, Taco Bell, Pizza Hut, and KFC, the three business units spun off by PepsiCo to form Tricon and later Yum! Brands, went so far as to share common facilities across the three restaurant chains. Essentially, Tricon would build one location to house all three restaurants. The stores were able to share storage and administrative space, as well as common overhead expenses like utilities and insurance. In so doing, the costs to each was reduced, increasing individual profitability for each and so the profitability of the whole.

Activity sharing often takes the form of administrative or "backroom" consolidation. A highly diversified firm with a variety of unrelated business units may still share common legal resources, common human resource management, or common insurance resources. When IBM acquired the management consulting division of PricewaterhouseCoopers, for instance, it installed its own human resource and information technology practices and systems, enabling it to leverage many of its own existing activities and resources to service this new business unit. By so doing, it was able to eliminate some costs of the new division while still retaining its revenues, thereby helping to create new value for the corporation. Firms that acquire new units may choose to consolidate their advertising expenses by using a single provider, so taking advantage of their increased bargaining power. In the same way, a firm may decide to consolidate its purchasing function in an effort to get better prices or terms from vendors. In any of these cases, the focus of activity sharing is to increase resource utilization and so reduce the cost of the activity to the business units involved. The result is greater earnings for the businesses and for the corporation as a whole.

Returning to Competitive Advantage

Any one of these approaches can yield competitive advantage for the firm and so lead to strategic success. However, at a general level, they all contribute to success in the same basic way, strengthening the value of the whole by increasing the net competitive advantage of the units. Moreover, that competitive advantage will be built upon one of the two generic sources of competitive advantage described in the last chapter—either differentiation or low cost.

To illustrate, consider again the example of Honda, whose competitive advantage is based largely on differentiation. Its products are highly desirable in relation to those of most of its competitors and, as a result, demand is somewhat inelastic. As such, its prices and margins are often higher on comparable products than those of its competitors. What is important to understand, though, is how Honda is able to extend its expertise and brand in order to create that differentiation across the full range of its products. It does this largely by transferring skills and sharing resources along the value chains of its business units. In engineering and design, in market research and advertising, even in areas like HR and R&D, Honda leverages a **core competence** in engine technology and quality manufacturing to produce a range of different products that are seen as being largely differentiated in their respective and different industries. That sort of synergy is a resource that is highly valuable, unique, and extremely difficult to imitate or substitute. As such, it has become a key feature of Honda's competitive advantage and financial success.

At the same time, some combination of these approaches may just as easily yield low-cost-based advantage. Consider the example of PepsiCo and its Taco Bell subsidiary. Taco Bell was able to earn extraordinary revenues and profits by serving food that was quick, consistent, and inexpensive to a highly elastic customer base. How was PepsiCo able to promote and accelerate this? Again, by sharing resources, transferring skills, and allocating capital more efficiently. As a growing business, Taco Bell needed investment. However, as a small, relatively unknown business, such capital was largely unavailable and unaffordable. Yet, once it was a subsidiary of PepsiCo, it had access to an enormous pool of capital that could be allocated internally. The result was a growing chain, with the ability to better leverage PepsiCo's core competencies in marketing and branding. Those skills and resources fed upon one another, enabling Taco Bell to grow large and familiar, facilitating greater leverage in purchasing and greater consistency and recognition in the market. All of this together meant Taco Bell could provide ubiquitous and highly standardized products at very low costs. Thus, it was through the valuable, rare, and largely inimitable synergies created by PepsiCo's corporate strategy that Taco Bell was able to achieve such a strong, low-cost-based competitive advantage and to produce such extraordinary financial results.

CONCLUDING THOUGHTS AND CAVEATS

Related and Unrelated Diversification

In 1974, Richard Rumelt published what is still considered by many the seminal work on diversification and corporate-level strategy. In it, he provided a framework for categorizing different types of diversification. Using three values—the specialization ratio, the related ratio, and the vertical ratio—Rumelt's framework placed firms into one of nine categories: single business, dominant-vertical, dominant-unrelated, dominant-constrained, dominant-linked, related-constrained, related-linked, unrelated business, and conglomerate. Over the years, this elaborate framework has been abbreviated into two general categories, related and unrelated diversification. Textbooks, articles in the popular press, even comments by business managers often contain references to related and unrelated diversification. Along with those references are implicit judgments about the value of each such that related diversification is generally considered to be better than unrelated diversification. There are a number of reasons for this, some of which are sound, others of which are not.

Perhaps the biggest contributor to this view is the past experiences of conglomerate diversifiers. As described earlier in the chapter, conglomerate diversification typically offered fewer obvious opportunities for synergy because few if any linkages were attempted across the value chains of the different business units. Rather, the principal source of value added from conglomerates was thought to be cash-flow stability, the reduction of financial risk, and the associated reduction in cost of capital. That benefit, however, offered little in the way of new value to shareholders, who could diversify their own risks themselves and do it with few real transaction costs. Thus, most conglomerate diversifiers failed to produce the synergy or new value needed to sustain the organization. Beyond this, though, there is also a bias against unrelated diversification connected to the results of Rumelt's study. Rumelt found that, generally, related diversification produced better results than other types. He speculated that this may have to do with the ability of related diversifiers to transfer managerial expertise or to share various assets and skills. Because of their similarity, related diversifiers were simply able to achieve synergy more readily than non-related diversifiers.

While the contribution of Rumelt's work is undeniable, and while the common view of related and unrelated diversification may be grounded in his findings, it is important to note that related diversifiers do not always succeed and that unrelated diversifiers do not always fail. Rather, in every case, the success of a diversification is a function of the synergy that the firm is able to realize. As illustrated through figures 7.2 and 7.3, and as explained throughout the chapter, diversification success is really about the creation of new competitive advantage and new profitability at the business unit level. There are certainly instances where this occurs in related diversification. However, there are also many examples of its occurring in unrelated businesses as well. The key in each case is the ability to share some resource, skill, or activity along the value chain, so that the net earnings of the business units are increased. While the possibilities for this sort of sharing may be more readily apparent and more easily achieved in related firms, they exist nevertheless in unrelated ones as well.

Market Selection

As discussed throughout the chapter, the key to successful corporate strategy is the creation of new value through the interaction of the corporation and its business units. A successful corporate strategy produces an organization that is worth more than the sum of its parts. But what of firms with unsuccessful corporate strategies? Can a corporation be worth less than the sum of its parts? The answer is yes, a firm can indeed be worth less than the summed value of its business units. When diversification imposes new costs over and above the new earnings generated by the business units, the value of the firm as a whole will necessarily decline. Firms that find themselves in that position will often become targets of an acquisition, in a process that looks very much like a market form of natural selection (Hughes & Singh, 1987). Market selection refers to the tendency of the market to penalize inefficiency and the underutilization of valuable assets. In such cases, the market actually provides an incentive for firms that are worth less than the sum of their parts to be purchased, broken apart, and reorganized into a more efficient and more valuable form.

One mechanism by which this selection process occurs is the **hostile takeover**, and the principal actor in such takeovers is often called a **corporate raider**. The latter term is unfortunately pejorative, as it has been linked to a variety of notorious characters such as Ivan Boesky and the fictitious Gordon Gekko, from the movie *Wall Street*. While these corporate raiders, along with the function they perform, are often cast in a negative light, in reality they fulfill an important function, identifying poorly managed firms and then facilitating the reallocation of underperforming assets to more productive and valuable uses.

Indeed, the incentive for a corporate raider is the value that can be realized through the elimination of inefficiency. Typically, a raider will spot a corporation that is not creating new value. Because the corporation is failing to create value in excess of the costs that it is imposing, it is necessarily worth less than the summed value of its individual business units. A raider can then buy the corporation at its fair market value and break it apart, selling off its various units and their assets individually, and still realize a substantial gain. Of course, the loser in this transaction is typically the corporate management and staff. With the business units all sold, there is no longer any need for corporate administration. Thus, corporate

Box 7.2
Corporate Raiders

A Mixed Record of Good and Bad

Corporate raiders became a familiar feature on the business landscape in the 1970s and 1980s. These raiders made their money by buying controlling interests in struggling companies and then selling off the assets or business units of those companies at a profit. They would move quickly and stealthily, often buying a company from its stockholders against the will of the company's managers. They would then dissolve the company and liquidate its assets. The practice was often viewed negatively, as a number of raiders went after large and well-known firms, such as Unocal, TWA, Revlon, and Disney.

Most of the raiders claimed to be protecting the interests of the shareholders. Nevertheless, they were often accused of a more sinister motivation—unmitigated greed. Indeed, raiders did often make tremendous amounts of money at the expense of thousands of jobs and several well-known companies. In 1987 the corporate raider was depicted in a fictionalized character named Gordon Gekko (played by Michael Douglas) in the popular Academy award-winning movie *Wall Street*, which told the story of Gekko manipulating the stock market and violating U.S. securities law in an effort to take control of Blue Star Airlines. Gekko's motivation was to profit from the company's overfunded pension plan while eliminating the jobs of people at the airline.

management generally resists these sorts of takeovers, arguing that the value of the individual units will not be greater than the value of the corporate whole. And sometimes they are right. However, the mere threat of a takeover is often enough to motivate management to be diligent regarding synergy and value. Stockholders simply will not long tolerate a firm whose efforts at diversification are costing more than they earn. Thus, the process of market selection is, over time, an effective judge of corporate strategic success.

The M-Form Organizational Structure

One of the most vexing issues in corporate strategy is the dual responsibility it creates for the business units and the business unit managers. On the one hand, the units must add to the value of the corporate whole. Some will do this directly, through the revenues and profits they create, while others will do it indirectly, through their relationship to the other units. Within Disney, for instance, there are individual business units competing in the theme park, movie, and television industries. The strategies of these businesses are simple enough to understand and evaluate and the performance of each is simple enough to measure. But how should these revenue-producing business units be compared with Disney's more creative, non-revenue-producing business units? The creative arm of Disney, known for years as the "Imagineering" group, sells its products primarily to the other Disney divisions, enabling their competitiveness but generating no outside revenue and earning no direct income on its own. Moreover, the various units within Disney support one another through co-branding of the characters and stories and through shared promotion of many of the firm's products. While this sort of activity and resource sharing is good for synergy, it is not always good for the performance of the business units themselves. Thus, there is an inevitable tension between the demands of the corporate-level strategy and the pressures of the business-level strategy.

It is probably unrealistic to think that these tensions can ever be fully resolved, even with the best strategy, management, and accounting methods. Business unit managers are most easily evaluated on the performance of their units. So, understandably, they want to be as successful as possible at competing within their own industries. However, operating as if they were single businesses may not be what is best for the corporation as a whole. Suppose, for example, that the Pizza Hut management had believed the restaurant chain would perform best by serving Coke products rather than Pepsi. Even if such a move were to benefit Pizza Hut, it would likely hurt PepsiCo as a whole. Thus, the business units within larger corporations must be managed to serve two masters. They must try to compete effectively, within their industries, as a function of their business unit strategy, while also serving the greater interests of the corporate whole. To facilitate this, business units are often managed in a semi-autonomous fashion, operating independently, within the constraints and mandates of the larger corporate strategy. The structural mechanism that facilitates this state of semi-autonomy is called the "M-form" organization.

The M-form is a label given to the structure of many multi-divisional corporations (Williamson, 1975). An M-form structure (illustrated in Figure 7.3) has a headquarters and a series of semi-autonomous business units. Each of these units operates under the mandate of the larger corporate strategy, sharing resources as required, for instance, to benefit the corporate whole, but also with its own management and its own strategy competing within its own industry. Georgia Pacific, for example, has several separate divisions, including building products, pulp and paper, even real-estate management and development. Each of these business units has a dual charge, to add value to the corporate whole and to compete effectively within its industry.

To facilitate this dual responsibility, corporate strategy and structure must provide a number of infrastructural support mechanisms. Most significant among these is an accounting and compensation system that effectively tracks the real value added by the business units to the corporate whole, independent of the individual business unit's profits. Such contributions may come through the sharing of a resource, such as the brand name of another unit, or the transfer of a skill, as would be the case where one unit provided engineering expertise to another. Regardless of how the value is added, the challenge is to account for it accurately so that its contribution can be effectively measured and rewarded. In the absence of such mechanisms, business unit managers have little incentive to support the corporate strategy. Indeed, they may find that in trying to create synergy they actually hinder the performance of their units. As such, they may choose not to pursue synergy. The M-form, then, is an important tool in helping firms to manage both the vertical and the horizontal relationships required for an effective corporate strategy.

Organizational Culture

One of the frustrating realities of corporate strategy is that synergy is much easier to envision than to realize. Indeed, in case after case, firms believe that they can diversify and create new value, only to find that the envisioned synergy never materializes and the corporation consumes more value than it creates. While this occurs for a number of reasons, one of the main reasons is that the corporation cannot get the business units to change as necessary to fulfill their new roles. One of the main culprits in this common problem is the culture clash of the organizations.

One well-known example of this occurred when the German automobile maker Daimler announced that it would sell its U.S.-based partner Chrysler to the private equity firm Cerberus Capital Management, who later sold the company to Fiat as part of a bankruptcy proceeding. The initial sale reversed a 1998 merger that was undertaken amid great optimism but which never produced the benefits envisioned. Indeed, Daimler originally paid over $36 billion for Chrysler. Yet, in the end, it realized just $7.4 billion on the final sale. What was especially startling is that, even with the staggering loss, Daimler's stock rose when the sale was announced, suggesting that the two companies were better off apart than together. How could a deal that once seemed so promising end so poorly?

Several things contributed to the result. In the years after the merger the slump in Chrysler's performance was worse than expected, as legacy costs associated with its pension and healthcare expenses rose more quickly than forecast. A rise in oil and gasoline prices also contributed to the performance decline, since Chrysler's strength was in larger, but less fuel-efficient cars, which became less attractive as gas prices spiked. Ultimately, though, the deal fell through, with the performance of both companies suffering, because the anticipated synergies between the two never materialized. Those synergies, which would have enabled Chrysler designers to benefit from Daimler's engineering and technology competencies and the dealership networks of both companies to offer a full range of different types of vehicles from both manufacturers, required a level of cooperation and relationship that simply never occurred.

While it is reasonable to question whether such cooperation was ever practical to begin with, it was certainly anticipated by the management of both firms. Indeed, top-level executives at both companies trumpeted the partnership with enthusiasm. Daimler's competencies in design and engineering were supposed to have increased the efficiency and quality of Chrysler's line-up. Meanwhile, Chrysler's familiarity with the U.S. market, combined with its large dealer network, was supposed to provide Daimler the opportunity for increased penetration of the U.S. market. Both firms' dealers were supposed to have benefited from the expanded number of new offerings. Daimler's dealers would be able to sell the popular Jeep brand, which was owned by Chrysler, as well as the full range of Chrysler trucks. Chrysler dealers would have also been able to sell Mercedes cars, and so garner a larger share of the luxury car market. On paper at least, there were many points of intersection where the value chains of the two firms could be linked and where there would be opportunities to share resources. Nevertheless, the deal ultimately failed because so little of what was true on paper translated into reality.

Chrysler's culture was oriented largely towards marketing and volume sales, while Daimler's culture was based on precision and efficiency. Efforts by Daimler managers to introduce new processes were often rejected because they slowed development time, limited scalability, or necessitated higher prices. At the same time, many of Daimler's employees viewed Chrysler with suspicion. There was little regard for Chrysler's products and often little respect for its managers or suggestions on marketing. The dealer networks were each highly suspicious of the other and viewed one another as competitors. Neither group wanted to see the other selling its products and undercutting its presence in the local marketplace. Thus, on virtually every dimension, there were cultural and human impediments to the synergies that had seemed so achievable when the merger was designed.

These sorts of issues are often relegated to lower levels of management when major deals like this one are struck. Too often, in fact, they are considered just the mundane work of implementation, barely worthy of the attention of upper management, whose time is best spent on more important issues like financing or market positioning. However, as the old saying goes, the devil is in the details, and these sorts of cultural details can be the essence of strategic success. Without synergy, corporate strategy fails. And without some means of bridging the culture divide between the combined organizational units, there is likely to be very little synergy.

Multi-Point Competition

Because a corporation consists of multiple business units which compete in different competitive environments, it stands to reason that some corporations will have business units that compete in multiple yet similar industries. Indeed, this is actually quite common and for understandable reasons.

Consider the example of a hypothetical business unit that is part of a larger corporation, from which it derives synergy. That derived synergy will likely provide this business unit with substantial competitive advantage over any independent competitor. Bryan Foods, for example, is a subsidiary of Sara Lee, from which it draws synergy in the form of market power and bargaining leverage. That bargaining power may translate into a number of tangible benefits for Bryan Foods. Its products may get better placement or it may obtain better terms from its advertising providers or financial suppliers. Whatever the exact form of the benefits, they will make Bryan Foods a much more formidable competitor than any single business firm that does not benefit from similar corporate synergy. To compete effectively against Bryan Foods, then, a competitor would need to be diversified in much the same way, so that it too could leverage the synergy from its corporate parent. So, over time, many if not most of the firms in that industry would have to diversify in a similar fashion or be forced to exit the industry altogether. The result of this process is a set of corporations that often compete across a number of different business units and product lines.

Multi-point competition is a complex but fascinating phenomenon that has been the subject of considerable academic research (Baum & Korn, 1996; Gimeno & Woo, 1996). One interesting observation from this research is a phenomenon called **mutual forbearance** (Karnani & Wernerfelt, 1985), which occurs when firms, competing in multiple different markets, decide to compete less vigorously as a result of their broad interdependence. Increasing aggressiveness in one market could lead to increased competitive intensity across the full range of the different markets and product lines. As a result, rather than risk intensified competition that could hurt them both, the firms will often choose to tolerate one another. The logic for this forbearance reflects a sort of competitive parity principle, where corporations have so much exposure and so much to risk across the breadth of their multiple business units that they opt to accommodate rather than to provoke their competitors.

Multi-point competition can also lead a corporation to remain in a business or an industry long after the attractiveness of that industry has faded or to enter an industry that would otherwise seem unattractive, as a way to defend against potential competitors. Certainly, as business has grown increasingly global, there are more and more instances where firms bump into one another through different product or geographic units. Thus, the strategist will want to be cognizant of the full range of implications of his or her initiatives. What may seem a good idea for a business unit may well produce problems for the corporation overall. And what the larger corporation needs may not always be in the best interest of particular business units.

SUMMARY

Corporate-level strategy can best be thought of as the strategy for dealing with multiple business units. As reviewed in the preceding chapters, strategy at the business unit level deals with how to compete in a particular business and business environment. Corporate-level strategy, on the other hand, deals with the value of the corporate whole. The ultimate challenge of corporate-level strategy is to satisfy what Porter (1987) called the "better-off" test. In other words, to be successful, the corporate strategy must somehow create new value through its multiple businesses and business units.

While a simple concept, this better-off test has proven to be a very high standard in practice. Indeed, corporate strategy and diversification seem to fail as often as they succeed. The reason for this has to do with the economic realities of corporate strategy. As explained in the chapter, adding business units, whether through organic growth or acquisition, imposes new costs and new pressures. With all else being the same, units would run more efficiently and more profitably without these new costs and pressures. The key to success, then, comes in the things that the corporation does that are not the same. Creating an internal capital market that can allocate resources more efficiently and with better information and insight can lower the overall cost of capital and make the business units more profitable. Combining resources or linking value-chain activities across the units so that they are more competitive in their various industries can make them more profitable. Even sharing expertise within the corporation such that underperforming business units can be restructured and turned into sources of greater profit can increase the value of the corporate whole. These various different types of activities are all sources of synergy, which is the key to success in corporate strategy. Moreover, synergy is a very real resource, which is valuable and rare, as well as very difficult to imitate and substitute. A successful corporate strategy, then, enables a strong and sustainable competitive advantage.

KEY TERMS

Business-level strategy is that part of a firm's strategy that focuses on how a single business or a single business unit will compete in its industry or business environment.

A **conglomerate** is a corporation that is highly diversified and involved in a number of unrelated businesses.

A **core competence** is a factor that can enable better products, services, and methods and that can be shared across different units or activities of a firm. They are embedded in the firm's resources and so are difficult to observe and imitate directly.

A **corporate raider** is a person who purchases or attempts to purchase a controlling interest in a company against the wishes of the current management. The raider will often then sell off the assets of the company and generate a substantial profit.

Diversification is a strategy for expanding organizational scope or reducing organizational risk by adding additional products, services, locations, or customers to a company's existing portfolio.

A **hostile takeover** is a change in ownership that occurs against the wishes of the target company's management and board of directors.

A **mode of entry** is the way in which a firm enters a new country or place or business. For example, it can enter by exporting, licensing, joint venture, or direct investment.

Mutual forbearance is said to occur when, because of their mutual interdependence, rival firms engage in tacitly collusive or non-competitive actions across a range of common market interactions.

Net present value is the current value of an investment's future net cash flows, discounted by the effects of time and risk, minus the initial investment. A positive NPV suggests a good investment.

A **profit center** is a business unit or department within a larger corporation that is treated as a distinct entity, with its own revenues, expenses, and profit.

Strategic business units (SBUs) are distinct and semi-autonomous units within a larger corporation. They will often operate in their own industry, with their own business-level strategy, and with full responsibility for their own revenues, costs, and profits.

Synergy applies in situations where different units cooperate to produce more than could be produced otherwise. Stated simply, synergy is said to occur when the whole is greater than the sum of the parts.

Time value refers to the current value of a sum of money to be received or paid at some time in the future, adjusted either for the growth that will occur through earnings or for the discount taken to reflect opportunity costs.

QUESTIONS FOR REVIEW

1   What advantages and disadvantages can you see for a firm such as PepsiCo to be in the restaurant business?

2   What is the difference between corporate-level strategy and business-level strategy? What is the practical value in distinguishing between these two levels of the strategic process?

3   How is corporate strategy like managing a portfolio of stocks, bonds, and other investments? How is it different?

4   Research suggests that most corporate strategies fail to achieve the value that they were intended to produce. Why is success in corporate strategy so difficult and elusive?

5   Describe the four approaches to corporate strategy discussed in the chapter. What are the differences and similarities across these general approaches?

6   What is synergy and how does it contribute to competitive advantage?

7   How does corporate strategy accentuate the value, rareness, inimitability, and sustainability of the firm's resources?

8   What is market selection and what are the positive and negative connotations associated with it?

9   Define multi-point competition. Why does it exist and how does it affect the strategies and competitive dynamics of the firms involved?

Companion Website

For a chapter review outline with links to videos and other valuable web resources, please visit the *Strategic Management* website: www.routledge.com/textbooks/amason.

Chapter 8

Strategy Implementation

Fit, Adaptation, and Learning

BILLIONS SERVED

If good strategy is reflected in performance over time, then few firms have had a better strategy over the years than McDonald's. The modern-day company took shape in 1954, when Ray Croc teamed up with brothers Dick and Mac McDonald to open the first location with the famous golden arches. By 1958, McDonald's had sold its 100 millionth hamburger. The stock went public in 1965, selling for $22.50 per share; by this time, there were over 500 locations across the U.S. Since these early years, McDonald's has grown and profited steadily, providing value for its customers, wealth for its owners, and a variety of opportunities for its employees. By 2009 the company had more than 31,000 locations in 118 countries, with system-wide revenues of over $54 billion and earnings of over $4.3 billion. Indeed, with over 1.1 billion shares outstanding, McDonald's share price ended 2008 at $62.19.

Yet, despite all of this success, the ride has been bumpy at times, prompting some to speculate that the firm's best days were in the past. For example, there have been any number of competitors who appeared for a time to be better positioned to the changing tastes and fashions of the day. Such was the case when Wendy's instituted a drive-through option or when Burger King began offering limited made-to-order service. More recently, competitors such as Chick-fil-A and Subway have promoted their products as healthy alternatives to the traditional offerings at McDonald's. And there have been other challenges as well, such as when McDonald's came under fire for the use of Styrofoam packaging or when Morgan Spurlock released the movie *Super Size Me*, criticizing McDonald's for its portion sizes and for the high levels of fat and sodium in its products. And when Starbucks began offering greater variety in food selections across its 11,000 stores, there was concern that McDonald's would suffer as consumers chose to move upscale for their breakfasts and midday snacks. Even the stock market has exerted pressure, suggesting at times that the firm had become a dinosaur, with little growth potential and upside for investors seeking competitive returns.

Despite these various challenges, McDonald's continues to thrive. Indeed, one could be reminded of the famous quote, often attributed to Mark Twain, "the reports of my death have been greatly exaggerated." Competitors and activists, analysts and professors have all reasoned at one time or another that McDonald's strategy was misaligned and out of touch with the environment, leading to speculation that its success was nearing an end. Yet, it continues to maintain its position as the leader in the fast-serve restaurant market, continuing to expand, to deliver good value to its customers, and to grow and profit as a result.

While this example may offer a number of lessons, perhaps none is more important than this: *strategy is ultimately about what you do to create value for your customers*. Competitors, activists, analysts, and the like are all important at some point. However, firms that stay connected to their customers, that continue to offer products and services their customers value and that do so at a profitable price, will maintain their competitive advantage and, as a result, continue to perform well. Recall from Chapter 1 that strategy may at times appear to be part plan, ploy, pattern, position, and perspective. However, what makes all of these facets of strategy meaningful is their link, whether immediate or eventual, to action. A ploy, for instance, would have little value if there were not some action implied so as to misdirect the competition. Similarly, plans are important because of their implication for action; otherwise they become little more than sources of frustration and cynicism. Strategy, then, is ultimately about action, about doing things that create value and so enable competitive advantage. Moreover, because the things that create value and enable competitive advantage will change along with the environment, so too must a firm's actions change as necessary to stay fit to the environment.

Those two issues, fit and change, are the subject of this chapter. Moreover, throughout the discussion of fit and change, a parallel and important distinction will become salient. That distinction is between the short term and the long term and the different types of thinking and actions that good strategists will use to prepare for and perform well in both. For now, it is enough to understand that a short-term focus will often be at odds with a longer-term focus. In the same way, long-term thinking will often conflict with shorter-term realities. Thus, there is an inevitable tension between the two, just as there will be an inevitable tension between the principles of fit and change. One is about immediacy and efficiency; the other is about flexibility and the creation of options. However, both are essential to success over time.

IMPLEMENTATION

As discussed in Chapter 3, implementation is an integral part of strategic management and is defined as the deployment and operation of organizational structures, facilities, human resources, and support systems, as necessary, to bring a strategy to fruition. The guiding principle of strategy implementation goes back to the work of Alfred Chandler (1962) and the idea that structure should follow strategy. Structure, in this sense, means all of the systems, processes, and functions of the organization. Structures take shape according to the design of strategy. Put simply, if strategy is the plan, then implementation is the execution.

This distinction between planning and execution, or between what theorists typically call formulation and implementation, is both intuitive and seductively simple. It stands to reason that some planning should precede action and that resource deployments should be guided by some thought and purpose. Over the years, though, implementation has come to be seen by students and practitioners as being less and less "strategic." Scholars spend much more time researching the analytical and creative aspects of formulation than the nuts and bolts of implementation. New managers are often encouraged by senior executives to think big and to think long term, and so not to confuse strategy with tactics. Strategy consultants have been the target of jokes, as in a television commercial for UPS Logistic Services, because they make grand propositions but do not "actually do" what they propose to do. The unfortunate result of all this is that both students and managers too often view implementation as less meaningful; implementation is what comes after strategy and is the work of others, somewhere lower in the organization.

The reality, though, is that formulation and implementation are intertwined in a very complex way. Each impacts the other and each exerts great influence over the performance of the firm. A well-formulated strategy should specify what a firm intends to do and how it intends to do it. However, even a well-formulated strategy is of no use if nothing ever actually happens. Something tangible must occur: some action must be taken, someone must do something for the intentions of a strategy to become a reality and so have their intended effects on customers, competitors, and competitive advantage. Implementation is that something; thus implementation is a key to strategic success.

In an insightful article, Mintzberg (1987) described strategy using the metaphor of a potter and a lump of clay. The potter starts with a plan for what the clay will become. Of course, the clay is unaffected by the plans. Rather, it is the actions of the potter that shape the clay. Just as importantly, those actions also lead the potter to adjust her plans. If the clay has a flaw, or if some accident leads to a surprise discovery, the potter may reconsider her plans and undertake something different than what she intended originally. By illustration, Mintzberg makes the point that there is always an initial plan—what we would call the formal strategy. Nevertheless, the reality of the outcome emerges from a process of doing and learning. The clay is shaped by the potter but the potter also responds to the clay, acting to convert her plans into reality and learning how best to achieve her objectives, given the details of the situation, as they unfold.

While a bit esoteric, this picture is still closer to the reality than most textbook depictions of formulation and implementation. Indeed, the illustration makes especially clear two important points. First, implementation requires some action or some change of assets from one purpose or state to another. Plans aside, the potter gets the outcomes she wants only by getting her hands dirty; it is action, then, that converts plans to reality. Second, strategy is simply a means to an end; it is not an end unto itself. No one should be surprised when the strategy changes, most especially the strategist. Rather, good strategists expect it. It has been reported that Mike Tyson, the famous former world champion boxer, once said: "Everyone has a plan, until they get hit." His quote reflects the celebrated insight that no battle plan survives its contact with the enemy. No one can anticipate every contingency and every change in circumstance; in fact, no one should try. Instead, good strategists must prepare to respond as needed as the situation changes.

Thus, if strategic management is all about performance, good strategists should be obsessed with implementation. Implementation is how plans are converted to reality and how firms interact with the environment, so as to learn about new opportunities and threats. Going back to the example, McDonald's has created a record of sustained success by doing things that actually deliver value to its customers, lower costs for its franchisors, and drive traffic to its stores. Most of these things resulted from learning, either from customers or from competitors. That learning then had to be converted into the sorts of action that produced real and tangible results. Redesigning its facilities to provide drive-through service was an action requiring specific and new investments and changes in procedures. The initiative to build and market the McCafe coffee shops in the restaurants also required real menu changes, fresh marketing campaigns, and the addition of new equipment. Over time there have been many such changes, some of which resulted from creativity and innovation, some of which were simply responses to the marketplace. Yet all were driven by the desire to build and sustain competitive advantage.

A Second Level of Fit

As discussed throughout the book, strategic success is a reflection of fit. Until now, fit referred to the alignment or congruence between the competitive environment and the strategy. For example, Ryanair is a discount airline serving 150 destinations across 26 European countries. With high consumer satisfaction, steadily increasing traffic, and a history of strong profitability, Ryanair has a strategy of being the lowest cost and most reliable discount carrier in Europe that seems to be working well. It works, though, because it fits the environment. That Ryanair is successful tells us, for instance, that there is a portion of the market for air travel that is highly elastic. It also tells us that there is a substantial and underserved group of travelers who were either unwilling or unable to fly with other non-discount carriers. Ryanair charges for things like luggage, priority boarding, and refreshments in flight. That passenger traffic remains strong despite these charges suggests that most customers are willing to accept them, provided that the savings are passed back in the form of low ticket prices. For now at least, the success of Ryanair in this market and at this time is undeniable. And that success is the best evidence of the fit between the strategy and the environment.

But there is a second level of fit, where the idea is the same but the pieces are different. This is the fit between strategy and all of the elements of the organization's structure and operations. Different strategies require different types of organizational structure and action. It was in observing the relationship between how strategies evolved and how that evolution necessitated changes in structure that Chandler (1962) reasoned that structure should follow strategy. Other early organizational theorists, such as Burns and Stalker (1961) and Lawrence and Lorsch (1967), drew similar conclusions from their own observations. Organizations that performed well over time were organized and operated in way that fit their strategy. In essence, when form was fit to function, good performance was the result. The principle of fit, then, applies at two levels—between the environment and the strategy, but also between the strategy and the organization. Incongruence anywhere along the chain threatens the ability of a firm to deliver value to the customer and, thus, threatens performance.

In the abstract language of theory, this notion seems more complicated than it need be. So, to illustrate by example, let us return to the case of Ryanair. Its strategy of low cost and reliability is well formulated and fit to its environment. Thus, to succeed, Ryanair needs to implement its strategy as designed; in essence, it needs to convert design into reality. The question is, how?

Using the example, it is clear that one imperative of this low-cost, high-accessibility strategy is a route structure that facilitates high load factors and short turnaround times. Over its history, Ryanair has built a route structure precisely for those purposes. It serves major cities or population centers where there have been few options. This facilitates high load factors, which lowers cost per unit. Moreover, the route system operates on a point-to-point basis. There are no connecting flights and no transferred baggage; there is no responsibility for missed connections or for scheduling beyond a single flight. Planes are loaded at the point of origin and unloaded at the destination, with no accounting for connections. This simplifies the scheduling and servicing on the ground, lowering administrative costs, reducing risk, and increasing reliability. It also facilitates faster turnaround by reducing system-wide delays, allowing the planes to spend more time in the air, making more trips per day than the competition. This increases asset utilization, further enabling lower ticket prices.

Ryanair is decidedly no frills: snacks and beverages are sold, not given away, and, unless a customer pays for premium seating, there are no classes of service. This minimizes time at the gate, facilitating reliability and asset utilization. The limited cabin service also fits with the many short-haul flights in the route system. The fleet consists of 196 planes, all Boeing 737s. While this plane is efficient for short- and medium-range routes, the real advantage comes in having only one type of aircraft; only one set of maintenance routines, mechanics, and tools is needed. There is also only one procedure for servicing the aircraft at the gate. Again, this facilitates lower costs, quicker turns, and greater scheduling reliability. Ryanair uses discount prices to encourage online booking and check-in, so as to reduce staffing and administrative costs. It also offers discounts for advance purchase to facilitate scheduling.

Even its indirect activities reflect its strategy. In the case of marketing, for instance, Ryanair attracts customers by positioning itself as an alternative to the more established, major carriers like British Airways or Lufthansa. To build awareness and position itself as the counter to these established carriers, Ryanair uses quirky and unorthodox advertising, at times courting trouble for its racy and off-beat campaigns. But this approach facilitates the purpose, leveraging a smaller budget while building an "us against them" reputation. Finally, even its employment practices reinforce the unique and low-cost strategy. Ryanair builds performance incentives into its salary structure, encouraging its employees to find new savings and efficiencies. It also uses its strategy in recruiting in an effort to attract workers suited to the culture, thereby reducing the costs associated with staffing.

When considered in detail, it is easy to see why Ryanair is successful. Its strategy is well fit to its environment and the organization itself is well fit to the strategy. Where that sort of multi-level fit exists, good performance follows. But it is important to remember two things. First, the principle of fit goes both ways. While effective for this strategy, these structures and practices would work less well elsewhere. Indeed, the very same structures and practices would likely be less effective if employed by Lufthansa. Lufthansa has a large, transcontinental route structure and a variety of different aircraft suited to its various routes and needs. Imagine the chaos and dysfunction that would result if it were to try and use only one type of aircraft. Second, implementation works through a combination of elements. There is no single part of Ryanair's implementation that carries the load, no single facet of the operation that is by itself the key to competitive advantage. A competitor cannot simply copy Ryanair's quirky advertising campaign and hope to be equally successful. This echoes the point made in Chapter 5 that competitive advantage emerges from a complex sequence of actions and events.

McKinsey 7-S Model

Notwithstanding that complexity, though, the example serves to illustrate the importance of fit between strategy and the various levers of implementation. Figure 8.1, showing the McKinsey 7-S model, is meant to reinforce the point again. Developed in the late 1970s by a group of consultants at McKinsey & Co. (Pascale & Athos, 1981; Peters, Waterman, & Phillips, 1980), the 7-S model is a depiction of the various facets within a firm that are likely to affect its performance. The model reminds us that these seven factors are all connected, either through direct causal linkages or through indirect consequences. And so the model illustrates how performance is attributable to more than just a good strategy, more than just good human resources practices or good logistics. Rather, performance results from all of these things, working together in combination, to produce value for the customer.

While robust in its implications, the model is often dismissed for its simplicity. In reality, though, it is a powerful analytical guide that can help to diagnose dysfunction or to design structures and practices to complement a strategy. Its use involves some intuition and judgment and can at times seem tedious and unstructured. It

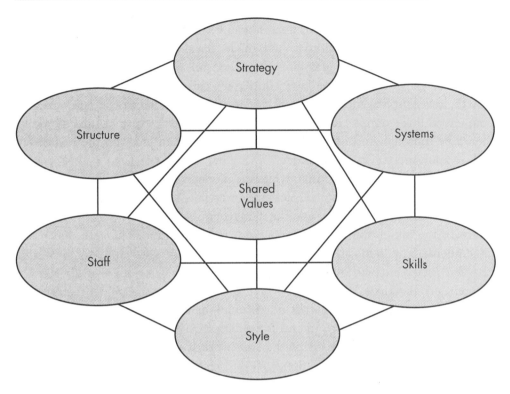

FIGURE 8.1 The McKinsey 7-S Model

involves working through a variety of linkages which are often straightforward in isolation but which can produce indirect effects that are subtle and complex. Overlooking these indirect effects can lead managers to decisions about structures or systems that can seem reasonable at a high level but that can produce unintended and indirect effects detrimental to success.

Such was the case at Home Depot in 2005, when new CEO Bob Nardelli undertook a restructuring that moved away from the style of the past to a less personal and less costly way of doing business. While the new approach yielded savings and profits in the short term, the long-term consequences were unforeseen and ultimately damaging. Home Depot's growth and success had long been built on superior service. That service was delivered through a staff of knowledgeable and experienced employees, working with a large and varied inventory. Sales associates would listen, advise, and teach, and then draw upon the in-stock inventory to provide solutions that customers might never have found on their own. Over time, customers grew to expect that Home Depot would solve their problems, even when they themselves did not know exactly what they needed.

While this system may have been more costly in terms of compensation and staffing levels, it did produce the customer value and sales volume that were at the root of Home Depot's competitive advantage. As a result, while Nardelli's changes produced short-term savings and a subsequent improvement in profits, they also undermined the foundation that had made the firm successful. As a result, customers slowly began to gravitate away, choosing alternatives that were either cheaper or provided better service. Ultimately, this migration led to diminished growth, lower profits, and lower stock prices, which then led to Nardelli's resignation. Given this example, it is important to remember that use of the 7-S model should be thorough and detailed, with full consideration given to the realities of each relationship, direct and indirect.

It should be acknowledged that, while the model is powerful in its implications, there is nothing magical about the actual items (skills, staff, style, etc.). Indeed, it is likely that the number of items and the items themselves were chosen intentionally to create the alliteration, which helped to make the model familiar and easily remembered. The items are just broad categories. There is certainly some overlap between them and without doubt different terms that would work better for different organizations. What is important, though, is that the model represents a robust set of activities, characteristics, or functions common to virtually all firms that are necessary for strategy to become reality.

Structure, for instance, refers to the way work is organized and the way that products, processes, and information flow through the firm. For Ryanair, structure includes things like the route system, the terminals and ground infrastructure, and the aircraft inventory. Systems take in things like the online reservation system and the procurement systems that deliver fuel to the planes and schedule the flight crews and maintenance. Staff involves people from the managers to the baggage handlers, while skills are all the abilities of those people, the attributes that go into their selection and training, and the institutional memory of how things get done. Every strategy requires certain skills for its effective implementation, and those skills are a reflection of the people the firm hires as well as the training and development it provides. Style refers to the personality of the organization. Every firm has a personality. Ryanair has a very clear style that reinforces its strategy and that is recognizable to customers. Moreover, it is a style that is cultivated intentionally and deliberately, as necessary, to support the strategy and the other elements of the model. The final element is shared values. Shared values can also be called culture, which is simply the core of what the people in the firm believe. At Ryanair, there is a strong shared value of low cost, of being distinct from the more traditional carriers, and of making air travel fun and easy. To create value for customers, given the choices, alternatives, and expectations created by the environment, and to produce good performance, these seven elements must complement one another as well as the strategy.

As a result, whether building new strategy, optimizing existing strategy, or diagnosing poor performance, the 7-S model can provide a clear and cohesive guide. A good strategist will review continually the linkages and relationships depicted in the model in an effort to improve, to identify potential problems, or to work through the implications of changes in strategy. For McDonald's, the strategy has always been to be the option of first choice for consumers searching for a quick and inexpensive, and yet reliably tasty, meal. To facilitate that strategy, there must be the right locations, the right menu, and the right procurement and preparation procedures, all matched to the right marketing, financial, and HR systems. As the environment changes, and as customer tastes change along with it, so must the menu change as well. Changing the menu, though, will necessitate changes in procurement and preparation procedures as well as in the marketing and store layout. When all of these parts work together, good performance follows. Conversely, when performance is poor, the cause can usually be traced to some inconsistency or lack of fit in what the firm seeks to do and what it is actually doing.

In concluding the discussion of fit and of the 7-S model, then, two issues need to be reinforced and understood. The first is that many of the important determinants of performance are subtle and indirect, embedded in the linkages among the elements of the model. Thus, 7-S analysis can be complex and even tedious, requiring detailed evaluation, imagination, and expert judgment. Chrysler, a former member of the "big three automakers" and a stalwart of the American car industry, went bankrupt because it was not designing and producing cars that consumers wanted to buy in sufficient numbers and at sufficient prices to provide a sustained profit. Given that, why could Chrysler simply not invest more in engineering, design, and efficient manufacturing facilities? The answer is that the problems are rarely the result of just one or two elements working in isolation. So addressing problems like these is never as simple as adjusting just one or two elements. Chrysler certainly wanted a strong design and engineering group that developed good cars. However, simply hiring bright people might not be enough to make that desire a reality. Other issues would have to be addressed as well. For example, were the engineers given the right incentives? Was the connection between the design and manufacturing functions direct and efficient? Was top management sufficiently well connected to identify the right products and get them to market quickly? It is likely that multiple breakdowns in numerous areas undermined Chrysler's strategy and success. Thus, just as competitive advantage is embedded in a complex and interacting set of resources and actions, so does effective implementation depend upon a combination of events and factors. The challenge is to understand all of those linkages and their implications and to use that understanding to create a firm that can deliver on the promise of its strategy.

The second thing to remember is that, because of all this complexity, fit can always be improved. Just as competitive advantage can always be strengthened, so too can the various connections across the firm be refined and strengthened. Indeed, one way to put relentless pressure on the competition is by continually tightening the fit among the elements of the 7-S model. Ryanair is constantly looking for ways to make its operations more efficient, so that it can lower ticket prices even further. Understanding that its market is highly elastic, Ryanair understands that its customers will continue to buy only for so long as it continues to be the best alternative. Thus, it is always interested in ways to turn planes quicker, to move passengers and luggage more efficiently, and to reduce the overhead associated with technology, HR, and infrastructure.

SHORT-TERM FIT, LONG-TERM FLEXIBILITY

But better fit alone cannot guarantee long-term success. Indeed, there are subtle trade-offs and hidden consequences in this principle of fit that have vexed managers and academics for years. As recounted earlier in the text, history is full of examples where firms that once held dominant positions in their industries and that once performed well above the average somehow managed to slip and lose their advantages to upstart competitors. These firms often were the best positioned, with the best fit both internally and externally. Yet their competition found a way to overtake them, to lure away their customers and, in some cases, to drive them out of business. Given this, it has been argued that success is somehow paradoxical and difficult if not impossible to sustain over time (Amason & Mooney, 2008; Miller, 1992).

The idea that performance is somehow paradoxical was introduced in Chapter 2. However, a full discussion of the topic has waited until now because the issues are most clear when viewed in the context of implementation. The connection between fit and change, strategy implementation, and the paradoxical nature of performance mirrors the relationship between short-term and long-term thinking. Often, doing what is necessary for the short term means sacrificing some flexibility in the long term. Alternatively, building for the long term may involve forgoing some benefits in the short term. A good example of this is research and development spending. Most investments in R&D constitute expenses in the current period; yet the benefits of those expenses are not likely to be realized until much later. And those future benefits are speculative, involving some risk and uncertainty. Indeed, research shows that R&D spending does not guarantee future profitability (Foster, 2003). Given the delay and the uncertainty in the benefits, it stands to reason that financial pressure would often lead to reduced R&D spending (Demirag, 1995). Managers facing intense competition or serious financial distress will find it difficult to justify speculative expenses like R&D, and so often pare them back in an effort to conserve cash and address more immediate problems.

Of course such decisions, while potentially necessary in the short term, may have dire consequences in the longer term. Indeed, the *Wall Street Journal* reports how many executives in 2009 struggled to maintain R&D investments, fearful that cutting research and development would leave them with obsolete products or technologies and poorly positioned to compete in the future. History shows that many major innovations—things such as the iPod and iTunes or the composite turbine blades in jet engines—resulted from research and development that occurred during economic downturns. Given the lesson of examples such as these, many consultants and academics have advised that firms should be most aggressive during periods of economic distress, so as to seize the initiative and outmaneuver the competition (Rhoades & Stelter, 2009). Such advice, though, while easy to give, can be difficult to take when sales are dropping, cash is tight, and the future is uncertain. After all, investing for the long term makes little sense if you cannot survive past the short term.

Thus, the conundrum between maximizing returns based upon current resources and capabilities and creating value for the future by investing in new resources and capabilities is a familiar one. It is also a problem with no simple solution. Certainly there are anecdotes where speculative investments, made despite more immediate needs, produced great innovation and success. But such investments involve great uncertainty which can place a firm at risk. On the other hand, there are just as many stories of firms that missed opportunities by playing it safe. Worried about cash flow and profits, managers stood pat, only to watch later as competitors overtook their market with new products and services. So there is no formula, no rule, by which managers can know exactly how to balance these two imperatives. Nevertheless, they must both be served: firms must do what is necessary to profit and thrive in the short term. However, they must also invest in new resources and capabilities if they hope to survive in the long term.

The Paradox of Success

The dilemma maps onto two specific challenges in strategy implementation. The first is to make sure the organization fits the strategy as it exists in the current competitive environment. As discussed earlier, that involves aligning the elements of the 7-S model both to the strategy and to one another. But, more than just that, it also involves continually fine-tuning and refining the alignment, working to improve, to tighten the fit, and to strengthen the competitive advantage of the firm. The second challenge, though, is to look beyond the current strategy and the current environment in an effort to build new capabilities and new strategies for the future. As discussed elsewhere, environment change is inevitable. Thus, if they hope to sustain a competitive advantage over time, firms must change too by developing new assets, new resources, and new capabilities.

The problem is that these two processes—strengthening fit in the present and developing capabilities for the future—are largely incompatible. Tightening the fit between the strategy and the various parts of the organization requires eliminating unnecessary effort, reinforcing successful routines and practices, and relentlessly pursuing efficiency and consistency. Strengthening fit means identifying and consolidating the practices that contribute to competitive advantage while eliminating virtually everything else. Unfortunately, though, building new capabilities requires a different type of effort altogether—experimenting with new, unfamiliar, and often unproven practices. It requires speculative investment in the development of new ideas and novel resources that may one day prove valuable but are likely to provide little immediate benefit.

The challenge of improving fit involves a short-term focus and an immediate set of imperatives and rewards. Increasing efficiency and consistency in structures and systems can yield all sorts of benefits in areas like the costs of current products and services, the speed of moving products to market, and the ability to measure and respond to customer feedback. These are the sorts of benefits seen in the example of Ryanair. Meanwhile, cultivating future resources and capabilities involves a longer-term focus and a less tangible set of imperatives and rewards. Environmental change is uncertain. Managers are unsure which capabilities to develop or which resources to acquire. New products and services can fail to achieve all that was hoped and new technologies can fail to deliver all that was envisioned. Building for the future, then, will involve investing in some hits and some misses. Across a range of speculative and uncertain initiatives, some will succeed while others will not. Finding those winning new technologies, products, and services will mean enduring the losses and frustrations associated with some failures. While necessary for innovation and development, those losses will place a real drag on short-term fit and efficiency. Speculative and uncertain investments in the future will divert energy and effort away from the current competitive advantage, hampering competitiveness and fit in the present. However, while eliminating speculative and uncertain initiatives can improve short-term fit and performance, it can also leave the firm unable to adapt to the future.

Exacerbating the problem is a subtle dynamic known as **path dependence** (Nelson & Winter, 1982). The basic idea of path dependence is simple: current decisions reflect outcomes from decisions made in the past (see Figure 8.2). The idea is illustrated in a quote by Winston Churchill, who once said: "we shape our buildings, thereafter they shape us." The point is simple and powerful: the design and construction of a building reflect the intentions of its builders. Once constructed, though, the building becomes a fixture that constrains future plans. In essence, then, rather than structure following strategy, structure begins to determine it.

A similar observation was offered by Sam Walter Foss (1858–1911), in his poem "The Calf Path" (see Box 3.2, p. 73). This amusing story illustrates a pervasive behavioral principle: people tend to follow the path of least resistance in reasoning and decision making. The tendency is less about lethargy, though, than about efficiency and certainty. In an effort to capitalize on experience and familiarity, to economize on effort, and to reduce uncertainty and risk, people rely on known patterns and precedents. A number of psychological and organizational processes, like **problemistic searching**, **satisficing**, **filtering**, and **framing** (Cyert & March, 1963; Dutton, Fahey, & Narayanan, 1983), combine to produce this pattern. And

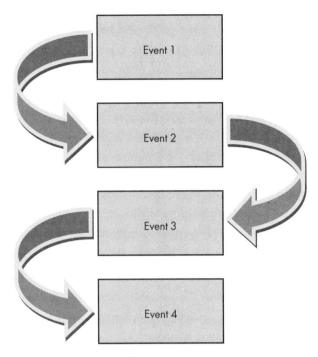

FIGURE 8.2 Path Dependence

as the poem illustrates, the pattern will often produce suboptimal decisions and ultimately poor performance. What is so vexing is that path dependence can masquerade as sensible and even strategic decision making. Indeed, in the normal course of managing it makes good sense to follow established precedents, rely on proven practices, and stick to familiar frameworks. So doing reduces uncertainty, increases efficiency, and promotes reliability and consistency. However, this sort of thinking reinforces the status quo and limits the consideration of options and alternatives.

Problematically, then, managers can seek to maximize fit and efficiency, doing what seems right at each and every step and making decisions based on the best examples and the data available from the current strategy and environment. And yet, in so doing, they can create and reinforce processes that, over time, will produce suboptimal decisions which can leave them unable to compete effectively in the future. This phenomenon has contributed to a number of surprising missteps by well-known firms. Microsoft, for example, despite its great technical expertise and overwhelming financial strength, has a history of missing opportunities in web-based functions. It was a late entrant in the browser, media, search, and advertising businesses and so lost considerable market share and margin to faster-moving competitors. The pattern, though, is less about reluctance on the part of Microsoft than it is about a business model based mostly on preloaded operating systems and applications. This business model has served Microsoft well and so has become central to its strategy. In essence, Microsoft's past decisions and practices now limit its actions and view of the future. As a result, it has often been slow to recognize and capitalize on new opportunities.

Another example would be Compaq, the computer hardware manufacturer that was acquired by Hewlett Packard in 2002. Compaq saw tremendous growth and profitability in the 1980s and 1990s and by 1995 was the recognized leader in personal computers and servers. Its strategy was to offer superior quality, with prices below the competition, so as to become the preferred supplier to the large retailers who supplied most consumers. It did this by engineering and building many of its own components, which provided quality and reliability, while pricing and promoting aggressively to build volume and the scale economies. Compaq was very successful in this, and sales and profits grew dramatically.

The environment, though, continued to evolve; new entrants emerged, offering more options and newer designs. Consumers grew more elastic and component suppliers adapted and improved, offering greater reliability at even lower costs. In addition, the technologies used in managing internal functions like ordering, supply chain, and delivery improved to the point that new business models became possible. One such model was introduced by Dell. In an increasingly elastic market, Dell chose to outsource its components. It also developed an online ordering system that allowed customers to design machines built to their own tastes and specifications. Dell then synched this ordering system to its manufacturing and procurement, enabling lower sales costs, lower inventory costs, and less waste. The combination of these elements enabled it to produce computers that were reliable and largely customized, but less expensive than those sold by other manufacturers. Compaq in particular suffered in terms of market share and profitability as it struggled to compete with Dell's direct, efficient, and flexible business model.

Ultimately, though, Compaq could not escape the burden of its past. With so much invested in engineering, plant, and equipment, with so much of its reputation and advantage built on its proprietary designs and equipment, Compaq was unable to shift to a strategy that could compete with Dell. By the year 2000, many of its assets appeared old and out of date and so were unattractive to other manufacturers. Compaq also had substantial inventories in both finished product and components. Much of that inventory was now obsolete and so would have to be discounted if it was to be converted into cash. Finally, because of its competitive disadvantage, Compaq was unable to generate, through its own operations, enough funding for the retooling necessary to compete in the new environment. As a result, it was largely stuck in its old strategy, able to devise a new and better alternative but unable to adapt to take advantage of it. As its prospects for the future declined, Compaq's stock price fell, to the point that it was soon acquired by HP.

This pattern is common and can be seen in a variety of different examples. Industry leaders like Kodak, General Motors, and K-Mart missed opportunities in product and technology that were later seized by new competitors—Fuji, Honda, and Wal-Mart. Firms such as Ryanair and Southwest gained footholds because larger and more established incumbents—Lufthansa, American, and British Airways—chose to reduce coverage areas, leaving underserved gaps in the market. Many well-managed and successful firms made conscious decisions to maximize returns from their current strategy by tightening fit and efficiency, leveraging already strong positions in an effort to reinforce existing competitive advantages. In so doing, however, these firms overlooked new and emerging products, technologies, and business models that would later prove a substantial threat.

Such is the case in the music industry, where the RIAA (the Recording Industry Association of America) has spent years fighting to protect its revenues and profits from the threat posed by online music downloading. While some of these downloads may be illegitimate and even illegal, no one can deny that the technology that made them possible has revolutionized the way consumers think about and acquire music. Moreover, it is all but certain that, whatever the future of the industry may be, the trend is towards reduced market power and lower revenues and profits for major recording labels like EMI, Sony, and Warner. It is also seems clear that, barring some significant change of heart and strategy, these incumbent firms are not likely to be the ones to transform the marketplace and lead the industry into the future by capitalizing on the new and revolutionary technologies.

Exploitation versus Experimentation

This tendency for strong and established firms to look inward and focus on ways to strengthen their current advantage while failing to develop new products and processes for the future has been noted by scholars (Hedberg, Nystrom, & Starbuck, 1976) and has been called the **curse of incumbency**. Incumbent firms are often larger and more bureaucratic than their smaller and more entrepreneurial competitors. As a result, they may be slower and less flexible, with more vested in the continuation of the status quo than newer rivals. Larger and more successful firms have a natural **inertia** that is not displayed by smaller, newer, and less successful firms. While providing some advantages, the size and tradition of these large incumbents can prove to be a liability over time, as they can restrict creativity and the creation of new options.

One way that size and tradition limit creativity and flexibility is by influencing the way that managers frame and make decisions. Indeed, researchers have noted how success can create a sense of creeping defensiveness in the minds of top managers (Amason & Mooney, 2008; Fredrickson & Iaquinto, 1989). To understand this tendency, consider this principle: the more successful a strategy is, the less attractive any alternative strategy will appear in comparison to it. The analogy of picking low-hanging fruit is appropriate here. It is quite natural that, so long as there is low-hanging fruit available, no one will want to invest additional energy trying to pick the fruit at the top of the tree that is harder to reach. Rather, a sensible person would make that extra effort only after the easily picked fruit has been taken. Managers often view alternatives to a successful strategy in much the same way. The current strategy is familiar, well understood, and easily implemented. Any alternative to that current strategy will be more difficult, involving change, additional effort, and the risk of failure. So, as long as that current strategy is successful, there is a tendency to continue exploiting it, rather than exert the time and effort looking for something else. Over time, as new alternatives emerge in the form of new products, markets, technologies, and business models, managers will begin to view those alternatives as threats to the status quo, rather than as opportunities for learning, innovation, and change.

This phenomenon relates to **prospect theory** (Kahneman & Tversky, 1979), which deals with decision making and risk and the effects of context on the evaluation of alternatives. At the heart of prospect theory is an S-shaped value function (see Figure 8.3). This function depicts the values associated with all the potential outcomes to a decision, from large losses to large gains. The most important feature of this function is that it is not linear. As discussed in Chapter 2, while outcomes are typically quantified in standardized units (such as U.S. dollars, for instance), the actual values associated with different outcomes can be quite different. For example, a firm such as Johnson & Johnson, which is accustomed to profits in the hundreds of millions of dollars, would be disappointed in an annual profit of a mere $1 million. Yet some other firm, with a small operation or a history of losses, might be thrilled with a profit of $1 million. Thus, where the firm starts—the reference point on Figure 8.3—affects how it values its outcomes. This reference point moves, based on historical precedent and future aspirations. The higher the reference point, the more difficult it is to have outcomes that feel like gains and the easier it is to have outcomes that feel like losses. In the world of sports, for instance, teams that are used to winning, like the New York Yankees, have little patience for even modest performance. Because the reference point is so high, anything short of winning the pennant feels like a disappointment.

The second important characteristic of the value function is its asymmetric S-shape. This suggests two things. The first is that, beyond some point, marginal gains and losses become increasingly less important. For example, in the early years, each new location was very important to McDonald's, affecting growth and profitability significantly. As the firm grew large and successful, though, the value of each additional new store grew increasingly small. In the same way losses can seem devastating at first. When a firm fails to meet sales or earnings projections, for instance, analysts and investors react quickly and negatively, selling the stock and depressing the price. But over time, as a firm continues to absorb losses, the effect diminishes; losses cease to be a surprise and come to be expected. At that point, the value or significance of each additional loss is low.

The second important implication is that, near the center, where the outcomes are nearest to the reference point, people will work harder to avoid a loss than to

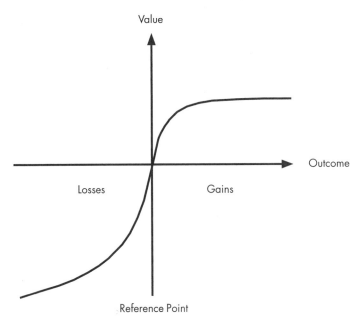

Value

Outcome

Losses

Gains

Reference Point

FIGURE 8.3 Prospect Theory and the S-Shaped Value

achieve a gain of similar size. Kahneman and Tversky (1979; Tversky & Kahneman, 1981) confirmed this across a large number of observations and experiments. In case after case, the research revealed a tendency to safeguard against losses before pursuing gains. What this showed was that, for a manager near his or her reference point, given a choice between making $750,000 but potentially losing $500,000 versus making only $250,000 but potentially losing nothing, he or she will frequently choose to make less if that choice also shelters against the loss. In essence, then, most managers will work harder to avoid a loss of some amount than they will work to achieve a gain of the same amount. The only time this is not true is when they are so far below the reference point that additional losses seem unimportant. At that point, there is an incentive to risk even a great deal in an effort to produce even a small turnaround in performance.

Taking together the effects of incumbency with the tendencies illustrated by prospect theory, it is easy to see why success can be so difficult to sustain. Indeed, it may well be that, as firms become established, large, and successful, they are, without knowing it, sowing the seeds of their own demise. Firms and managers can grow dependent upon the strategies and practices that produced their success. In so doing, they can fail to invest in experimentation, to take the chances needed to learn, and to notice when events create new opportunities. As a result, history shows that the most successful firms are often the least likely to undertake novel courses of action, to introduce radical innovations, and to engage in the sort of creative destruction of the status quo that can bring about new competitive advantage and spawn new industries (Ghemawat, 1991; Schumpeter, 1942).

This pattern has been called the paradox of success (Miller, 1992). It is subtle, embedded deeply in the process of strategy implementation, and of tremendous importance to the ability of a firm to sustain its competitive advantage. It is pervasive in the sense that it reflects subtle natural tendencies, shared by virtually all managers and firms. Finally, it is an ongoing conundrum with no simple solution or fix. There is no formula a manager can apply to know exactly how much emphasis to place on fit and the exploitation of the current competitive advantage versus how much to place on innovation and experimentation, as necessary, to develop potential advantages for the future. Rather, managers must simply sort this out, day by day, doing what is necessary in the short term to sustain success and provide resources, while also investing those resources for the long term in an effort to prepare for change before it is thrust upon them.

When Less is More

In their article on the paradoxical tendency for successful firms to stagnate over time, Hedberg, et al. (1976) offer suggestions on how the pattern can be broken. Their advice is both counter-intuitive and somewhat esoteric. Yet it is also highly valuable for what it illustrates and quite practical, when fully understood. The crux of the advice is this: do only what is necessary in the short term to gain competitive advantage and to maintain success. Any additional effort, beyond what is minimally necessary for ongoing survival, should be directed towards the future and towards the cultivation of new alternatives, options, and ideas. Hedberg and his colleagues offer six specific prescriptions designed to prevent the paradoxical tendency outlined above. These prescriptions, which were mentioned briefly in Chapter 3, are discussed in more detail below.

The first is for *minimal consensus* on the part of the firm's decision makers. Contrary to common and conventional wisdom, firms can suffer from too much consensus. Managers can become too insular and distant. They can restrict the flow of information and limit the sources from which they receive information. In so doing, they may sharpen their focus, reduce their disagreements, and maximize their own efficiency. However, without knowing it, they may also be cutting off the very sources of creativity and insight that can stimulate innovation and new ideas. While some minimal level of consensus among managers and key decision makers is necessary, the idea that cooperation is synonymous with consensus is counter-productive and dangerous, providing the illusion of satisfaction and success in the short term but stifling initiative and opportunities for learning in the future.

The second prescription is for *minimal contentment*. As with the others, this one may seem counter-intuitive and unnatural. Managers spend their careers trying to provide stability for their firm and its constituents. And most stakeholders, including employees, suppliers, and owners, desire some level of satisfaction and contentment. What possible advantage could there be in fomenting discontent? To understand, it is important to comprehend problemistic search. The term was introduced earlier and is defined at the end of the chapter. It applies in this context because the search for alternatives is typically motivated by discontent. When a gap exists between the current and the desired state, when there is pressure to improve upon current performance, or when there is a sense of restlessness and uneasiness with the status quo, decision makers are motivated to take the risks and make the efforts necessary to learn. Where there is too much contentment and too much comfort, there is little incentive to change.

Great champions in sports—people like Tiger Woods, Lance Armstrong, Roger Federer, and Tom Brady—often cite the key role of hunger in sustaining their motivation. That intrinsic desire to improve and excel is especially important when there is no obvious or immediate threat from the competition. Without it, complacency begins to emerge and the firm loses its edge. So there is an advantage to never being fully content and to constantly pushing for more and better results.

The third prescription is for *minimal affluence*. Firms and managers are typically judged on their financial success. So, as affluence rises, discontent declines. With affluence comes the ability to build slack resources. Slack resources, which were defined and discussed briefly in Chapter 3, enable a firm to absorb mistakes and to insulate itself against shocks from the environment. Firms with slack resources have a buffer that can be used to absorb mistakes and to mitigate oversights. Deep pockets protect a firm from immediate threat and provide the luxury of time when responding to change. As a result, affluence can have the unintended effect of making a firm less aware of its surroundings. With a cushion of affluence, changes in the competitive landscape will arouse less urgency. Early signs of dissatisfaction among the customer base may be met with little more than a shrug, while promising new products and technologies get lost amid the bureaucratic shuffle.

Of course, some affluence is necessary. Firms must have resources to operate in the present and to invest in the future. Affluence can buy the best talent, the best technologies, and the best locations. Affluence can enable rational and reasoned decision making, supported by all the research and data necessary for an informed decision. Experimentation and learning cost money, and so affluence can provide for both while also offering greater margin for error. Affluence, then, is a good and important resource. The danger is too much affluence. As odd as it may seem, too much affluence in the short term can hinder the cultivation of wealth in the longer term. Thus, managers must decide how much affluence is absolutely necessary, and then keep no more than just that.

The next prescription is for a firm and its management to have *minimal faith*. Hedberg, et al. explain that "an organization should plan its future but not rely on its plans" (1976: 59). This statement can appear at first to be doublespeak, the sort of nonsense that is too often associated with academic impracticality. On closer consideration, though, the point is both valuable and practical.

Planning is a useful exercise for a number of reasons. It can force management to think rigorously and systematically about the future. It can push managers to consider cause and effect relationships in the industry and the importance of various goals and objectives. However, plans can never remove all of the uncertainty from the future. There will always be surprises: events will unfold in a way or at a pace different from what was anticipated, long-held assumptions will prove faulty, and new revelations will emerge that change the landscape on which the plans were based. Thus, too much planning or planning in too much detail can be counterproductive. Much like the hypothetical building in the Churchill quote, plans can take on a life all their own. Shaped in one context and for one reality, they end up shaping behavior in another.

It is better, then, that managers plan but do so only minimally: set direction, articulate goals, provide the guiding principles and the ongoing support and attention, but otherwise allow the details to evolve over time. This is another application of the logical incrementalism discussed in Chapter 3. Planning is an important process, but if the plans are articulated in too much detail, and if they are held to too rigidly, they can become like a straight-jacket, restricting flexibility and limiting the ability of the firm to respond and adapt as the changing circumstances warrant.

The fifth prescription is for *minimal consistency*. While unorthodox, it is nevertheless logical in the context of strategic management, because the environment is inconsistent. To maintain the sort of fit described throughout the book, a firm must adapt constantly and appropriately. It must reassess its market, its competitors, its resources, and its business model regularly. It must search out new technologies and products and it must listen to its customers, anticipating their motivations and adapting in response. With the ferment of new competitors, innovations, products, services, and technologies, and with the continual evolution in customer tastes, preferences, and patterns, change in the environment is constant. Thus, firms are under continual pressure to keep up by changing themselves as well. In essence, the only way to stay fit to the environment is to adapt and change with it.

But change can be difficult and uncomfortable. It can increase uncertainty and reduce efficiency, it can undermine the value of existing resources, and it can dilute focus and energy. In short, change can make a firm appear inconsistent. But consider the alternative: when a firm fails to change, pressure from the environment builds up. This pressure may build slowly, so that it is barely perceptible, or it may build quickly. Ultimately, though, it will force a change by the firm. The only question is whether the firm will be able to survive that change and respond. Often, the answer is no, because the change is simply too dramatic and unfamiliar.

The sixth and final prescription is for *minimal rationality*. Rationality is defined by Allison as "not just intelligent behavior, but behavior motivated by a conscious calculation of advantages, a calculation that is based on an explicit and internally consistent value system" (1971: 13). While scholars and managers have long realized that the sort of rationality described here is unrealistic in practice, it nevertheless remains an ideal in the minds of many. Specialization and the division of labor are rational practices, designed to limit redundancy and increase asset and knowledge utilization. Lines of authority are made clear to minimize conflict and to reduce the likelihood of miscommunication. Objectivity is emphasized and hard data are valued over intuition and subjective judgment. Clear directions are provided and sought, so that there will be no misunderstanding of what is to be done and what is being expected. Indeed, professors, managers, consultants, and investors spend much of their time trying to design and enforce greater rationality, so as to produce greater efficiency and better results.

The problem with all of this is that creativity and imagination will often seem less rational than other, more productive options. Thomas A. Edison's famous quote "we now know a thousand ways not to make a light bulb" illustrates this well. To reach his objective, Edison had to endure a long string of failures. While he chose to view these failures in positive terms, they still represented real losses of time, effort, and money. Of course, it is now easy to look back, to see this investment in relation to the outcomes, and to applaud Edison's determination and vision. However, what if he had not succeeded? Indeed, one could hardly blame Edison had he decided that, after a mere 900 failures, his time would be better spent on other matters. The true value of creative insight and innovation is rarely obvious to those steeped in the values and practices of the status quo. Indeed, an overly developed sense of rationality can drive these creative energies out of a firm, leaving an organization that may do things right but may not do the right things. This distinction, between doing things right and doing the right things, was noted and explained by Peter Drucker (1966). Firms can be well managed, follow the best practices, apply the best models, and so avoid blunders and mistakes. Yet those same firms can overlook creative alternatives; they can miss key opportunities and forego chances to seize new advantage by focusing too heavily on their own practices, process, and consistency. That is the hazard of rationality and that is why strategists must view it cautiously.

ADAPTATION AND LEARNING

The ultimate goal of these prescriptions is an organization that can learn and adapt, that can redesign itself in an ongoing and continuous way, and by so doing stay focused on the bulls-eye of a moving target. Strategy implementation involves building structures, systems, skills, and shared values that complement the strategy. But implementation must also provide for the continuous redesign of the organization, as necessary, to stay fit to an ever changing strategy.

Strategy, though, does not change for its own sake. Rather, it changes to maintain fit with the environment. Fit between the strategy and the environment is the key to competitive advantage. As discussed elsewhere, providing value to customers over and above what is available from other products and services is the essence of competitive advantage and success. To do well over time, firms must create that sort of value for their customers both in the present and in the future. Implementation, then, involves two equally vital imperatives. The first is to insure the creation of value in the present. The second is to enable the sort of learning and adaptation necessary for the creation of value in the future. It is only by accomplishing both that strategy and competitive advantage maintain currency and relevance in the marketplace over time.

Competitive advantage, then, is closely related to the processes of adaptation and learning (Duncan, 1974; Fiol & Lyles, 1985). Yet these processes are rarely connected to the nuts and bolts of strategy implementation. Rather, adaptation and learning are often viewed as academic topics, of concern to theorists and consultants but of little tangible value to practicing managers. That view, while understandable, is unfortunate. Organizational learning and the adaptation that follows are natural by-products of strategy implementation and essential contributors to competitive advantage and performance. When practiced effectively, strategy implementation should stimulate creativity and innovation. It should provide previews of emerging changes and prepare the firm to adapt. To visualize this better, return to Figure 3.1, p. 49. Virtually all depictions of the strategy process show feedback paths. These loops are meant to symbolize how information on the results of a strategy feeds back to the beginning of the strategy process. Whether called feedback, strategic control, or learning, the effect is the same—to incorporate the best, the most relevant, and the most current information into the formulation of new strategy.

The best source for such current, relevant, and high-quality information is the front line of the firm, where the feedback is the most immediate and tangible. After all, who better to provide input on the current products and services than the customers and those who interact with them most directly? Who better to notice operational shortcomings and to make improvements than those most involved in operations? Who better to spot emerging technologies and competitors than those who are in the marketplace every day? That front line of the firm, where strategy is converted into action, is also the best place to experiment with alternatives, to try new things, and to refine current offerings.

This sort of experimentation is the first step in learning. Creativity is encouraged, innovations in products and processes are attempted, new combinations are tried, and the responses are evaluated. All of the resulting information then feeds back into the crafting and development of new strategy. This approach to implementation enables the firm to learn, in process. It enables ongoing adaptation and evolution, without ever requiring a radical overhaul of the firm's structure and systems. Moreover, it allows all this to happen naturally, on the basis of information that comes to the firm through its normal activities.

But this sort of thing can happen only if the firm is minimally committed to the status quo, willing to reexamine things continuously, able to get outside of itself and so view the world realistically, and then willing to change even before the need to change becomes urgent. It is this process of continuous learning, adaptation, and change that will emerge from the prescriptions outlined earlier. A firm that can resist the pressure towards excessive rationality, consensus, and consistency can take advantage of the information that flows naturally from its own operations. Once it has achieved minimal affluence, it can direct resources towards experimentation and innovation, rather than just building slack to buffer the current advantage. By feeding information learned through implementation directly into the strategy-making process, the firm can capitalize on first-hand awareness of the environment. With the ability to experiment and learn, the firm can begin the processes of planning and adaptation before it is forced to change by pressure from the outside. As a result, the firm can understand and be ready for the future even before that future fully arrives. Indeed, when done well, and when integrated throughout the whole of the strategic process, implementation, learning, and adaptation can sow the seeds of truly sustainable competitive advantage.

CONCLUDING THOUGHTS AND CAVEATS

Dynamic Capabilities

Much of the academic discourse in strategic management over the past two decades has dealt with sustainable competitive advantage. Competitive advantage is the object of strategy and the best indicator of enduring performance. In every instance and setting, firms should seek to build greater competitive advantage by creating greater value. However, the creation of value and the pursuit of competitive advantage cost money. They involve investment in resources, time, and effort and also risk, as these investments are by their very nature speculative and uncertain. Thus, the sustainability of a competitive advantage is important. Advantages that can be sustained provide greater returns, as their benefits persist over longer periods of time. For example, a firm may develop or purchase a technology that can be used to create value in the marketplace. The advantage derived from that technology can be protected with a patent, extending the life and the earning potential of the advantage. Even the patent has a value, directly related to its duration and to the value of the technology it represents. In much the same way, every competitive advantage has a value, directly related to its value and durability. Advantages that cannot be easily imitated or substituted are more valuable than others, because they represent returns that can be sustained for longer periods of time.

However, the intensive focus on sustained competitive advantage has led to an unintended and unproductive mindset among students and practicing managers. Specifically, students and managers alike often get caught up in the pursuit of singular, inimitable, and non-substitutable resources, as necessary, to provide a sustainable competitive advantage. Much like 49ers in a modern-day gold rush, there is a perception that, by finding just the right resources or staking out just the right positions, a firm can gain advantages that can be sustained indefinitely.

While this is an attractive idea, it is important to understand that these sorts of resources and positions are little more than fool's gold. With sufficient time and effort, every resource can be either substituted or imitated and, given the continuous drag of competition and market evolution, every advantage will eventually erode. As a result, sustainability should be seen in continuous rather than categorical terms. In other words, rather than asking if an advantage can be sustained, managers should be asking for how long the advantage can be sustained. In essence, managers should ask: What is the window during which the advantage will function and what is the earning potential of the advantage during that time? Moreover, the advantage should be seen in terms of its ability to promote future advantages. Managers should ask themselves if an advantage will enable the firm to create new options that will facilitate the sort of ongoing redesign discussed earlier. This sort of ongoing process of redesign, as necessary, to move the firm from strength to strength and from advantage to advantage reflects its *dynamic capabilities*.

Dynamic capabilities are defined as the "ability to integrate, build and reconfigure internal and external competences to address rapidly changing environments" (Teece, Pisano, & Shuen, 1997: 516). In essence, they are the firm's ability to learn, adapt, and change as necessary to stay fit to the environment, even as the environment changes. These sorts of capabilities are not bound to specific tangible assets, nor are they applicable only in particular settings. Rather, they transcend resources and strategies and deal instead with how resources and strategies are used. To return to an issue discussed in Chapter 2, firms have value over and above the value of their assets. Tobin's q was a measure of that value added by management and strategy, over and above the book value of the firm's assets. Dynamic capabilities are analogous to the knowledge, thought processes, and structure that govern how the firm's assets are used and how strategy is applied in the day to day. By way of analogy, if tangible resources and assets are bricks, then dynamic capabilities are the mortar in between. This mortar, however, has the special ability to liquefy, harden, and then liquefy again, as necessary, to change the shape of the wall to meet the changing environment.

The dynamic capabilities perspective, then, places less value on the sorts of resources that show up on the balance sheet than on how those resources are used and how a firm learns and adapts. The environment is constantly changing and so every advantage is ultimately at risk. So the challenge for managers is not to find the elusive resource that can never be imitated or to develop the strategy that is so unique and powerful that it will never be defeated. Rather, the challenge is to cultivate the sorts of mindsets, processes, and paths that will enable the firm to learn and adapt before change is forced from the outside. Such capabilities will enable the firm to sustain competitive advantage by changing and to create value by continually learning, adapting, and moving forward.

Real Options

Much of what this chapter has presented regarding the future value of implementation can be understood in terms of options. Stated simply, an option is the ability to do something in the future. For example, a prospective buyer may purchase an option on a piece of property. The option is not ownership; rather it is the right to purchase later. For the price of the option, the owner may withdraw the property from the market, agreeing to give the prospective buyer the right to decide on the purchase at some point in the future. In the same way, firms can take options on the future. A firm might obtain a patent on some product or some piece of technology that is yet to be fully developed or commercialized. The product or technology may or may not prove valuable in the marketplace. However, as long as it holds the patent or rights to this product or technology, the firm has the option of moving forward with it. The product or technology may or may not prove very valuable at some point. For now, though, just having the option represents some value. Moreover, while it holds that option, the firm is able to refine and improve the product or technology. It is also able to learn about the market, to begin educating potential customers, and to influence the pace at which the process moves forward.

Thus, the value of the option derives from two sources—the actual commercial value of the product or technology in the future and the value of the learning and information that can be acquired as the option is being developed. It has been argued, then, that the value of any firm is a combination of the value of its current operations and resources, as well as the value of its options on the future (Luehrman, 1998). That future option value can be cultivated and managed, just like the current operations and resources. Given this, the option value of the firm should be an integral part of the firm's strategy. This is what is known as the *real options* view (Scherpereel, 2008) and is a relatively recent development in the academic literature on strategic management. However, it is extremely important to the pursuit of sustained competitive advantage and to the long-term value of the firm (Ferreira, Kar, & Trigeorgis, 2009).

The real options approach is a little different than the traditional approach to developing and managing strategy. Students and managers are traditionally taught to think about strategic initiatives and the range of strategic alternatives in terms of net present value (see Chapter 2 for a review). Alternatives are assessed in terms of risk and potential cash flow, and managers select and invest in those initiatives with the highest net present value. In so doing, though, they also choose not to invest in the others. The real options view changes this approach. Rather than seeking to eliminate potential initiatives, it suggests keeping the options open until there is better information on which to base a go or no-go decision.

Of course, no firm has the resources to invest in everything. Thus, seizing every initiative and trying to fund every potential alternative is simply not possible. Rather, the firm invests modestly in many different projects, thereby purchasing options on those projects into the future. Those options are then managed, just like an investment portfolio. Moreover, as time moves forward, the firm learns about the market for such future options; it also invests in the refinement and development of these emerging products, markets, or technologies. As the firm has better information on the future potential of each option, it can choose to reallocate its resources, doubling down on the best options and discontinuing or selling the others. The result of all this is a pipeline of options that move systematically from the farfetched to the probable and from the highly risky to the highly certain.

Interestingly, the research on the subject has been promising and suggests that the value of a portfolio of strategic alternatives will be higher over time if a firm adopts this approach than if it selects and cuts too quickly, using just net present value. Of course, both approaches are highly dependent upon the process by which they are managed and the knowledge of those who manage them. The real options approach, then, is no silver bullet. Adopting this approach can no more guarantee success than can acquiring any particular resource or following any particular strategy. Rather, the value in the real options view comes from its effect on strategic thinking. Recall that the sort of continuous learning and redesign of the firm described earlier requires a reprogramming of the strategists and the strategic process. Adopting a real options approach to strategy development can be a mechanism for accomplishing that sort of reprogramming.

The thinking is that, as managers view their jobs as the creation and management of options to yield an ongoing stream of emerging, high-value initiatives, so will they internalize the processes of learning and adaptation. In this view, strategy becomes less about analytical precision and efficient execution and more about the ongoing process of continuous evolution and change (Mintzberg, 1987). However, the change is no longer a speculative and clumsy process where managers try to guess about and make bets on the future. Instead, it is a process where the firm, through the cultivation of options and the implementation of its strategy, actually learns its way forward (McGrath, 1997, 1999). When done well, this process yields a continuous stream of competitive advantages, creating an ongoing harvest of value and performance.

Problems with Present Value

Net present value analysis was discussed in Chapter 2 and is a common and widely accepted practice for evaluating performance and for assessing alternative strategies.

It uses discounted cash flow to produce standardized values of future events, so that those events can be compared to one another directly and assessed in present terms. While it is a powerful and sound analytical tool, NPV does have a subtle and potential problem.

Recall that NPV works by discounting future cash flow based upon uncertainty and the opportunity cost of the investment capital. This sort of discounting is reasonable and sensible and is meant to guard against poor investments. Risky propositions must produce large returns to justify investment, and even good returns may not be sufficient if the capital can be allocated to better purposes. Thus, a good manager will carefully weigh potential initiatives against the risks and against the opportunity costs. But recall the principle mentioned earlier: the more successful a particular strategy is now, the less attractive an alternative will look in comparison to it. Moreover, given that an existing and successful strategy is likely to be well practiced and well understood, the risks associated with any alternative strategy will be higher almost by definition.

As a result, NPV analysis has a built-in bias favoring the status quo in those instances where the status quo is successful. In other words, successful firms that apply NPV analysis to the range of their various strategic alternatives will almost always find that their best course of action is to increase investment in the current strategy, reinforcing their core competencies and buttressing the existing competitive advantage. And the more successful the current strategy, the stronger this bias will be. As a result, highly successful firms will find it very difficult to try new things, to justify experimentation, and to promote innovation. This is part of the mechanism underlying the curse of incumbency (Chandy & Tellis, 2000), discussed earlier.

Two things about this phenomenon are especially interesting. First, it is intriguing how the potential for bias in the use of this analytical tool parallels the effects of prospect theory on decision making. Recall the S-shaped value curve discussed earlier in this chapter. That portion of the curve above the reference point, in what is called the domain of gains, is flatter than the portion of the curve below the reference point. Thus, marginal gains are less valuable than marginal losses of comparable size. What this means is that decision makers will often work harder to avoid a loss than they will to achieve a gain of the same amount. Moreover, note that, at a point beyond the reference point, the curve flattens almost completely. In this region, the effect of current performance or of the current resource position is so strong that even a large potential gain offers little incentive to change the status quo. While it is a difficult thing to imagine, history is replete with examples of firms that chose the profitability and security of the status quo over attractive new alternatives. These events are often chalked up to complacency or some sort of fat-cat syndrome, where companies rest on the laurels of past success and executives, blinded by hubris, refuse to acknowledge threats to their hegemony.

But a closer look suggests a more subtle and pervasive problem. The second issue of interest here is whether our analytical methods are reflecting and amplifying our own biases. For instance, it is easy to imagine how NPV analysis might reinforce the effects of prospect theory on decision making. A firm could perform so well that, in comparison, virtually no alternative to the current strategy would appear attractive. So long as that firm had the ability to increase investment in the current strategy and to double down on its existing competencies and advantage, no stream of future cash flows from any alternative strategy would produce a positive NPV. The opportunity cost of the capital would simply be too high. So it might be that, rather than being complacent fat cats, many executives apply good reasoning and analysis and choose quite rationally to forego new strategic alternatives because the numbers actually favor the status quo. If so, then it is all the more important that students, professors, consultants, and managers work to reprogram themselves and the strategy process. The challenge is to learn to apply the best logic and the best analyses available while also institutionalizing processes like real option development and cultivating dissensus and discontent, as necessary, to blunt the effects of subtle biases that can lead to complacency and drift.

A Means to an End

Balancing the short-term demands of fit, efficiency, and performance along with the longer-term need for innovation, adaptation, and learning is a complex and ongoing challenge. It is not the sort of problem that can be easily solved with a simple policy or a single action. Nor is it the sort of issue that can be addressed once and thereafter forgotten. Rather, it requires a different way of thinking, a complete reprogramming of the strategic process and the firm's strategists. Beginning with the mission of the organization and then working through to the strategy and its implementation, resolving this dilemma requires seeing the firm as a means to an end rather than an end unto itself. But, if the firm is merely a means to an end, what is the end that is actually being pursued? To put it succinctly, the end is the creation of value. Firms are to create value for their customers and, in so doing, to create value for their owners, employees, and other stakeholders. As explained in Chapter 1, managing the firm's resources to create value is the essence of strategic management and what is expected of good managers. Meeting that expectation, though, requires seeing the organization as a tool for the creation of value rather than a result unto itself.

Unfortunately, seeing the firm as just a tool for the creation of value is easier said than done. Indeed, as Hedberg and his colleagues (1976) describe, firms are often built as monuments to their own greatness and success, with elaborate architecture and structures designed to insulate those on the inside from the outside world. They build slack resources in the form of cash reserves, stock repurchases, redundant capacity, excess infrastructure, and reputation. They then often use that slack to filter information that threatens the status quo, to resist even the most inevitable changes, and to buffer themselves against the very environmental forces that are essential to their success. How many instances have there been where industry leaders acquire potential new competitors, rather than learn from and respond to them? How many firms and industries have lobbied for subsidies or for legislation that would protect and benefit their positions, rather than adapt to inevitably evolving economic forces? It is no secret and no surprise that managers often choose to see the firm as an end rather than a means, and so they work to consolidate their positions, to reduce ambiguity, to promote predictability and clarity, and to provide a large measure of security and consistency for themselves and those around them. This can seem natural and reasonable, in the short term.

Unfortunately, though, it is a shortsighted approach. Ultimately, the value of the firm is enhanced when it creates the most value for its customers. Thus, the creation of value both now and in the future is the responsibility of managers in the present. Understanding this, many have begun to focus on sustained competitive advantage as the key to long-term value. But the quest for sustained advantage is complicated by an ever changing environment, by the shifting aspirations of customers, and by an evolving technological landscape. New competitors emerge and old competitors fade away. Customer desires develop and alter as demographics change and as products and services go from being novel to being routine. New technologies are created and new processes emerge, affecting the cost, availability, and attractiveness of all sorts of goods and services. And yet managers often struggle to find that key inimitable resource or that enduring brand or product feature that cannot be substituted. Such quests are destined to end in frustration.

Rather, the key to sustainable advantage is the ability to learn and adapt ahead of the demand and the competition. Firms that create an ongoing stream of real options, that build and invest in dynamic capabilities, and that maintain their hunger for new value creation and growth are actually able to create and enjoy multiple, temporary advantages. Each periodic advantage reflects a fit between the environment, the strategy, and the firm at a specific point in time. Each periodic advantage leads to revenues and profits, which can be invested in the creation of more options and the cultivation of greater dynamic capability. Thus, while the firm is enjoying the benefits of one resource, one position, and one advantage, it is simultaneously investing in the development of resources and positions that may lead to other advantages in the future.

This ongoing process will necessarily involve change on the part of the firm and those within it. A firm may be a leader in an industry for a time but later sense the need to transition out of that industry and into something else. A firm may enjoy a substantial advantage in one particular environment but later decide that the time is right to evolve into something different. The firm may change its products, technology, people, or strategy. But what does not change, what endures across every form that the company may take, is the pursuit of value. Understanding that, a firm and its managers become better able to implement strategy in the present and to learn and adapt as necessary for the future.

SUMMARY

This has been a chapter on strategy implementation. Implementation contributes to competitive advantage in two crucial ways. First, it is the process of converting strategic intent into tangible action. Thus, it involves organizing and managing the nuts and bolts of the firm in such a way that the strategy functions as it was intended to do. Organizational structures and systems, along with processes, practices, style, and culture, must work together for strategy to create value and produce competitive advantage. Just as strategy must fit the environment, so too must the firm fit the strategy. That internal coherence—between the strategy, structure, systems, skills, staff, style, and shared values of the firm—was illustrated with the 7-S model. Each of these elements is important in its own right. However, they are all much more important as part of a larger whole. The fit of that larger whole is essential to the effective implementation of strategy. Strategy that is well fit to the environment and that is supported by coherent alignment of these elements will produce competitive advantage and superior performance. Moreover, where there is little or no competitive advantage and where performance is poor, the cause can be traced to one of two causes—either poor fit between the strategy and the environment or poor alignment between the organization and its strategy. Understanding the 7-S model and learning to apply it to different strategies and organizational configurations, then, is a key skill for every strategist.

The second way that strategy implementation contributes to competitive advantage is by providing the sensory inputs to the firm. As it implements strategy, learning to create value and refining the processes for delivering it, the firm also gathers information about the environment. This information is immediate and practical and customized to each firm and each environment. In implementing its strategy, McDonald's is perfectly positioned to learn about its customers and to experiment with new products and delivery models. Through implementation, customers and potential customers are engaged as a resource for identifying new opportunities, new competitors, and new technologies. As a firm like Ryanair implements its strategy, it should also be gathering feedback on what works and what fails to work, on what customers like and what they object to, and on what changes are likely as the industry evolves. This information should then be an input for innovation, new product and process development, and the formulation of new strategy. This process of "learning by doing" is designed to keep the firm ahead of changes in its environment, enabling it to learn, adapt, and redesign itself as necessary to sustain competitive advantage.

Unfortunately, this sort of introspective and ongoing redesign is difficult to achieve and manage. It is often at odds with the nuts and bolts of implementation and is most challenging in highly competitive environments and in the most successful firms. This is a paradox that relates directly to the conundrum of long- and short-term thinking. To thrive in the short term, providing the value customers demand while outperforming competitors, firms must use their resources efficiently, tightening the fit between the strategy and the firm and strengthening their own internal alignment so as to eliminate waste and to maximize return on investment. This sort of efficiency, however, leaves little room for creativity, innovation, and novelty. These things, by their very nature, are uncertain, inefficient, and speculative. As the quote by Thomas Edison illustrated, the pursuit of creativity and novelty involves certain failure on some things, as needed, to learn about others. Even in the best of cases, learning about the future and developing the right products, processes, and strategies for it will involve diverting some resources and some attention away from the present and away from the current competitive advantage.

Resolving this dilemma, and so satisfying simultaneously the demands of both the short and the long term, involves reprogramming the strategy and the strategists. Rather than seeking to maximize internal commitment, consensus, consistency, affluence, rationality, and faith, firms and managers should seek to minimize them. While still doing what is necessary to create value for customers and to develop competitive advantage, firms and managers should also cultivate a healthy sense of insecurity, discontent, and urgency. They should constantly seek better products and processes, challenge their own assumptions and priorities, and try to improve upon the status quo. Rather than defend their own advantages, they should look to overthrow them, before some competitor does. Paradoxically, then, to create the greatest value the firm must be its own fiercest competitor, constantly feeding new information gathered through implementation back into the formulation of better strategy. Fail at this, and the firm will eventually drift out of favor and relevance, losing touch with customers and being surpassed by innovative competitors. Succeed in this, and the firm will move from strength to strength, maintaining its alignment with the environment and sustaining its competitive advantage.

KEY TERMS

Curse of incumbency is the term used to describe a group of factors affecting large and established firms. Because of things like size, bureaucracy, and established practices, such firms can be rather inflexible and slow in responding to pressure or seizing emerging opportunities.

Filtering is a cognitive process by which individuals organize and attend to information from the environment. Because no one can gather and interpret all the available information, they attend selectively to particular issues, filtering out what is thought to be irrelevant and internalizing that which is thought to be significant.

Framing involves the categorization of complex issues under simple and discrete labels for the purpose of easing communication and decision making. Two common examples of frames used by managers are opportunity and threat.

Inertia in organizations refers to the tendency for established strategies, practices, and routines to be repeated over and again, such that forces for change are mitigated and the organization continues, reliably, to move in the same direction and to function in much the same way.

Path dependence is analogous to the simple principle that history matters to the present. More formally, though, it suggests that current decisions and economic conditions are at least partly constrained and affected by the sequence of decisions and events that preceded them.

Problemistic searching is the tendency for people to look for solutions only once problems have been identified, rather than searching continuously for opportunities to improve.

Prospect theory was developed by Kahneman and Tversky (1979) and deals with decision making under conditions of uncertainty or risk. Its basic premise is that the starting condition, or reference point, of a decision maker influences the valuation of the potential outcomes.

Satisficing is a common occurrence in decision making and is the tendency to accept adequate solutions, rather than to continue searching for solutions that could in fact be optimal.

QUESTIONS FOR REVIEW

1   What does the example of McDonald's illustrate about the principle of fit and the importance of implementation for long-term performance?
2   What is the distinction between implementation and formulation? What purpose does it serve to make this distinction and what potential harm can it cause?
3   What is the tension between short-term fit and long-term flexibility? Why does this tension exist and what sorts of problems can it create?
4   Why is success paradoxical and what forces contribute to this phenomenon?

5 What is the connection between this paradox of success and adaptation and learning? How do adaptation and learning contribute to sustained competitive advantage?

6 What is meant by a real options approach to strategy, and how does this approach resolve the paradox of success and contribute to sustained competitive advantage?

7 How does the use of net present value (NPV) analysis reinforce subtle biases in managerial decision making? What is the danger in relying too heavily on this analytical tool?

8 When done well, strategy implementation should serve two important purposes. What are they and how does each contribute to performance over time?

Companion Website

For a chapter review outline with links to videos and other valuable web resources, please visit the *Strategic Management* website: www.routledge.com/textbooks/amason.

Chapter 9

A General Framework

Strategy, Entrepreneurship, and International Business

A BROAD VALUE PROPOSITION

The Executive Assessment Institute (EAI) is a small, boutique consulting firm specializing in talent management, strategic leadership, and leadership development. It is based in North Carolina and has just five full-time employees. EAI's client list includes Fortune 100 firms in the automotive, healthcare, and computer fields, as well as entrepreneurial ventures in photo optics, private equity, and sustainable energy. While many of its clients are based in the U.S., many others are headquartered in places like Finland, Denmark, Germany, and Japan. Some are publicly held, with stocks traded on the NYSE and NASDAQ, while others are privately held, funded either by their own operations or through venture capital.

How can such a small firm service such a broad and varied array of clients? To understand, it is important to recognize that even firms that are different in many ways still share some basic things in common. Indeed, at a fundamental level all firms are much more similar than they are different. For example, all firms survive by creating value for customers, over and above what those customers can find elsewhere. That value leads to transactions, and those transactions translate into revenues and profits. This basic dynamic is true for all types of organizations. Large existing firms create products and services all the time, which they hope will lead to transactions, revenues, and ultimately profits. But new ventures face the same challenge. They generate capital by creating an expectation of value for their investors. That expectation of future revenues and earnings translates into financing, which provides the venture with the cash flow it needs to survive. Even non-profits must create value for someone, and that value translates into donations or other forms of volunteer resources, which enable the organization to continue operating. So all firms share the same basic imperative to create value and to translate that value into revenues and profits, or some form of cash or resource flow, as necessary, for them to continue operating.

Recall from Chapter 4 that all firms are open systems and so can be viewed in terms of a simple, input => transformation => output model. All firms gather resources and then transform those resources to produce outputs in the form of goods and services. It is from understanding this open systems model that we derive the principle of fit, discussed throughout the book. Firms that fit their environments perform better than those that do not. In fact, firms that do not fit their environments simply do not survive for long. So the imperative of fit is common to all types of firm. Because they are open systems, their survival depends upon their fit with their environment. Finally, all firms have value chains, reflecting the ways in which they source their inputs, conduct their transformations, and manage the flow of their outputs. While the details of the different value-chain processes and operations will vary from firm to firm, the basic functions are always present.

These are just some examples of the many basic similarities shared by all types of firms. The point, however, is this: by understanding the workings of these basic dynamics and functions, which all firms share, a student could understand a great deal about any firm, even if that firm was unfamiliar. In the same way, a manager who understands the similarity in these basic characteristics could come into a new firm and understand a great deal about it in a very short amount of time. And, in the same way, a consultant could work with many different firms, providing real value to each, by focusing on just those basic processes and operations that are present in and important to them all. This is how a firm like EAI adds value. EAI leverages its understanding of two things—strategy and the value of human capital—in providing service to all sorts of firms in all sorts of places. Every firm has a strategy and every strategy depends heavily on having the right people to manage it. As we know, strategies must change and evolve with the environment. That change and evolution require that the strategist create options for the future, make hard decisions about resource allocations, and connect the analytical and intuitive aspects of strategy formulation to the practical nuts and bolts of implementation. Every firm, then, whether large or small, public or private, international or domestic, must somehow fit its strategy to its environment and then connect that strategy to its organization and to its people.

Assisting firms to make those connections is the value proposition of EAI. Its consultants help firms develop the right kinds of talent for their own competitive environments and strategic challenges. They help firms construct models that guide the selection and succession of key executives. They help top executives diagnose dysfunction in their management teams and structure those teams to make better decisions. EAI has assisted venture capitalists to assess the potential of new ventures and of new venture teams and aided large multinationals in developing the organizational capabilities needed to facilitate success across a range of diverse markets. And it has done all this by offering a value proposition that is of importance to every firm. So, by understanding some essential linkages that are important to every firm, EAI has been able to service a wide array of clients and produce value across a wide range of settings.

A HIGHLY GENERALIZABLE DISCIPLINE

One of the challenges every strategist faces is learning to apply the general framework of strategic management across the breadth and variety of settings where it has value. From large, publicly held firms to entrepreneurial new ventures, from companies with single businesses in single locations to highly diversified multinationals, all firms and managers practice some sort of strategic management. Moreover, across all of these various and different settings, the specific applications and workings of strategic management's principles, tools, and models will appear somewhat different. Thus it is tempting to think that the practice of strategy itself somehow changes from firm to firm and from setting to setting. While certainly true to an extent, such thinking can also lead to problems. Indeed, it is important to understand that strategic management is a highly **generalizable** discipline, with a fundamental logic and framework that can be translated in some measure to every firm, every industry, and every setting.

Take, for example, the concept of competitive advantage. As defined in Chapter 1, competitive advantage exists when a firm produces value for customers sufficient to motivate an exchange above the firm's costs. This basic mechanism is essential to profitability, essential to the survival of the firm, and based on a few simple elements, present in every transaction. For every type of product or service and customer there will be some level of use value, some exchange value, some consumer surplus, and some profit or loss. Moreover, every transaction will be influenced by the finite resources of the buyer, the alternatives available in the marketplace, and the unique attributes of the producing firm. Because all of these elements are present in every transaction, competitive advantage will hold the same meaning for every firm; it will be the key to success and survival in every setting, public or private, large or small, domestic or international. Firms with a competitive advantage will perform better than firms with no advantage, and firms with no advantage will not be successful. That is why Jack Welch, former CEO of General Electric, once said, "If you don't have a competitive advantage, don't compete." While settings differ, that basic truth remains the same.

This is true for all the processes, concepts, and tools introduced in this book. For instance, firms of all different shapes and sizes are affected in much the same way by bargaining power. All else being equal, firms with great bargaining power will perform better than those without it. Intel has substantial power over its customers because of its name, reputation, and market share, and it uses that bargaining power to generate sales and earnings. The same is true of other types of businesses and industries as well. Good and reputable surgeons benefit from great bargaining power. Patients will often wait longer and pay more for a specific practitioner if they believe that practitioner is the best. Automobile makers like Honda and BMW have great bargaining power because of their brand and their reputations for quality and reliability. That bargaining power enables them to sell cars at higher prices and with fewer incentives than their competitors, enhancing the bottom line. Even universities derive benefits from bargaining power. With more applicants than it can accept, a university can be selective in admissions, charge more in tuition, and ask more in terms of preparation than if it had fewer applicants. Bargaining power, then, along with its tendency to benefit those who have it and penalize those who do not, is a constant across settings. As a result, understanding how bargaining power works and how it is gained and lost is a powerful tool that can transcend any particular context.

Indeed, concepts like value creation, competition, buyer elasticity, scarcity, asset specificity, customization, resource attractiveness, imitation, efficiency, option value, and fit are at work in every business, every industry, and every type of market, and they affect the performance of every firm. These concepts hold value for every business, in every setting; so it behooves the strategist to understand them and to know how to apply them. The problem comes in translating the concepts from the abstract to the practical and from the classroom to the specific setting of interest. This has long been a stumbling block for many and has limited the ability of students, managers, and professors alike to reap the full benefit of strategic thinking and management. Too many managers view strategic principles merely as academic concepts that may work for others but that could not work for them. Their businesses, they often think, are just too complicated and too unique. Students and professors often make the mistake of thinking one way in the classroom but then a different way in the business world, as if one part of the brain is used for academics while another part is used to actually manage. Realizing the full benefit of strategic management means understanding its generalizability and so learning how to think strategically in every setting and across every type of firm.

However, there are just so many different settings that many find it overwhelming, and there are so many different conditions, contingencies, and nuances that no one can be an expert in them all. So the field of strategic management has fragmented into a number of various subdisciplines, reflecting a wide range of specific issues, situations, and settings. In related fashion, the practice of strategic management has fragmented too, with experts in different industries, in different technologies, and in different types of firms. While all of this specialization offers some advantages, it also comes at a cost. That cost is that we lose the ability to understand quickly and to apply the generalizable principles of strategic management across different settings. For every student and manager, then, the challenge is to assess the context and situation in an effort to understand what is similar and what is different, so as to be able to take the best from the logic of strategic management and apply it to the unique and particular setting of interest.

That translation process, from the general to the specific, is the underlying theme of this chapter. This theme will be used to connect two particular issues—entrepreneurship and international business—to the generalizable framework of strategic management. These two topics are extremely important and so have given rise to their own unique body of academic research, their own vocabulary, and their own set of practicing specialists. However, because both deal with and directly impact firm performance, they are inextricably intertwined with the larger framework of strategic management. So it is helpful to think of both entrepreneurship and international business as special topics or areas within the larger field of strategic management. And so, with a good grasp of strategic principles and thinking, both topics can be better and more easily understood and better leveraged to greater benefit.

ENTREPRENEURSHIP

Defined strictly, entrepreneurship is the initiation, organization, and operation of a business venture for the purpose of earning a profit. This definition reflects the origins of the word *entreprendre*, a French word that means "to undertake" or "to initiate." The term "entrepreneurship," though, has grown to take on much broader connotations and now includes a host of issues involving innovation, private equity, new venture management, and small business management. Researchers who study entrepreneurship examine a range of varying issues, among them characteristics of entrepreneurs and entrepreneurial teams, strategies of new ventures, franchising, environmental influences on venture success, the commercialization of new technologies, resource protection, and firm capitalization. Most business schools offer various courses in entrepreneurship, at both the undergraduate and the graduate level, and many business schools have entire programs and faculty devoted exclusively to entrepreneurship.

In both theory and practice, entrepreneurship is interdisciplinary. With scholarly roots in both economics and management, the field draws from finance, marketing, and other disciplines as well. The earliest interest in entrepreneurship arose in economics, through the work of Joseph Schumpeter (1942). Recall that Schumpeter's concept of creative destruction was discussed elsewhere in the book, in relation to innovation and change. Innovation and change are important to all types of firm but are especially salient here, as the creatively destructive force in economic systems that Schumpeter identified was entrepreneurship. At a macroeconomic level, creative destruction was the collective manifestation of many individual entrepreneurs, acting to seize opportunities in the environment that had previously gone unrecognized. Entrepreneurs were able to discern gaps of unsatisfied demand and untapped potential. They then marshaled the resources and launched the businesses to provide innovative products and services to fill those gaps. Sometimes it worked: the gap materialized as expected and the new products and services were valued and purchased by the customers. Other times it did not work and the venture failed. That risk, though, of initiating and organizing was borne by the entrepreneur.

When it worked and the venture was successful, the result was both creative and destructive. The new ventures provided better value to customers, which led to new revenues and profits. In so doing, though, they set new standards, established new norms, and created new industries and markets. These new ventures, with their new products and services, destroyed the status quo along with the competitive advantages of many existing firms. This phenomenon was of great interest to economists, who saw entrepreneurship as an ongoing source of economic growth. With each successful occurrence, entrepreneurs created new value for themselves and the economy, inspiring others to look for similar opportunities and creating the conditions in which new gaps could arise.

The recognition of entrepreneurship and the realization that it often led to the creation of new firms attracted interest and scrutiny from management scholars, who were concerned less with the economic and societal impact of entrepreneurship than they were with the normative issues associated with the operation, management, and performance of the new firms. Those interested in entrepreneurship examined issues such as how entrepreneurs organized their businesses, how they could be made more successful, and how they should be managed to yield the greatest success (Sandberg, 1986; Vesper, 1980). As a result, entrepreneurship came to be associated with strategic management. Indeed, at one level the two are almost indistinct. Strategic management is concerned with the whole enterprise and with performance at the level of the firm; the same is true of entrepreneurship. Thus, entrepreneurship, along with the range of issues related to new venture management, can be considered a subdiscipline within the larger framework of strategy.

Parallel Models

Through observation and study, researchers have identified a series of key steps in the entrepreneurial process. The consistency of these steps has been validated through anecdotes and evidence and distilled into models used in teaching entrepreneurship. While the specifics of different models will vary, the basics remain largely the same and are illustrated in Figure 9.1: (1) opportunity recognition, (2) feasibility analysis, (3) business plan development, (4) gathering key resources, (5) securing investment, and (6) launching the venture. That structure maps neatly onto the strategic management framework introduced earlier in this book (see Figure 3.1, p. 49).

To illustrate, consider that the entrepreneurial process begins with opportunity recognition. Academics have debated whether the entrepreneur actually creates the opportunity or simply identifies an opportunity that was there all along. In reality there are likely cases of both. In the bigger picture, though, it is important to see the pursuit of this opportunity as the purpose of the entrepreneur. Recall that the process of strategic management also begins with a statement of the mission or purpose for the firm. In both cases, that purpose can be explicit and formalized in written statements or implied and understood through action and

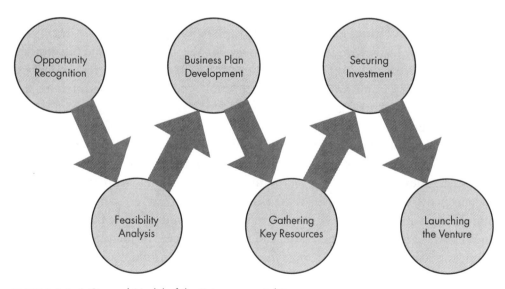

FIGURE 9.1 A General Model of the Entrepreneurial Process

common direction. However, in both instances the strategies of the firms, new and existing, will be directed by this basic purpose.

Next in the entrepreneurial process is the feasibility and environmental analysis. The challenge here is to evaluate the opportunity in light of the environmental forces. Will customers really value and buy the new product or service? Will the anticipated demand continue over time? Can a competitive advantage be achieved and sustained in light of anticipated competitor reactions? The whole approach is very similar to the sort of analysis depicted in the larger strategic model. Entrepreneurial ventures would certainly want to assess the state of the macro- and competitive environments, and they would do well to employ models like Porter's five forces model and the product/industry lifecycle. Moreover, it is important to understand that, when doing this analysis, both entrepreneurs and existing firms are looking for the same sorts of things—evidence of opportunity and sustainability, insight into the elasticity and strength of the demand, and clues about the behavior of competitors, customers, and suppliers. Both are interested in identifying a space or a position within the environment that their firms can fill and, in so doing, generate revenues and earnings.

Having identified a position in the environment and ascertained its potential for competitive advantage, both new and existing firms begin an assessment of their own resources and capabilities, in light of the conditions identified through the environmental analysis. In the strategic process, this happens as part of the resource-based assessment and involves the use of the value chain. In the entrepreneurial process, it happens during the development of the business plan and through the prioritization and securing of the key resources. In the world of entrepreneurship and new venture management, focus on the business plan is ubiquitous and intense. A business plan is an articulation of the strategy and is used to secure financing and support; it specifies how the new firm will make money by detailing how the venture will capitalize on opportunities in the environment. As a result, any good business plan will include an analysis of the resources and capabilities of the venture itself. Not surprisingly, that analysis will resemble the value-chain analysis described in Chapter 5 and take into consideration the resources needed to support the strategy, along with some assessment of the value, rarity, imitability, and substitutability of those resources going forward. A good business plan, then, will fulfill the same requirements as the basic competitive analyses described in chapters 4 and 5. Both are designed to assess the opportunities and threats in the environment, both should capture the strengths and weaknesses of the firm or venture, and both are designed to articulate how the firm will make money through specific activities in a specific competitive environment.

With the business plan complete and the conceptual part of the strategy in hand, the next step in the sequence is implementation. For entrepreneurs, that often means promoting and selling the plan to investors. As mentioned at the beginning of the chapter, these new firms require resources even though they may not yet have a product or service to sell. So, rather than rely on revenues, they rely on capital supplied by investors. In the world of entrepreneurship, these investors—often called **venture capitalists** or **angels**—supply the necessary cash flow, allowing the venture to operate while it develops and gets to market its products and services. It is important to remember, though, that these investors are motivated by economic opportunity. Put simply, they expect to make a profit from their investments. Moreover, because they frequently have a variety of other opportunities, they are typically very deliberate and sophisticated in their assessment of every new firm. They study prospective entrepreneurs and their management teams closely, examining the technology and resources of the venture, considering the opportunities and threats in the environment, estimating the value of the competitive advantage both now and into the future. Like any investor, what they want is a strong return. So they search diligently, studying the business plans of prospective ventures, analyzing them for future growth and profitability. When they are convinced the opportunity is right, they invest, providing capital, connections, and expertise in return for a portion of the equity.

While the process of obtaining new venture investment is complex, involving a great deal of specialized effort and knowledge, it still reflects the same basic elements of any other form of investment. There is the expectation of a positive return. Thus, the new venture must offer the prospect of future cash flows. There is an understanding that the investment must be competitive. Just as a private investor can choose among a variety of stocks, bonds, and real estate, so too can a venture capitalist choose among a range of different entrepreneurs and new ventures. Finally, there is a horizon over which the investment will be held and a terminal value if it is sold. All of these elements factor into the value of any investment. As explained in Chapter 2 and elsewhere, that value can be estimated using net present value (NPV) analysis. So, while an entrepreneurial venture is a unique type of investment, it is still helpful to see it in terms of its net value, just as a good strategist views his or her firm in terms of its net value. It is also helpful to think of the venture itself, along with its management, its resources, and its capabilities, as a product that the investor buys. As with all transactions of this type, there is an exchange value or price. In this case the price reflects the amount invested and the amount of equity provided in return. There is bargaining power at work in this exchange reflecting the relative desire of the two parties to reach a deal. Finally, there is competitive advantage; high potential ventures, with strong prospects, quality resources, and good potential, attract more investment and at better terms, while less attractive ventures must give up more in order to get less.

When viewed this way, the various steps in the entrepreneurial process make sense in more than just mechanical terms; they also make sense in larger strategic terms. Entrepreneurs ultimately face the same challenge as any other strategist: they must design a strategy that creates and delivers value, despite the opposition of competitive forces and the friction of organizational processes; they must craft a plan that identifies the opportunity while addressing the threats; they must identify the sources of value and rareness and then acquire the resources necessary to bring their strategy about; and they must take into account the potential for responses from the competition and the dangers of imitation and substitution. And they must do all of this in such a way that all the other potential stakeholders— investors, business partners, suppliers, and employees—will see and understand the potential the new venture represents. Finally, then, they must deliver on that potential, creating value in the form of transactions that lead to revenues and profits. Viewed in this way, entrepreneurs are simply strategists who happen also to be operating under special circumstances and so grapple with a variety of special challenges unique to their setting.

New Complexities

Most of those special challenges associated with entrepreneurship fall broadly into a category known as the **liabilities of newness** (Stinchcombe, 1965). Newness, in most any endeavor, carries with it some unique problems related to unfamiliarity and the lack of example or precedent. Entrepreneurs create new products and services or offer existing products and services in new places or in different ways. As a result, they often face greater uncertainty and ambiguity than the managers of other types of business. Introducing new products or services means educating customers; it may also mean creating new processes, training new workers, or retraining existing workers in new methods. It may mean developing new supplier networks, introducing new business models, or educating investors on the risks and prospects of a new business model. The unique nature of the setting requires that entrepreneurs be good strategists while also dealing with heightened uncertainty on their own as well as on the part of others.

Not surprisingly, many of the special issues and topics that have been studied by scholars in the field of entrepreneurship are reflections of these special challenges and liabilities. **Franchising**, for example, is an organizational form that enables growth by leveraging the financial resources of multiple independent owners, while also providing those independent owners access to a recognized name, to proven systems, and to tested products and services. **Licensing** is a mechanism whereby new firms can commercialize an invention or a piece of intellectual property without incurring the risk and uncertainty associated with market research and product development. Research into the various roles of venture capitalists reflects the fact that these individuals can and often do contribute more than just money to the success of their ventures. Having invested with other entrepreneurs and in other new firms, these VCs will often have expertise and connections that can be leveraged to reduce uncertainty and to improve the chances of venture success.

For the purposes of this book, though, and for the purpose of learning to apply the strategic framework and to think strategically, it is helpful to view entrepreneurship as a special case of strategic management. Returning to the example at the beginning of the chapter, EAI is an entrepreneurial venture, set up to fill a niche and to leverage a new and unique set of resources. Its success reflects the fit between the environment and a set of resources that are valuable and rare. Its continued success will depend upon the ongoing value of those resources in the face of potential imitation and substitution as well as the changing needs and tastes of the customers. Like any other firm, EAI must develop and nurture its competitive advantage through its day-to-day activities. It must sell services to clients who are seeking their own best interests; it must deliver value over and above its costs and over and above the prices that it is charging; and it must do all of this while creating new options for new competitive advantage in the future. In reality, then, EAI's continued success will be a reflection of its strategy and the ability of its managers to learn, adapt, and implement the right strategy at the right time.

As mentioned earlier, specialization by academics and managers has become a necessary reality in the face of overwhelming complexities throughout the business world. However, specialization can be a double-edged sword when an intense focus on how things are different prevents us from seeing how they are still the same. Such is the situation here: while it is different and specialized in many ways, entrepreneurship is still simply and best understood as a special application of strategic management. It is still about fit, still about resources, still about creating value and competitive advantage, and still about providing a return on an investment. While the terminology and issues may change, and while the challenges may be somewhat specialized, those basics remain very much the same.

INTERNATIONAL BUSINESS

There is an old saying that only two things are truly certain: death and taxes. Perhaps it is time to add a third item to this list of inevitabilities. Specifically, the world of business is becoming increasingly global. Table 9.1 provides a list of the world's 25 largest companies in 2009, based on revenues. Of those listed, 13 are from Europe, seven are from the United States, and five are from Asia. Just four years earlier, in 2005, this list consisted of 11 from Europe, ten from the United States, and four from Asia. Consider how different this list would have looked 20 years earlier and how different it may look 20 years from now. In addition, consider that there are many other large and well-known companies with names such as Pemex, LG, Petrobras, Samsung, Tata, Yukos, and Telefonica from countries like Mexico, Brazil, Russia, India, Spain, and South Korea among the Fortune Global 500 that are growing rapidly as leaders in their industries. And the birth of new industries may yet provide even more impetus for other new firms to expand and grow into global giants.

Table 9.1
The World's Largest Companies, 2009 and 2005

	2009	2005
1	Royal Dutch Shell	Wal-Mart Stores
2	Exxon Mobil	British Petroleum (BP)
3	Wal-Mart Stores	Exxon Mobil
4	British Petroleum (BP)	Royal Dutch Shell
5	Chevron	General Motors
6	Total	DaimlerChrysler
7	ConocoPhillips	Toyota Motors
8	ING Group	Ford
9	Sinopec	General Electric
10	Toyota Motors	Total
11	Japan Post Holdings	Chevron
12	General Electric	ConocoPhillips
13	China National Petroleum	AXA
14	Volkswagen	Allianz
15	State Grid	Volkswagen
16	Dexia Group	Citigroup
17	ENI	ING
18	General Motors	Nippon Telegraph & Telephone
19	Ford	AIG
20	Allianz	IBM
21	HSBC Holdings	Siemens
22	Gazprom	Carrefour
23	Daimler	Hitachi
24	BNP Paribas	Assicurazioni Generali
25	Carrefour	Matsushita Electric

The amount of international business transacted by firms such as these, along with many others, is growing rapidly. Fifty years ago, international trade was barely more than 1% of world GDP. By 2006, it represented nearly 30%, and that proportion continues to grow. Direct investment in foreign assets by firms and individuals, called **foreign direct investment** (FDI), has also risen drastically over the past 30 years to the point that it is over 25% of world GDP. This same period has seen an explosion of treaties, agreements, and new organizations intended to facilitate international business and trade. Perhaps the most significant of these was the establishment of the euro as the standard currency among the majority of nations in the European Union. The euro is now accepted and used in over 20 countries, making trade between individuals and businesses in those countries virtually seamless. Indeed, even with the recent debt crisis in Europe, experts fully expect that the euro will continue as one of the world's most widely accepted currencies. In addition to the European Union and the euro, a number of other trading agreements and associations have impacted international trade. The North American Free Trade Agreement (NAFTA) created a free-trading bloc among Canada, Mexico, and the United States. A similar arrangement evolved in Southeast Asia, where ten countries are members of the Association of Southeast Asian Nations (ASEAN). These nations established the Asian Free Trade Area, or AFTA, which is designed to leverage bargaining power and to facilitate trade and economic growth. Similar sorts of trading blocs exist in South America (Mercosur) and Africa (AEC). Owing to the desire for a world body to promote, monitor, and facilitate international trade, the World Trade Organization was created in 1995 for the purpose of liberalizing world trade. The WTO now has 153 members—80% of the 192 nations recognized by the United Nations.

From these observations, two things are abundantly clear. First, the trend towards the **globalization** of business is pervasive and ongoing. Certainly there has been international business and trade across national borders going back thousands of years. But the last two centuries has seen the level of that trade grow exponentially, both in absolute terms and as a proportion of overall economic activity. Even now, the world can be viewed as a series of regional economic blocs (Frankel, 1997), and many believe that this regionalism represents movement along a continuum, away from fragmentation and towards true globalization. While there will surely be periodic instances and momentary episodes where the level of international business declines, the overall trend is undeniable and likely to continue. The world is moving closer and closer to becoming a single market where goods and services are made and sold with little regard for national borders. As the experience of the **Eurozone** has shown, there is a continuing trend towards **transnationalism**, where national identities are blurred and pose increasingly smaller constraints on the conduct of business.

Given this, the second implication that can be drawn from all of this is that international business will be an increasingly important and common concern for strategic managers. Much like entrepreneurship, international business has often been viewed as so unusual and complex that it was the province of only the largest companies and only the most sophisticated and dedicated specialists. Today, however, international business is more and more a normal and everyday part of strategy, of increasing importance to the success of every firm and a challenge of every strategic manager.

International business is defined here as transactions between individuals and businesses that cross national borders. A wide range of issues are implied by this definition. Things like currency values and trading policy, along with cultural differences and attitudes, are significant parts of the international business landscape. Other issues, too, like patenting and intellectual property protection, asset ownership and taxation, conflicting labor practices, protectionism and government regulation, and accounting rules on activities conducted in multiple countries, with other currencies, and according to different laws all fall within the boundaries of this broad definition. Taken together, these issues all affect the performance of international firms, as well as the competitive environments of most non-international firms. Given this pervasive influence, international business must somehow fit into the larger framework and logic of strategic management.

As discussed earlier, though, strategic management is a highly generalizable discipline. So, while there is much about international business that is specialized, technical, and complex, there are also many issues that parallel the basic framework and logic of strategy. Understanding these common themes and leveraging these basic similarities can facilitate better management, with better performance as a result. This section, then, outlines some parallel issues along with some common implications meant to help students and managers translate across the contexts, from the basics of strategic management to the practical realities of international business and then back again.

International Strategies

One important parallel comes in the area of basic strategy and competitive advantage. Recall that competitive advantage derives from one of two sources—low cost or differentiation. As discussed in Chapter 5, these generic strategies are really reflections of market conditions and demand elasticity. In situations where customers have strong preferences for a particular product, service, or supplier, their options are limited; they are less willing to substitute and more willing to pay a premium price. Thus, there is opportunity for competitive advantage based upon differentiation. In other situations, where customers have little or no preference among the suppliers of a particular product or service, their options are much broader; they are more willing to substitute and less willing to pay a premium price. Thus, in cases like this there is opportunity for competitive advantage based on low transaction costs. Across the range of all products, industries, and transactions, every competitive advantage can be described and understood in terms of these two basic dimensions.

Not surprisingly, the same is true in the international context: elasticity of demand, along with issues like product substitutability and bargaining power, still shapes strategy and competitive advantage. In the international context, though, the scale and complexity of the market is much greater. Thus, the opportunity emerges for two different kinds of generic strategy. Each of these—the **global strategy** and the **multi-domestic strategy**—leverages the same principles as discussed in Chapter 5 but does so in a way that is unique to the international context. Both reflect basic realities about the international market and about how firms compete within it.

To illustrate, consider Vodafone, the largest provider of mobile communications in the world. Based in the United Kingdom, Vodafone has over 300 million customers in more than 60 different countries, among them the United States (where it operates as Verizon), Chile, Turkey, New Zealand, Russia, Egypt, Italy, and Germany. In 20 of these countries, Vodafone owns much of the infrastructure needed to support its network. In the others, it operates through a series of partnerships. In all of them, though, it uses the same or similar technologies to deliver the same basic services, with the same basic contracts and business models. In essence, Vodafone is a global company, with the ability to treat the entire world as one huge marketplace, an approach which affords it tremendous economies of scale. Those scale economies facilitate its competitive advantage by providing seamless usage across regions, a wide range of plans and options, and a broad spectrum of devices and functionality. More importantly, all of this capability and flexibility lowers the transaction costs for customers, who often have many other options for the same basic services. These customers benefit from the range of options and so are frequently elastic, able to shop from among a number of different suppliers and to choose the one that offers the features, equipment, functionality, and price that bests suits their needs. Vodafone's global strategy, then, leverages the same principles as the basic low-cost strategy. It is often the easiest choice, the choice offering the most options, the choice with the lowest price, and the choice with the greatest capability at a particular price point. Taking into account all of these things, it is the choice that meets the needs of the customer at the lowest overall transaction cost. By expanding its low-cost strategy globally and doing what it does on a worldwide scale, Vodafone is able to expand the size of its market, the scope of its capabilities, and the scale of its economies dramatically and exercise great competitive advantage over firms that lack similar size, scope, and scale.

The global strategy, then, follows an economic logic that is very similar to the low-cost strategy, leveraging things like efficiency, scale economy, and portability to offer products and services that appeal to elastic customers. But it does so by treating the world as a single, large, and seamless market where one product or product category can be adapted easily to suit all of the global demand. Standardization around one basic model provides enormous scale advantages, lowering costs per unit dramatically. Standardization and scale enable firms to source their materials at lower costs. Vodafone has enormous bargaining power over the suppliers of its equipment, the firms that deliver its advertising, and the institutions that finance its operations. It even has bargaining power over the governments and partners in the countries in which it operates. And it uses all of this bargaining power to lower its costs and to make its products and services more accessible and attractive to more and more customers, enabling greater competitiveness in an industry marked by high elasticity of demand.

Many other international firms have adopted the same approach. Numerous large financial institutions, for example Citigroup, ING, and HSBC, have followed a similar path of trying to provide a seamless presence and consistent service across a wide range of national borders. The automobile industry has evolved towards global competition where a very few large manufacturers—Ford, Toyota, Hyundai, GM, Volkswagen, and Honda—control the vast majority of the world's car and light truck market. These firms leverage common technologies, designs, and platforms to gain tremendous operational efficiencies. Their size gives them enormous bargaining power over their suppliers and they enjoy tremendous scale economies, as necessary, to gain market share and profitability in an industry where substitutability and bargaining power of the buyer are high. Indeed, in every industry where the conditions are ripe for low-cost-based competitive advantage, there are also opportunities for a global strategy. In the airline industry and in petroleum production, in basic food commodities and in cement, even in industries as different as steel and computer assembly, there is the opportunity for advantage by employing a global strategy. Those opportunities reflect the realities of the markets, products, services, and customers. And, just as those same basic forces drive domestic competition towards low-cost strategies, so too do they drive international competition towards global strategies.

Consider, though, how different this is from a multi-domestic strategy. A good example of this approach can be seen in a firm such as Johnson & Johnson. Like Vodafone, Johnson & Johnson is large, with tremendous international reach. Based in the U.S., it operates in nearly 60 countries, including Malaysia, Argentina, Russia, France, China, Israel, and Brazil, with millions of customers and billions of dollars in sales and infrastructure spread across the globe. However, as opposed to Vodafone, which produces just a few basic products, J&J produces hundreds of products in the areas of pharmaceuticals, consumer goods, and medical devices. Moreover, it operates through 250 semi-autonomous subsidiaries, organized into groups based upon product and geographic similarity. Both domestically and internationally, J&J seeks to be a premium provider. When its products have direct substitutes, it focuses on adding value through quality, reliability, service, and innovation. And it is reluctant to sacrifice price or margin simply to gain market share.

However, when operating with so many different products in so many different markets, the challenge of this approach is enormous. Across a huge spectrum of tastes and preferences, across a maze of laws and regulations, amid myriad different cultural norms and histories, J&J must position its brand and its many products as unique and different and so worthy of a premium price. To do this, it must do two things. First, it must recognize and understand those differences in all of the various different countries and regions in which it operates. Second, it must adjust its strategy to meet the specific needs of each of those various and different markets. In essence, it must see the world as a patchwork of different markets, each with its own characteristics and variations and each warranting its own strategic variations. This approach yields a host of different small strategies tailored to the contours of the local marketplace but together all part of the larger corporate whole.

As with the global strategy, the multi-domestic case is uniquely international. As the name implies, it involves operating in multiple different domestic environments. However, this strategy leverages some of the same principles as a domestic strategy based on differentiation, as it seeks to segment the demand and to match products and services to individual tastes and preferences. A multi-domestic strategy leans towards customization and away from standardization, again in an effort to appeal to the unique and varied preferences of different regions and groups. In doing all of this, a multi-domestic strategy seeks to capitalize on familiarity and loyalty, which can reduce elasticity of demand, increasing prices and margins. But doing all of that necessitates local information on the preferences and tastes of the different regions and customer groups as well as the systemic flexibility to provide products appealing to a wide array of tastes. For example, it requires the dexterity to design, make, and sell one type of product for the Chinese market and yet a very different sort of product for the South American market. And it requires the discipline to allow the business units in all of those different regions to evolve and adapt their own unique strategies, as necessary, to appear differentiated in their own domestic contexts. This is the challenge that Johnson & Johnson faces, and this is the reason for its complex corporate-level strategy and structure.

Here, again, many other firms have adopted the same approach. YUM! Brands (discussed in Chapter 7), for instance, incorporating Taco Bell, Pizza Hut, Long John Silvers, A&W Restaurants, and Wingstreet, operates more than 36,000 restaurants in 110 countries around the world. While based in Dallas, Texas, over 35% of its locations—nearly 13,000 restaurants—are located outside the U.S. Moreover, many of these international stores are owned and run by local franchisees or joint-venture partners, who have moderate levels of autonomy over things like store concept and design, as well as over menu variations and supply chains. As a result, each of the different brands can take on a uniquely local flavor appropriate to its location and customers. So a Pizza Hut in St. Petersburg, Russia, for instance, may feel very different from a Pizza Hut in Paris, France, and a KFC in Shanghai, China, may look and feel very different from a KFC in Oxford, England. The result is a strategy adapted according to local knowledge and preference, a strategy designed to build familiarity and loyalty within particular markets, so as to support higher prices and margins. Indeed, anywhere that there is the opportunity for this sort of customization, there is the opportunity for a multi-domestic strategy.

The music industry, for example, is worldwide. Yet, the leading firms in the industry—firms like Sony, EMI, Warner Music, and Vivendi—follow multi-domestic strategies, promoting artists and producing music that is tailored to specific national and regional tastes. The same is true in healthcare, where myriad laws, regulations, and payment practices necessitate wide variation in medical devices, pharmaceutical products, and service delivery practices to suit the local markets. The prepared food and food products industries are often multi-domestic, given the wide variety in tastes and regulations in different countries and regions. Grupo Bimbo, for instance, is a worldwide leader of baked goods. Based in Mexico City, it has annual sales of $10 billion and operations in 18 countries, including Mexico, Brazil, Argentina, Peru, the U.S., the Czech Republic, and China. It markets over 150 different brands and delivers to 1.8 million locations daily. Yet, while Bimbo is a huge organization, its operations are still largely local, as necessary, to match local tastes and to assure freshness and high-quality service.

Generally speaking, then, where there is opportunity for differentiation-based competitive advantage, there is likely to be opportunity for a multi-domestic strategy. Both leverage individual differences and preferences; both capitalize on organizational flexibility and customization so as to satisfy unique, local pockets of demand; and both seek to leverage inelasticity in an effort to increase profit and margin. So, just as a global strategy maps onto a set of economic principles similar to those underlying a low-cost strategy, the multi-domestic strategy maps onto a set of economic principles similar to those underlying a differentiation strategy. As a result, understanding those basic principles can help a manager to understand better and function well in both domestic and international contexts.

Of course, all global strategies are not entirely low-cost based and all multi-domestic strategies are not based purely on differentiation. As illustrated in Figure 9.2, all international strategies and every competitive advantage combine some elements of both. This figure should be familiar as it was adapted from Figure 6.4 (p. 158). Indeed, it is offered to illustrate the same point, only this time in a different context: that every strategy is a combination of two basic and generic motivations. Whether in a domestic or an international setting, even the most cost-conscious consumers will have some desire to have their individual preferences met. Thus, firms like Vodafone, Cemex, or Dell, all of which have strategies that are largely global, may still offer some measure of local customization or be willing to make some small accommodations, as necessary, to adapt to regional or national tastes. At the same time, even those customers with the greatest desire for customization and local responsiveness will still care about costs and still factor them into their purchasing decisions. Thus, firms like Johnson & Johnson, Grupo Bimbo, and Vivendi may still look for opportunities to standardize and to leverage scale economies to reduce their costs. International firms, then, seek to design strategies that fall somewhere along the curves in Figure 9.2, blending together elements of both approaches to fit their specific markets and to produce competitive advantage. Position A would represent a focus that is almost entirely global. To this firm, the world is one large and homogeneous marketplace, and so its products and services would be highly standardized, enabling scale economies and lower costs per unit. Position X, on the other hand, would represent just the opposite. To this firm, the world looks like a patchwork of distinct and different markets. Thus, its products and services would reflect local tastes and adaptations, enabling premium pricing and higher margins, but offering fewer opportunities for scale economies.

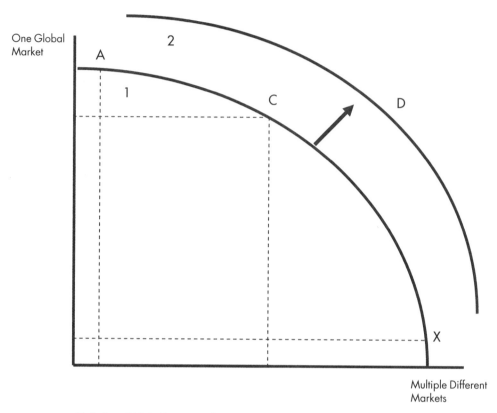

FIGURE 9.2 Global and Multi-Domestic Strategies

Firm C in the figure would represent some point in between the two, somewhat less attractive to the most elastic customers than Firm A and somewhat less attractive to the most inelastic customers than Firm X. However, depending upon the nature of the market, this position could still be advantageous, by offering modest local responsiveness while still providing a reasonably low transaction cost. More importantly, though, virtually any position on curve 2 would offer advantages over a position on curve 1. Recall that changes in technology, practice, and capability can enable firms to offer more of both lower costs and greater differentiation. The same is true for these generic international strategies. The creation of a common currency, the availability of a new technology, or a reduction in barriers to trade could all represent a shift in the horizon of possibilities from curve 1 to curve 2. That shift would enable some firms to provide greater levels of customization and local responsiveness, while also better leveraging economies of scale and so providing lower transaction costs. Such a position would clearly be advantageous and valuable, at least until it was imitated or encroached upon by competitors.

The lesson in all of this, then, is that the same basic economic principles that guide strategy development in a domestic context should also guide strategy development in the international context. The international context is decidedly larger and more complex, offering greater opportunity and greater potential risk. There are many more variables to consider and more competitors to monitor. But there are also more customers and more options for sourcing supply. However, amid all this added complexity, the same basic forces are still at work, and so the sources of competitive advantage remain largely the same. As a result, the two generic international strategies, global and multi-domestic, correspond both logically and practically to the two generic strategies discussed earlier, low cost and differentiation.

Implementation and Fit

Beyond just the nature of the strategy and competitive advantage, though, there is another level of similarity between the basic strategic framework and international business. That similarity lies in the relationship between strategy and implementation. Recall from Chapter 8 that strategy should drive the shape of the organization. Just as form follows function, so should the attributes of the organization reflect the imperatives of the strategy if the strategy is to work as intended. This was the point of the 7-S model and the rationale underlying the idea of fit between strategy and things like structure, skills, style, staff, and shared values. Given the importance of this principle to organizational performance, it should come as no surprise that the relationship is just as important in the international context as it is in the domestic one. Success still depends upon having the right capabilities, the right people, and the right organization for the strategy.

So, to continue with the examples of Vodafone and Johnson & Johnson, it is clear how these two firms are different in terms of structure and approach and how those differences reflect differences in their strategies. Whereas Vodafone is largely centralized, Johnson & Johnson is highly decentralized. Where Johnson & Johnson employs specialists across a broad spectrum of technologies, functions, and disciplines, Vodafone is much more focused, specializing in a much narrower band of technologies, products, and services. Vodafone's marketing, contracting, billing, and accounting systems are also likely more streamlined and simpler than those of Johnson & Johnson, given its more limited product offerings and business models. Both firms, though, are tremendously successful and both would hold considerable advantages over almost any purely domestic competitor. Thus, by combining good understanding of basic strategic management principles with the enormous opportunities of an increasingly worldwide marketplace, both firms have been successful.

To return to the example at the beginning of the chapter, it should come as no surprise that even a small firm like EAI can be successful internationally. It simply has to match its capabilities to the nature of the opportunity, leveraging the logic and principles of strategy to create value for its customers around the world. As a small boutique firm, EAI emphasizes customized service. Thus, it interacts with each prospective client directly, designing solutions for each specific situation and problem. There is relatively little effort given to standardization or to leveraging economies of scale; each client and each problem is unique. This approach may limit growth and overall volume. At the same time, though, it builds loyalty, limits substitutability, and promotes premium prices and margins. And, just as with larger organizations, EAI's success depends upon how well its systems, people, skills, and capabilities fit its strategy. Just like Vodafone and Johnson & Johnson, EAI benefits from the expanded opportunities of an increasingly worldwide marketplace. However, it too must develop strategy appropriate to its position and that market, and it too must construct the sorts of structures and systems needed to support that strategy. Whether in a global or a domestic market, these relationships are universal.

These parallels and similarities notwithstanding, no one should underestimate the complexity of the international marketplace. Cultural, legal, economic, even geographic distances can extract a tremendous toll on a firm's strategy and success. Ghemawat (2001) provides an insightful and instructive discussion of the various costs associated with these different dimensions of international distance and concludes that, even in an increasingly small and integrated world, distance still matters. Every manager, every student, and every academic would do well to heed this advice. But fear of such costs should never overshadow the size of the opportunity. International competitors that follow the principles of strategic management will often enjoy substantial advantages over purely domestic firms. Thus, international business is a reality for virtually every manager, if not now then in the not so distant future. The challenge is to understand what is similar and what is different, to adapt and apply what is similar, and to identify and account fully for the costs of what is different. While a full examination of all of this is beyond the scope of this book, the matter is nevertheless central to performance and so fully within the purview and responsibility of the strategist.

SUMMARY

Throughout the book, various chapters have ended with a series of caveats. These comments were meant to give additional breadth and depth, to offer some exceptions or special conditions, and to provide a measure of practical relevance to the concepts, tools, and frameworks presented. This chapter, and the next one as well, will be somewhat different. The reason is that they deal with what are essentially exceptions and special conditions. In essence, both chapters focus entirely on issues that are supplemental to the larger framework of strategic management. Each of the topics—entrepreneurship and international business in this chapter and strategic leadership in the next—is a discipline unto itself as well as an important part of the larger strategic management process. Each can be an important contributor to a firm's performance, but each is also sufficiently unique to justify its own vocabulary and its own scholarly identity and to be practiced by its own set of specialists. While this specialization offers advantages, it also comes at a cost. That cost is seen in the form of redundancy, unnecessary complexity, and the inability to generalize across settings, the result of which is a more complicated landscape for students and less effective management overall. Thus, the purpose of this chapter has been to illustrate that, while these topics are specialized and important, they also share in common two essential things. They are all drivers of firm value and they are all among the responsibilities of strategic management.

For the sake of this chapter, then, entrepreneurship is all about creating value and providing a good return on investment. It seeks pockets of unsatisfied demand and looks for opportunities to apply innovative methods and technologies. It requires planning and positioning, formulation and implementation, as well as learning and adaptation. Entrepreneurs create new ventures, and those ventures have value chains through which products and services are created and distributed to the environment. Those ventures that succeed do so because they develop a competitive advantage, giving customers a reason to buy at a price above the venture's costs. And that competitive advantage enables revenues, profits, growth, and a positive return for the investors. So it is important to see that, even though it is called by a different name, entrepreneurship is inseparable from the practice of strategy. Even inside of large and well-established firms, the energy, vitality, and creativity of entrepreneurship can be harnessed to promote growth, to provide incentives, and to sustain competitive advantage. This harnessing of entrepreneurial energy and thinking inside of existing organizations has been called **intrapreneurship**. But giving it a different name does not make it fundamentally different. Whether we label it intrapreneurship, entrepreneurship, or strategic management, the challenge is still fundamentally the same: to create value that will lead to competitive advantage and to sustain that competitive advantage in the face of a changing competitive landscape. So it is important to understand how entrepreneurship and strategy are fundamentally linked and then to leverage the understanding of each in the practice of the other. Labels notwithstanding, it is inevitable that good entrepreneurs will also be good strategists and that good strategists will understand the importance of entrepreneurship.

The same is true of international business. While involving a host of specialized concerns and technical issues, success in international business still rests on the basic precepts of strategic management. Substitutability, bargaining power, and elasticity still characterize the competitiveness of the environment. Rare, valuable, and inimitable resources still drive uniqueness and competitive advantage across firms. And disconnects between the strategy and the various elements of a firm's systems, style, structures, and staff still represent the greatest threats to success. What then happens, as a firm moves from a domestic approach to an international one, is that a new layer of complexity is added. Processes that worked in one market may not work in another. The drivers of a product's value in one place may be very different than the drivers in another. Potentially everything about the way a firm goes to market and manages its own structures and affairs may change as the landscape of laws, practices, and preferences change. But those changes do not alter the basic formula of success. In every context, whether domestic or international, in just one country, in two countries, or in dozens of countries simultaneously, success is still a function of value creation for customers and value capture through revenues over and above the firm's costs.

Ultimately, then, the point of this chapter has been the same as that of the entire book: better management and better organizational performance. Recall from Chapter 1 that performance is the crux of business and business education. And the ability to drive performance and deliver results is the goal of every business student, every manager, and every investor. Strategic management is nothing less than the single most valuable framework for understanding, directing, and delivering that performance. However, in addition to being valuable, it is highly generalizable. Indeed, as this chapter has illustrated, the basic framework and logic of strategic management can be applied to understand and to operate better in both entrepreneurial and international contexts. In both settings the challenge remains the same. Thus, in both settings the fundamental logic and basic principles of strategic management continue to apply.

KEY TERMS

Angels are typically wealthy individuals who invest their own funds to finance entrepreneurial ventures in the earliest stages of development.

The **Eurozone** consists of the 16 European countries that are both members of the European Union (EU) and have adopted the euro as their official currency.

Foreign direct investment (FDI) is the ownership of business assets by a foreign party, either an individual or firm.

Franchising is a business model where a franchisor, who owns a concept, brand, and set of practices, sells the rights to these assets to a franchisee, who pays in return an upfront fee and a royalty. This model facilitates rapid growth but involves shared ownership and profits, and so the potential for conflicts of interest between the franchisor and franchisee.

Generalizable is a term referring to the ability of a framework or principle to apply across a range of settings. Strategic management is a generalizable discipline because it provides a framework that can be useful across a range of firms, organizations, and settings.

A **global strategy** is a type of international strategy that leverages standardization and economies of scale in building competitive advantage across multiple countries. With a focus on consistency and per unit costs, it capitalizes on some of the same economic forces as a low-cost strategy.

Globalization is the name given to the homogenization of global markets, economies, and cultures. Notwithstanding some noteworthy ebbs and flows, the overall process and direction of globalization are undeniable over the course of time.

Intrapreneurship refers to the encouragement and cultivation of entrepreneurial thinking and behaviors inside of existing organizations.

Liabilities of newness refers to the various difficulties that arise from doing something new. Some examples are the lack of precedent, the lack of familiarity in a role, and the lack of legitimacy in the eyes of a supplier or customer.

Licensing is a means of commercializing a product, technology, or piece of intellectual property. In a licensing arrangement, the license holder grants another party, for a fee, the right to use, sell, or manufacture the licensed property.

A **multi-domestic strategy** is a type of international strategy that leverages customization and local responsiveness in building competitive advantage across multiple countries. With its focus on local preferences and branding, it capitalizes on some of the same economic forces as a differentiation strategy.

Transnationalism is the name given to a social philosophy where national borders are largely inconsequential and so offer little resistance to the movement of people, goods, materials, and information. Large multinational firms may have no distinct national identity and so are said to be transnational.

Venture capitalists pool funds from individual investors to invest in entrepreneurial ventures. While specializing in different types of firms at different stages of growth, venture capitalists are all accustomed to high risks, with the prospect of relatively short-term and large returns.

QUESTIONS FOR REVIEW

1 What is generalizability and what does it mean to say that strategic management is a highly generalizable framework?

2 What are some of the basic similarities between all types of firms, product, or service, large or small?

3 How can an understanding of these similarities help one to be a better strategic manager?

4 How is a business plan for a new venture similar to the strategy of an existing business?

5 What are the two generic international strategies and how do they reflect economic principles similar to the generic strategies of low cost and differentiation?

6 Describe some differences you would likely find in comparing the structures and systems of two firms, one of which pursued a global strategy and the other a multi-domestic strategy.

7 What is globalization? What role have regional trading associations played in the process of globalization?

Companion Website

For a chapter review outline with links to videos and other valuable web resources, please visit the *Strategic Management* website: www.routledge.com/textbooks/amason.

Chapter 10

Strategic Leadership
Leading and Governing

A LEADER IN BANKING

In 1982 Hugh McColl became president of North Carolina National Bank (NCNB). A year later, he added the titles and responsibilities of CEO and chairman. At the time, NCNB was a successful regional bank with operations in North Carolina and Florida, $12 billion in assets, $8 billion in deposits, and a market capitalization of $700 million. Over the next 18 years, McColl would remake the bank into the global financial powerhouse known today as Bank of America. And, in so doing, he would help to transform the entire banking industry.

The story of NCNB's growth has a number of chapters. In the early 1980s, for instance, banks in the U.S. were generally not allowed to operate in multiple states. NCNB was able to work around this limitation by exploiting a law that allowed banks to own non-bank subsidiaries, which, in turn, could own banks in other states. This provided a foot in the door for NCNB and McColl. By 1986 NCNB was operating in six southeastern U.S. states and had assets of nearly $20 billion. At the same time it was leading an aggressive effort to change the laws and regulations that would ultimately enable full interstate banking. Aggressiveness was a part of the NCNB culture, and McColl sometimes described the bank as a "hungry tiger" because of its ambition and acquisitive style. In 1990 NCNB and McColl completed their biggest deal to date with the acquisition of the failed First Republic Bank of Texas, which catapulted NCNB's assets to nearly $60 billion. A year later it acquired Atlanta-based C&S/Sovran, a bank that two years earlier had successfully fought off an attempted takeover by McColl. The combined bank was renamed NationsBank and was the fifth largest in the country. In 1998 NationsBank acquired BankAmerica Corp. of San Francisco and was renamed again—Bank of America— the first coast-to-coast banking franchise, with operations in 22 U.S. states. Although McColl retired in 2001, Bank of America continued to grow and prosper. At the end of 2009 it was the largest bank in the U.S., with total assets of over $2.5 trillion, a retail presence within easy reach of 80% of the U.S. population, and operations in more than 20 countries.

STRATEGIC LEADERSHIP

While much about this story appears now to be ancient history, it is important to note the significance of McColl in driving the changes that we now take for granted. His efforts and energy reflected a conviction that the business of banking should be transformed. Moreover, his vision of the future was infectious and motivating to the employees of NCNB and later NationsBank, as well as to the many investors, regulators, and competitors who also had bought into the idea that the industry was ripe for revolution and change. But McColl's leadership required more than just keen analysis and good execution. It required an ability to envision a future that was not yet visible to everyone else or even possible under the current conditions. It required an ability to convince others that he was right and so to convince them to join in his efforts. It required a keen understanding of the customers, the market, the industry, and the nuts and bolts of how to make things happen. On top of all of this, it required conviction and tenacity in the face of obstacles, especially from within the industry, where McColl's style and ambition often clashed with the traditional culture and approach. In essence, then, McColl's leadership required moving people in a direction in which they did not know they needed to move and taking them to a place that they did not know they needed to go. What McColl provided was strategic leadership.

Strategic leadership is best understood as the catalyzing force in the strategic process. In essence, providing strategic leadership means providing both the direction and the impetus for action, such that the desired results are achieved. Strategic leadership is about knowing the right things to do and then instilling in others the understanding, motivation, and energy to get those things accomplished. It employs all the tools of the strategic process, but it is more than just deduction and rational analysis. Rather, it is forward looking and forward reaching. It challenges the status quo, pushes the envelope of possibility, anticipates and creates a desired and different future, while also building support and buy-in throughout the organization. As illustrated in Figure 10.1, strategic leadership is a complex and multifaceted process, involving a variety of skills and inputs. However, it is still a process that is judged by its results. Stories about leaders like McColl are fascinating because of their outstanding results. Had McColl been wrong, and had he led his bank to ruin, few if any would commend him for his vision and leadership. But he did not fail. In fact, he radically transformed his organization and in so doing changed the

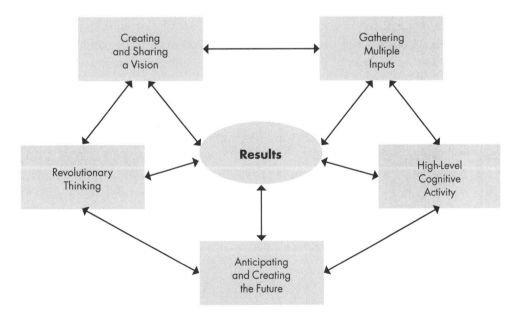

FIGURE 10.1 A Model of Strategic Leadership

face of an entire industry. It is that potential that makes strategic leadership such a fascinating and important topic and such a common feature in business books and business school curricula.

THE BASICS OF LEADERSHIP

To truly understand strategic leadership, it is important to have a basic knowledge of leadership in general. What exactly is leadership? A full and complete analysis of the topic would be beyond the scope of this book. Indeed, few issues have been studied so broadly, in such detail, from so many perspectives and across so many settings. However, leadership is generally defined as influencing others towards the achievement of a common goal. By implication, leaders are the individuals who exercise that influence, setting goals and directing others towards their attainment. Under the umbrella of such a broad definition, research on leadership has proliferated, with perhaps thousands of scholarly articles having been published describing the many different facets of leadership and often providing very different perspectives on its conduct and effects.

In an insightful review of the literature at the time, Pfeffer (1977) noted ambiguities in the actual definitions of leadership, along with ambiguities surrounding its effects and antecedents. More recently, Judge, Woolf, Hurst, and Livingston concluded that "not every scholar agrees on what is effective leadership or the behaviors that produce its effectiveness" (2008: 335). Other reviews of the research on leadership (Avolio, 2005; Yukl, 1989) conclude as well that it is a complex and multifaceted phenomenon, involving many layers of action, interaction, and response. As a consequence, studying leadership has proven to be a challenge and understanding leadership in all of its various forms and appearances has proven especially difficult. Indeed, like performance, which was discussed in Chapter 2, leadership transcends most simple definitions. Yet, just like performance, we can certainly recognize and appreciate it when we see it.

So, while various and different researchers, authors, and publications will emphasize different aspects of leadership, most will agree on the importance of a few basic dimensions. These would include (1) casting a vision or purpose, (2) communicating with and motivating others, (3) catalyzing innovation and change, and (4) driving for results. Each of these activities has been associated with leadership and each is essential to long-term value and performance. As a result, each is inextricably linked to strategy, to the exercise of strategic leadership, and to organizational performance.

Casting a Vision

Casting a vision or purpose is among the most familiar issues in leadership, and it is one of the first challenges of strategic management. Recall that the mission was discussed in both chapters 2 and 3 and depicted in Figure 3.1 as a first step in the larger strategic management process. While scholars and consultants will often make fine-grained distinctions between visions, missions, and the core values of an organization, practically speaking they all serve much the same purpose in the day-to-day reality of most organizations. That purpose is to provide a common principle or logic for the organization and its actions. Put differently, the purpose of the vision or mission is to answer the question: Why does this organization exist and what ideals govern its actions and approach to the future? For each organization, this purpose will be a little different. For example, Coca-Cola follows a simple mission—"to refresh the world" through its portfolio of beverages. For ING, the Dutch financial services giant, the mission is "to deliver its financial products and services in the way customers want them delivered." For Proctor & Gamble the purpose is "to provide branded products and services of superior quality and value that improve the lives of the world's consumers." All of these statements impart a general sense of direction that serves to unify, to build a common identity, and to guide decision making and action. For NCNB, it was to become the leading provider of financial services, first in its region, then across the country, and then around the world.

Of course, anyone can articulate a vision. So simply writing down some statement about the purpose of the firm is no guarantee of success. For leadership to have its desired effect, this vision must activate and energize the efforts of the organization and its various stakeholders. It must tap into the basic needs of the customers and into unseen opportunities in the environment. Indeed, leadership looks very much like entrepreneurship in this regard. Good leaders articulate a message that resonates with the needs of their constituents, providing something new and different that heretofore had not been obvious and available elsewhere. This message has meaning not just for the customers or constituents but also for the employees and internal stakeholders of the organization, serving to energize and rally their efforts. Employees of Wal-Mart used to love store visits by founder Sam Walton. He served as an inspiration, embodying the vision he cast for the company and visibly connecting the actions of rank-and-file employees to the corporate strategy and purpose. In casting a vision, leadership provides important value and momentum, both substantively and symbolically. It points the way forward, towards better opportunities, it provides guidance and direction for implementation, and it serves to motivate effort, connecting actions to outcomes and providing energy and enthusiasm.

The evidence is compelling that a well-crafted vision is important to organizational performance. However, simply understanding this is not enough. Indeed, true visionaries are rare and missions that deliver on all that they promise are illusive. To put it bluntly, casting a meaningful vision is easier said than done, and some will simply do it better than others. Thus, it helps for leaders or potential leaders to understand basic strategic management. At its core, strategy is about setting direction. The framework, models, and processes of strategic management are designed to facilitate that. Strategy, then, should serve the purposes of leadership, enabling the leader to better assess environmental conditions and to identify needs and opportunities. It should help leaders to understand organizational competencies and resources better, so as to leverage them to their fullest effect. And it should help to make clear the linkages between cause and effect, allowing every member of a firm to understand the relevance of their function to value creation and competitive advantage. Indeed, it is no exaggeration to say that good strategic management is the essence of leadership and that leadership is a key responsibility of strategic management. Nowhere is this more clear than in the role of casting a vision.

Communicating and Motivating

Of course, even the best vision is worth little until it is connected to the people and resources throughout the organization. As discussed earlier in this book, strategy cannot be separated from implementation because the two are judged together and by their final results. As a practical matter, it is simply not possible to have a great leader who does not deliver great outcomes. Thus, the vision, mission, and strategy are all inextricably linked to the communication and motivation that occur throughout the organization. Many great leaders have been noteworthy because of their communication skills and because of their ability to rally effort around their cause. Ronald Reagan and Barack Obama, U.S. presidents from different political parties, have both been praised for their abilities to communicate and connect with the voters in a way that inspires and activates. Founders Larry Page and Sergey Brin created enormous value and wealth not just because of the vision they cast for Google but also because of their ability to build and motivate an organization that could deliver on the promise "to organize the world's information and to make it universally accessible." Leadership is certainly about casting a vision, but it is also about building and managing an organization that can bring that vision into reality. Thus, it is also about communicating with and motivating others.

One prominent stream of academic research on leadership looks at the relationship between leaders and their followers. Called **leader–member exchange** (Diesnesch & Liden, 1986), this stream of research considers how leaders engage and motivate the support of their immediate followers. In this view, leadership occurs through a series of interpersonal relationships. Leaders likely have some symbolic influence at the organizational level, through their visions and public statements. However, most of their tangible effect is transmitted through their immediate followers. Thus the relationship between the leader and each member of this small circle is of key importance. Moreover, each of these lieutenants is also a leader of his or her own circle of followers, and so on throughout the organization. In this view, then, leadership can be seen as a series of interpersonal relationships, with leaders and followers taking on different roles and negotiating different responsibilities, as a function of their ability to influence, inspire, and deliver.

Because it focuses on individuals and dyads, leader–member exchange is often thought to be outside the scope of strategic management and of little importance to organizational-level performance. In reality, though, nothing could be farther from the truth. Indeed, the ability of a leader to connect with individual followers and to influence them towards the right goals is a key driver of success. Research and practical experience have both shown that strategic management is a shared activity (Hambrick & Mason, 1984). CEOs in virtually every major corporation rely on a trusted inner circle of managers—the **top management team**—who have substantial influence over the operation of the organization. This inner circle typically consists of vice-presidents, division managers, key board members, and various functional heads. Together they share the leadership of the firm, allocating responsibilities, promoting specific initiatives, and executing the vision through their various functional roles. Certainly the nature of the relationship between the CEO and these top management team members is strategically significant. Moreover, each member of the team likely has his or her group of followers, providing similar support and sharing similar responsibility.

As discussed in Chapter 8, the implementation of strategy can be viewed as a series of intra-organizational linkages and cascading responsibilities. One of the great deficiencies of many top managers is an inability to connect these dots, to understand the implications of a particular strategy to all those impacted, and adequately to divide, assign, and support the necessary roles and responsibilities. Too often, this detailed and tedious work can seem unglamorous and unworthy of a leader's time. However, the ability to make the necessary connections, to communicate the essential elements of the vision and strategy, and to relate those elements to the specific tasks of the various functions and roles within the organization is a key function of leadership. Leaders simply must be able to break down the strategy, to articulate it in terms of its operational implications, and to motivate every individual to make their needed contributions. This is true whether at Apple, Cisco, Home Depot, or Bank of America; none of these firms would be what they are today were it not for the contributions of many different individuals, all performing well in the roles outlined by their leadership and by the strategy. Thus, as a practical matter, it is impossible to separate leadership from the need to communicate with and motivate followers in the behaviors necessary to make the leader's vision a reality.

Catalyzing Innovation and Change

While individual behaviors are essential contributors to strategic success, they can also be a potential threat to innovation and change. Recall from Chapter 8 the discussion of path dependence and the paradoxical nature of performance. Successful behaviors can be repeated and reinforced to the point that they become ingrained habits that impede learning, adaptation, and change. Market leaders often defend the status quo against new technologies, fearing the loss of position and share. Key managers can grow defensive about new opportunities, as they fear an erosion of their own influence or as they seek to leverage existing investments to the fullest effect. These tendencies are a key challenge for leaders, who are to be catalysts for innovation and change.

Innovation and change are essential to strategic success. Without innovation, every firm will eventually stagnate and drift out of the mainstream of the market. And, without change, every capability will eventually grow calcified and obsolete, becoming irrelevant to customers and competitors alike and eventually losing all competitive value and advantage. Thus, innovation and change are keys to long-term success and imperatives of any successful strategy. Unfortunately, though, innovation and change do not happen by themselves. Rather, firms naturally develop their own inertia, with all the weight of habit and history reinforcing practices from the past. Leaders, then, must find ways to break this momentum and shift the energies of the organization into new directions. Moreover, they must do this when the need for such change is less than fully obvious.

Among the many responsibilities of leadership, this one is perhaps the most important and the most challenging, and yet also the least well understood (Heifetz & Laurie, 2001). Indeed, many who seek to be leaders fail to understand that the path to leadership is rarely traveled by the masses and rarely of immediate and obvious value when assessed in the present. For example, although it is now taken for granted, there was a time when air conditioning was viewed with suspicion. At the turn of the century, the gases used in air conditioners were often toxic and flammable, and malfunctions could easily result in serious injury or death. So, when firms such as GE, Frigidaire, and Carrier began working to develop the technology and market for residential air conditioning, they met with skepticism and little success and so had difficulty sustaining their efforts. There is also the case of Decca Records, which in January of 1962 auditioned but then declined to sign the Beatles. It is reported that a Decca Records executive justified the decision by stating that "guitar music is on the way out." Indeed, significant innovations are often discounted and unappreciated by those steeped in the conventional wisdom of the present. As the story of NCNB illustrates, many in the genteel and conservative banking industry were put off by Hugh McColl's ambition and aggressiveness. They thought his approach was bad for business and would be bad for the industry. Indeed, some competitors even advertised themselves as alternatives to the brash style of NCNB.

More recently, the manufacture and sale of hybrid drive automobiles was a considerable risk to those at the forefront of the technology. At least initially, consumers reacted negatively to the high prices, to the small size and limited power of the cars, and to their somewhat awkward appearance. Thus, many leading car makers chose to wait on the sidelines and not invest too much. Toyota, however, invested heavily, pushing the technology and design and promoting the vehicles despite their initial lack of acceptance. Of course, the Prius, Toyota's hybrid drive car, eventually became a resounding success, thereby affirming Toyota's efforts. However, that success came after Toyota's uphill battle for leadership.

As mentioned earlier, leadership is defined as influencing others towards a goal. Implicit in this definition is the fact that, at times, people need to be influenced. Leadership must take the initiative; it must set the course. If it does not, then people are likely to remain steeped in their routines and habits and content with the status quo. Without leadership to unite and motivate their efforts, people might never move towards even good goals. In other words, leadership involves influencing others towards a goal that they did not know they needed to achieve. Warren Buffett once said that "the chains of habit are too light to be felt until they are too heavy to be broken." The lesson is that the need for change is rarely obvious until it is too late to be effective. As a result, leaders must recognize the need for change sooner than others and so must also be prepared to shoulder the burden and the frustrations of going it alone, at least for a time. Here, again, leadership looks very much like entrepreneurship and very much like strategy. They both must anticipate and act based on expected realities and so both bear some risk of being wrong or of at least appearing to be wrong for a time. Had the price of oil not increased and had the concerns of climate change not focused attention on carbon emissions, Toyota might not have been so visionary in its development of the Prius. Alternatively, had Apple never introduced the iPod and had consumers never had the ability to take their music with them, satellite radio providers Sirius and XM might have blossomed into huge successes. Unfortunately for these latter two firms, the market did not evolve as they anticipated and the satellite radio industry struggled mightily. The simple yet harsh reality, then, is that leadership bears the responsibility for innovation and change, and that implies a significant burden and risk.

This key dimension of leadership overlaps with a basic principle of strategic management, discussed in Chapter 8. Recall that adaptation and change is a large part of the ongoing challenge of strategy implementation. Through interaction with the environment, a firm learns what works and what does not; through many trials and errors, firms introduce and perfect innovations, cultivating options and gathering information on which to base future strategies. This ongoing process of learning and adaptation is essential to success and so a fundamental component of strategy. However, it does not happen naturally. Rather, it must be catalyzed and directed and its value must be articulated. It must be institutionalized and promoted throughout the organization, encouraging managers at every level to innovate and take risks and reminding the organization's stakeholders of the hazards of inertia. Once again, then, good strategic management is the imperative of leadership. Leaders must take action to make innovation and change happen, even when so doing is unpopular or seems contrary to the conventional wisdom. They must cast the vision, communicate the purpose, and motivate and direct others towards a goal that will likely not be obvious or well understood. They must understand when to change and when to stay the course so that the organization produces greater value and grows more valuable as a result. Like every facet of strategic management, change and innovation are tools for furthering competitive advantage. So, a hallmark of good leadership is the ability to catalyze and lead innovation and change when and as necessary to move the organization forward, from strength to new strength, and from success to greater success.

Driving for Results

Focusing on success leads directly to the discussion of the final dimension. Leadership is judged by its results, both in the present and into the future. As discussed elsewhere in this book, tension between the short and the long term is natural and common. Should a firm invest and experiment with new innovations or should it streamline and focus its efforts in an effort to exploit an existing advantage? Should a firm go the extra mile and incur extra costs to satisfy its customers or should it hold its ground and make only reasonable accommodations in the face of mounting expectations and demands? Should a firm continue to leverage an asset until it is fully depreciated or should it invest now in a newer but more uncertain technology? These sorts of questions are pervasive in day-to-day management and yet significant to overall performance, and so they demand answers. Thus, they are opportunities for leadership as well as the sorts of moments where real strategy is made.

As mentioned, leadership and strategy are judged on their end results. But end results are typically a function of many small actions and seemingly obscure decisions. As discussed in Chapter 6, competitive advantage and organizational performance are manifestations of many discrete competitive episodes. Firms that perform well over time do so by doing well in these episodes. A strong competitive advantage and strong organizational performance, then, are the aggregated outcomes of many individual instances of good decision making, where value is created for individual customers and where lessons about the purpose, commitment, and values of the firm are taught and learned.

Linking all of those discrete episodes together and connecting them to the overall mission and strategy of the firm is the job of leadership. In his seminal work, Philip Selznick (1957) described this as the process of **institutionalization**. To an objective researcher or a detached theorist, a business is simply a collection of individuals and resources, performing routines and taking actions, based on the costs and benefits at hand. However, to real people, whether customers, investors, employees, suppliers, or competitors, a business can seem much more than merely that. Firms can take on a personality and they can have clear and discernible styles. Their products can have a nostalgic value and they can make lasting contributions to society. Firms can have an identity and grow into positions of familiarity and trust. In essence, through the consistency and value of their actions, firms can become more than mere collections of individuals, resources, and routines; instead, they can become institutions, whose place and value is recognized, understood, and even sought out by many. This process of institutionalization is a function of leadership and the exercise of good strategic management.

As with other things, though, institutionalization does not occur on its own. Rather, it must be organized and directed. Like a starter turning an engine, leadership must provide the impetus and the energy to move a firm from a mere collection of individuals and actions to being an institution, where every job, every office, and every routine is infused with meaning and purpose. This is what it means to drive to results, never to be satisfied or complacent, never to be content with wasted effort or with lost opportunities, always to look for new options and to be one's own toughest competitor. This drive must come from somewhere, because the natural inertia of the firm, along with the friction of bureaucratic necessity and individual habit, will be pushing against it. Firms can too easily settle into a peaceful routine, especially when they are in a secure competitive position. But that sort of peace can be misleading and that sort of settling can be dangerous. Roger Enrico, former CEO of PepsiCo, Inc., once credited competition from Coca-Cola as providing the energy that Pepsi needed to stay "original and lively" (Enrico, 1986). Without new challenges, without some recognized and unifying threat, without some common purpose to connect the different specialists, departments, and locations of an organization, work quickly devolves into a collection of routines, where no one provides extra effort and where creativity and initiative are quickly lost. Leadership should provide that drive, identifying the threats, outlining the challenges, and connecting the solutions to day-to-day decisions and actions.

Recall from Chapter 2 that the mandate for every strategic manager is to increase the net present value of the firm, both now and in the future. Focusing on value creation removes the tension between the short and the long term and provides a way to link discrete actions to long-term performance. Focusing on value provides a lens through which to assess the environment and to identify opportunities and threats. By focusing on value, strategists are better able to assess and evaluate their resources and capabilities, to organize their own structures and systems, and to create and evaluate new options. Following the basic logic of strategic management, every action should enable value creation and every decision should point towards competitive advantage.

Adding Value

To really appreciate the importance of strategic leadership, it is necessary to discuss one final issue. Leadership, like strategy, is marked by the value it adds, over and above that which is obvious and readily available to everyone. Recall from Chapter 2 the discussion of Tobin's q, which is a key measure of a firm's performance. Tobin's q is calculated as the market value of the firm, divided by the replacement value of the firm's assets. A higher number reflects greater utilization of the assets and greater value associated with their use. So, if two firms, Firm A and Firm B, have similar assets and yet Firm A has a higher Tobin's q, it would be fair to say that Firm A is using its resources to better effect. For example, Toyota and GM are similar companies in terms of their products, markets, and facilities. Yet Toyota has a higher market value and so a higher Tobin's q. What does that mean? It means that Toyota is better positioned, with a stronger brand and a stronger organization. It means that the past actions and decisions of Toyota's management created greater value than the past actions and decisions of GM's management. It means that Toyota has accumulated a more valuable set of resources and options by charting a course that was substantively different from that charted by GM. Put bluntly, it means that Toyota's leadership and strategy have been more effective. In essence, then, leadership and strategy serve a common purpose. While they may be different in various specific details, they are still complementary and part of the larger whole, like the right hand is different from but still complementary to the left. They interact to guide the firm in a way that enhances its overall value and they are judged in the same way, by the results that they produce.

Strategic leadership is simply a term that captures this close relationship. Leadership and strategic management are inextricably bound together, such that each is incomplete without the other. In large firms and small, in product firms and service firms, across all industries and settings, leadership is the driving force while strategy is the framework for analysis and action. Together they add intangible yet significant value to the assets and resources of the firm. They do this by providing a coherent vision of what the firm should be and by communicating that purpose, motivating and enabling others to work towards it. Together, they initiate change and innovation, as necessary, to keep the firm current, and they push for continued improvement and value in every transaction. Make no mistake, leadership matters, and it matters most when it is fully connected to the strategic process. Strategic leadership, then, represents the intersection of these two essential functions, leveraging both for the greatest effect on organizational performance.

CORPORATE GOVERNANCE

In the practical reality of modern organizations, talking about strategic leadership often means talking about the CEO. As the old saying goes, CEOs likely get too much credit when things go well and too much blame when things go poorly. That is because they are the visible face of the organization; they are the ones held most responsible for its performance and they are the ones who are expected to cast the vision, to establish the purpose, and to connect the strategy to implementation. They are also the ones to whom we look for answers when things go poorly and they can serve as handy scapegoats when there is no one else to blame (Fredrickson, Hambrick, & Baumrin, 1988).

While a singular focus on just one key executive at the very top of the organization may make sense in smaller firms or in newer, more entrepreneurial ventures, the picture is much more complex in larger firms. Indeed, despite their importance, CEOs are just one of several different actors in the overall management structure of most large organizations. There is also the top management team—that circle of senior managers just below the CEO in the firm's hierarchy. There are the many middle-level managers, whose understanding, consent, and involvement are so important to effective implementation and to strategic success (Wooldridge & Floyd, 1990). Finally, there are the owners or stockholders of the business, who may or may not be actively involved in its day-to-day operation but whose principles and expectations establish its direction and values. Imagine the result at NCNB had McColl not had support from all of these groups. Indeed, the success of NCNB and of McColl's leadership reflected a consistent philosophy and effort on the part of the stockholders, the executives, even the mid-level managers. It took all of these groups, working together and with the CEO, to produce the desired results.

To understand strategic leadership, then, as it is actually practiced and as it actually works in most large organizations, it is important to understand something known as corporate governance. Governance refers collectively to the processes, structures, and systems by which all of the various actors mentioned above interact and by which organizations are ultimately governed. Who has the authority to speak for the firm and to make key decisions? Who sets the agenda and the values that will drive the strategy? Who determines what level of risk is acceptable and what constitutes good performance? How are the goals and objectives of the firm established and in whose interests does the firm really operate? The answers to these questions describe how the firm is governed and identify the key sources of authority and responsibility in the strategic process. Given some recent and well-publicized scandals over corporate ethics, concerns over stockholder rights, and recurring frustrations over executive compensation, corporate governance has become an increasingly popular topic of academic research and political debate. But, even before this heightened awareness and increased scrutiny, governance was

**Box 10.1
Sarbanes–Oxley**

A Seismic Event in Corporate Governance

Enacted in 2002 and originally called the Public Company Accounting Reform and Protection Act, the Sarbanes–Oxley Act, or SOX as it has come to be known, was a response to a host of well-publicized corporate scandals in firms such as Enron, WorldCom, Peregrine Systems, and Tyco International, as well as the dramatic collapse of the accounting firm Arthur Andersen. The size, scope, and nature of these scandals was such that confidence in the U.S. stock market and in many public corporations was badly shaken. As a result, SOX passed both the U.S. Senate and House of Representatives by a combined vote of 522 to 3, and it was signed into law quickly by President George W. Bush. At the time SOX was described as—and it is still considered by many to be—the most far-reaching legislation affecting corporate governance, oversight, and accounting standards since the Securities and Exchange Act of 1933.

The law sets new standards of behavior and accountability for public firms, top executives, the board of directors, and auditors. It contains 11 sections, covering things like additional responsibilities of the board, the amount and quality of information that must be made available to the public, standards for accounting firms that audit public companies, and criminal penalties. Some of these specific provisions include restrictions on auditors taking positions in firms that were formerly their clients, personal loans from a public company to its executives, and altering, falsifying, or destroying documents in an effort to influence a bankruptcy case or securities investigation. SOX also led to the creation of the Public Company Accounting Oversight Board, a private, non-profit organization charged with overseeing the auditors of public firms in order to protect the interests of investors.

Debate continues on the overall effects of SOX. Advocates argue that it has been beneficial, restoring confidence in the capital markets by strengthening corporate governance, oversight, and the system of accounting controls. Critics contend that, these benefits notwithstanding, it has had a detrimental effect on the competitiveness of U.S. firms by burdening them and the entire financial system with an overly complex, onerous, and expensive set of regulations. One unintended consequence of SOX was the chilling effect that it had on venture capital. Venture capitalists often recoup their investments when the firms in which they have invested go public. The added burden of SOX-related regulation has led some firms to delay or to scrap altogether any plans for public offerings. In addition, other larger and more established firms have chosen to exit the public capital markets, choosing to return to private ownership, so as to avoid the costly and complex requirements of the law.

While certainly not all of its effects have been intended or beneficial, SOX still represents a major step towards open and honest corporate governance, which is essential for confidence in publicly held firms.

important because of its connection to leadership and strategy and its effects on organizational action and performance.

Public and Private Ownership

To understand governance, it is important to grasp some basic issues. Perhaps the most fundamental of these is the distinction between publicly held and privately held firms. This distinction was noted in Chapter 2, as publicly held and privately held firms will often employ different measures to gauge and report their performance. However, the distinction also has key implications for governance. Privately held firms are those where access to the ownership rights is closed to the public. Ownership of these firms can be by a single individual, by members of a family, or by a large number of individuals who are connected in some other way. However, the stock of privately held firms is not listed on any public exchange, nor is it available for public purchase. EAI, the small consulting firm mentioned at the beginning of the previous chapter, is privately held, controlled entirely by and operated in the interests of its owners. While privately held firms are commonly smaller than publicly held firms, large firms can be privately held too. For example, Chick-fil-A is privately held, yet it has nearly 1,500 restaurants and annual revenues of close to $3 billion. Some other privately held firms are even larger. Cargill, Inc., is a privately held commodities and food products firm with over $100 billion in revenue, more than 150,000 employees, and operations in 68 countries. Cox Enterprises is also a privately held, family-controlled media company, with interests in radio, newspapers, and cable television. It has over 77,000 employees and revenues exceeding $15 billion.

Even when they are quite large, privately held firms tend to have simpler governance structures than their publicly held counterparts. Because the ownership of privately held firms is less diffused, there is less opportunity for divisions among the interests of the stockholders. Also, because most or all of the stockholders share some relationship or connection, either as family members or as employees, they are better known to one another and so less likely to act in ways injurious to the group as a whole. Moreover, because there is often a closer relationship between ownership and management in privately held firms, there is less concern over **agency problems**. As a result, privately held firms are typically subject to less intrusive oversight and regulation, at least in the U.S. Indeed, one consequence of the increased oversight of publicly held firms resulting from the scandals that occurred in the late 1990s and early 2000s is that many public corporations were taken private by their management teams or by groups of private investors. So, while governance is still important in privately held firms, it is frequently less complicated because the number of owners is smaller, the interests of the owners are often more homogeneous, and the pressure from external regulators is lower.

As a practical matter, then, the management and leadership of privately held firms often reflects much more directly the desires and interests of the owners. Moreover, because of the limited number of owners, and because those owners typically share some common relationship or connection, their interests and desires are typically more homogeneous than in publicly held firms. In the case of Chick-fil-A, for instance, the purpose and values of the firm are a direct reflection of the values and desires of the founder, Truett Cathy. Even as the firm has grown and as the number of stockholders has increased to include employees, the basic values and focus of the firm have not changed. The reason is simple: all of the stockholders, or at least a large majority of the voting stockholders, remain committed to those same core values and to the same mission as established by the founder. As a practical matter, then, in privately held firms, leadership and ownership are closely related and owners influence directly and heavily the leadership of the firm.

On the other hand, publicly held firms are much more visible and complicated and so receive much more attention. Publicly held firms are those whose stocks are listed on public exchanges and so are accessible to public ownership. The largest of these firms may have billions of shares of stock outstanding, with the potential for millions of different owners. Coca-Cola, for example, has over 2.3 billion shares of stock in circulation. Microsoft has nearly 9 billion shares of stock outstanding, and Caterpillar has over 600 million shares of stock in the hands of its many individual owners. With potentially millions of different owners, each controlling different amounts of stock, and with those many different owners having different goals and objectives and exercising different levels of attention and involvement, it is easy to see why governance in publicly held firms is so important and how it can be so complex. It is also easy to see how the challenge of leadership in these firms is complicated by the presence of many different and varied interests and by the diffused and complex nature of organizational authority.

Agency Problems

The issue of greatest concern in the governance of publicly held firms is the separation of ownership and control; this is the agency problem referred to earlier (Fama & Jensen, 1983). Typically the principals or stockholders do not directly manage the firm themselves, despite the fact that they are its legal owners. Rather, the managers of most publicly traded firms are hired professionals, who act as agents of the owners. These professional managers control the firms but frequently bear few of the risks of ownership. As a result, their motivations, along with their orientations towards risks and rewards, can be quite different than those of the owners, thus creating the potential for **moral hazard**. As a result, managers may simply behave differently than owners because of the differences in their perceptions and motivations. Owners, for instance, might benefit from increased innovation, experimentation, and the cultivation of new options that could enhance the long-term value of the firm. Managers, on the other hand, might have a shorter perspective and so look to exploit an existing advantage, building market share and earnings in the present but doing so at the expense of longer-term investments. Alternatively, owners might entertain a takeover bid that offers a premium price for their shares. Managers, though, might see a takeover as a threat to their employment and so resist it, the premium price notwithstanding. The separation between the two also creates asymmetries in knowledge. Professional managers will typically have much better information about the firm and its activities than absentee owners. And the owners must rely on the managers for the information that they receive. Thus, a manager could be completely self-interested while effectively hiding that fact from the owners. This situation favors managers and creates a problem for owners. And so many of the issues in corporate governance deal with ways to overcome agency problems and make sure that agents or managers act in the best interests of the principals they represent.

Two key mechanisms by which this occurs are the oversight system, through which management actions are monitored and owners are kept informed of firm activity, and the compensation system, which employs incentives to align the interests of managers to owners. To understand how these systems function, it is important to identify some of the key roles and actors. The first of these key actors is the **board of directors**. Every corporation has a board, charged with the **fiduciary responsibility** of representing the interests of the owners in the governance of the firm. The board recruits, hires, and oversees the chief executive officer, who then sets strategy and is responsible for producing results that increase the value of the firm for its owners. The board is charged with monitoring this performance and making sure that the firm operates within the law and in the best long-term interests of the stockholders.

While simple enough in concept, these mechanisms can be quite complex in practice. Fueling this complexity are the number and variety of owners. Retirement funds and mutual funds, for instance, may invest heavily in a particular firm on behalf of their members. These **institutional investors**, as they are called, play an important role in governance by consolidating and giving weight to the voices of individual stockholders. They also exert pressure on firms, as their decisions to purchase or sell large blocks of a particular stock can substantially influence the perception and price of that stock in the marketplace. Other owners may represent themselves but control large blocks of voting shares. According to U.S. law, when the ownership of these large blockholders reaches 5%, they must be publicly disclosed, as large voting blocks can substantially influence board decisions and firm policy. Finally, firms can issue stock in different classes, some of which may include voting rights, some of which may not. Warren Buffett's Berkshire Hathaway, for instance, issues two classes of common stock, Class A and Class B. The Class B stock shares have 1/30th the value of the Class A stock shares but only 1/200th of the voting rights. Thus, there can be many different types of stockholders, with many different profiles and interests.

Of course, many owners are individual investors, with little expertise in the business, no direct knowledge of its operations, and little say in its strategy. Because these individual investors are seen as being so essential to the functioning of the capital markets and yet are so weak in terms of their influence, there is the Securities and Exchange Commission (SEC). Created by the Securities and Exchange Act of 1934, the mission of the SEC is "to protect investors, maintain fair, orderly and efficient markets, and to facilitate capital formation." The SEC enforces rules on ownership, voting rights, proxies, stockholder protection, and what firms can and must disclose to the public about their operations. Compliance with SEC regulations is the responsibility of the board, and various different committees within the board will typically be charged with different responsibilities.

For example, boards will generally have an audit committee. That committee will be responsible for hiring an independent auditor to review the firm's operations and financial performance. The audit committee will work with the independent auditor to make certain that all the information is current and correct and to disclose information, as necessary, to keep current and prospective owners informed about the firm's activities. The board may also have a governance committee, which will be accountable for nominating and overseeing the election of new board and committee members. This committee may be in charge of setting compensation and retirement policy for board members as well as policies for resolving disputes. The governance committee is essentially answerable for assuring the independence of the board, as necessary, for the board to fulfill its fiduciary obligations. Finally, boards will typically have a compensation committee, responsible for the compensation of the CEO and other key executives. This committee is charged with providing compensation sufficient to attract the best managers to the firm, while structuring that compensation so that it aligns the interests of the managers with the interests of the owners.

Compensation of the CEO and the other top executives is an especially controversial issue. However, it is among the most important responsibilities of the board. Ultimately, the board wants the CEO and other top managers to act as effective leaders of the firm. What that means is that managers should be good stewards of the value and resources entrusted them, while also being visionary and assertive in creating opportunities and building competitive advantage. Absentee owners expect that managers will focus on creating value, not just on maximizing earnings. To borrow a phrase from Peter Drucker, managers are to do the right things in addition to doing things right. Owners expect that managers will act in the interests of the owners, will behave appropriately, and will do all that is in their power and ability to leave the organization in a better position than it was when they encountered it.

To achieve its goals and to encourage this kind of leadership, the board will usually offer packages consisting of both present and deferred compensation, paid in the form of cash salary, incentive bonuses, stock, and options. The purpose of mixing various forms of compensation and then paying that compensation over extended periods of time is twofold. First, the board wants to hire the best and brightest managers to run their companies, as doing so is in the best interests of the stockholders. But, because of agency problems, these hired managers may not think and act like owners. Thus, incentive-based compensation, often in the form of stock or stock options, can serve to align the interests of managers with the interests of owners.

Here again, the actual process can be very complex and often produce unintended consequences. Many executives have received extraordinary sums as the result of bonuses, stocks, and options. For example, Michael Eisner earned over $700 million as CEO of Disney during the five-year period ending in 2002. And others have also received extraordinary sums. Richard Fairbanks, CEO of Capital One Financial, was paid $249 million in 2005, and Terry Semel, CEO of Yahoo, received $174 million in 2007. Many have argued that these sums are justified based on gains in the companies' stock values—gains which benefited the shareholders. Others, though, see these payments as evidence of agency problems gone amok (Dvorak & Scannell, 2009). And there is evidence that the highest-paid CEOs also have the highest-paid followers (Graffin, Wade, Porac, & McNamee, 2008), which may reflect disproportionate power and influence on the part of the CEO. All of this has contributed to an atmosphere of populist anger and a widely shared belief that effective oversight by many boards of directors is inadequate.

Governing the Board

Given the ability of the board to influence the firm, seats are often coveted. So maintaining the independence of the board can be a challenge. Board independence is a key feature of organizational governance. As mentioned earlier, boards have a responsibility to the shareholders and are supposed to represent those interests, independent of other influences. So maintaining independence is very important but also especially challenging when there is **duality**. Duality exists when the CEO and board chair are the same individual. While there are arguments for combining these roles, and while a majority of U.S. firms still operate with this duality, there are also strong arguments against it, and most European firms have abandoned the practice. The primary argument against duality is the challenge to independence. As the one most responsible for a firm's strategy and performance, the CEO cannot be expected to monitor his or her own behavior effectively. Quite the contrary, it seems more likely that a CEO would want to influence opinion in such a way that he or she looked good as a result. It would also seem that the CEO, as chairman, could influence the governance committee, or whatever group was responsible for the board and committee nominations—all of which could threaten the independence of the board and so its ability to execute its responsibilities. Corporate governance experts often distinguish insiders from outsiders when discussing board membership. Insiders are members who are also executives of the firm, while outsiders, as the name suggests, hold positions outside of the firm. The distinction speaks to the implied independence of the two groups. Insiders are likely more beholden to the CEO and so more inclined to support his or her agenda and policies. In cases where there is duality, a high number of insiders could be especially problematic, allowing the CEO and other insiders to manage the firm for their own benefit and in their own best interests, as opposed to the interest of the stockholders. Many shareholder watchdog groups, along with most institutional investors, use the number of outside directors as an indication of a board's independence, encouraging firms to increase the number of outside directors.

Certainly there is a trend away from duality and towards the increasing use of outside directors. While well intended, though, these moves may not necessarily increase the independence or quality of the board. As mentioned, there are advantages to duality and the use of inside directors. The role of a board member entails understanding a great deal about the business and its industry. There may be high levels of specialized and technical knowledge required, as well as a considerable investment of time and energy. Outside directors may simply lack the knowledge or time to do a thorough and adequate job. There may also be conflicts of interest, where outside board members represent key suppliers, customers, or other constituents. Board members may be obliged to other board members because of appointments to other boards. These so-called **interlocks** may compromise independence, even among outside board members. Thus, while the question of board independence is an important one, there is no single or simple answer that will satisfy the issue fully.

The Value of Good Governance

Of course, as important as governance may be, it is still simply a means to an end rather than an end to itself. Indeed, as has been discussed throughout this book, the real end is the success of the firm, measured in relation to its mission and purpose. Viewed in this way, governance is just one more responsibility of leadership and strategic management. Like international business and entrepreneurship, corporate governance is a highly specialized area, with its own vocabulary and requiring considerable and specialized understanding. Nevertheless, it is still just one of many issues of importance to strategic leaders and managers. And so it must be understood in the proper context. Good governance is necessary, but is not sufficient for good leadership to emerge and good results to occur. Good governance can contribute to the development of a competitive advantage, but it is not a competitive advantage in and of itself. Good governance creates conditions in which competitive advantage can grow, but by itself it cannot overcome a highly competitive environment, a poorly designed product, or a poorly marketed service, nor can it overcome a resource base that is outdated and easily imitated.

Rather, good governance is an intangible resource, something that interacts with and adds value to other things. Good governance enables good leadership and good management and undergirds a firm's reputation, providing assurance to suppliers, investors, employees, and customers. It facilitates trust and lasting relationships, it contributes to loyalty and commitment, and it can promote involvement, investment, and effort. It adds new value, over and above the obvious value of a firm's assets. It enables others to succeed, encouraging them with resources and autonomy and then monitoring the results to assure accountability. Beyond these affirmative benefits, good governance can also help to prevent disasters. Many of the scandals of the past decade that occurred in firms such as Enron, Adelphia, Global Crossing, Qwest, and Tyco can be traced to a lack of vigilance by the board of directors. And the lack of vigilance is a failure of corporate governance. As a result of these scandals, many firms failed. While some others survived, they did so only after great turmoil. For all these firms, though, there was great embarrassment and substantial economic loss. Better governance might have prevented all of this, providing value to many. Good governance, then, is like a healthy habit; it builds a stronger organization while also helping to prevent catastrophe. As a result, it is among the many important influences on strategic leadership and the many key responsibilities of strategic management.

SUMMARY

Ralph Waldo Emerson once said: "Do not go where the path may lead, go instead where there is no path and leave a trail." In this simple statement, Emerson captures the challenge of strategic leadership. Creating value is the imperative of every firm, large or small, public or private. Every firm must transform the available inputs into desirable outputs if they are to generate revenues sufficient for their survival. They do this by creating value for the customers, value that is distinct and attractive in its context and sufficient to motivate transactions at a profitable price.

But creating value is not easy. Indeed, customers can be fickle, with tastes that can change without warning. Customers can learn and adapt, adjusting quickly to changes in the available options and learning to take for granted those things that were once novel and exciting. Meanwhile, competitors are steadily pushing to create value for themselves. They will imitate the successes of others and offer substitutes where imitation is not practical. They will innovate as well and offer new products and services to customers all too happy to receive a better deal. There is pressure from suppliers, who seek constantly to increase their bargaining power and to extract and retain a larger portion of the revenue stream for themselves. And there is pressure from the environment, where changing demographic and economic conditions can undermine even the strongest competitive advantage and where evolving technologies and unforeseen catastrophes can change the landscape and alter the status quo quickly and irreparably. It is amid all of this activity, amid this constant ferment of evolving self-interest, competition, and technological capability, that firms must create value over and over again.

The challenge, then, is simply this: How to succeed in the face of such demands? Sustained competitive advantage really means succeeding while others are trying to bring about your failure. Given this stark reality, simply choosing to follow a trail established by others is insufficient. While imitating the successes of others can serve as a reasonable defensive strategy for a time, there is no long-term advantage in simply doing what others are already doing. The challenge is to create *new value*—value that will be appreciated by the customer, value that will appear unique in its context and that will trigger a desire to transact with the firm, over and over again. This will require doing things that are logical but not obvious, that leverage wisdom but are not conventional, and that move people and their organizations in directions in which they do not yet realize they need to go. Put simply, meeting the challenge requires leadership. It is the role of leadership to envision the possibilities, to catalyze the resources, and to focus and motivate the effort.

By its very nature, then, leadership is strategic. Leaders must understand their environments, the capabilities of their firms, and the opportunities and nature of competitive advantage. Leaders must recognize that there are times to change radically, times to change subtly, and times to stay the course. To be effective in building long-term value, leaders must appreciate the need for investment and the trade-offs between exploiting strengths in the present and building options for the future. They must understand human behavior and motivation as well as organizational structures, systems, and processes. But, more importantly, they must use all of this knowledge to get results and to provide a return that is better than that which investors can get elsewhere.

Empowering and enabling a leader to do all of these things is the governance structure of the firm. Governance, across all of its various levels and components, is the skeleton of the organization. Without effective governance there would be no financing to enable the acquisition of resources and no authority to enable the formulation and implementation of strategy. More than anything else, governance provides identity and direction for the firm. Identity simply means a sense of values and consciousness. What are the boundary conditions in which the strategy is made? What are the checks and balances that will govern decision making and the use of resources? Strategy gives a firm a personality that can be sensed and understood by the marketplace, and the origins of that personality lie in the firm's governance. Strategy is about deciding where to go and how to get there, and governance should be seen as a starting point in that process. What is the mission of the firm? What are its goals and how will it define and measure its own success? The answers to these questions will set the direction for the firm and govern the way it formulates and implements its strategy. Research has shown that patterns established early in a firm's development leave an **imprinting** effect on its people, processes, and structures for many years to come (Boeker, 1989; Kimberly, 1979). Governance controls the substance of that imprinted form, and so understanding it is essential to understanding leadership and to managing strategy.

This has been a chapter on strategic leadership. It has explored some of the basics of leadership and explained some of the details of how modern organizations are governed. It has also reinforced the inescapable reality that leadership is judged on its results. And that reality is what links leadership and strategy together. Strategic leadership, then, is leadership that produces results, at the highest level and in the overall interests of the firm. It is leadership that envisions, catalyzes, and enables the strategy of the firm and that, in delivering results, sets a pattern for others to follow. Indeed, the story of Hugh McColl and NCNB seems now like ancient history because it is a story of success. In leading his organization, McColl established a pattern that changed the entire industry. To borrow from Emerson, strategic leadership is about creating new paths—paths that will lead to value creation for the customers and competitive advantage for the firm.

KEY TERMS

Agency problems are the set of issues and complications arising from the separating of ownership and control—in particular the asymmetries in decision-making power and information between owners and managers.

The **board of directors** is the group of individuals who oversee a company or organization. In publicly traded firms, the board has the fiduciary duty of representing the owners in hiring the CEO, setting policy, and monitoring the activities of the firm.

Duality exists when the CEO of a firm is also the chair of that firm's board of directors. This one individual then holds these dual offices simultaneously.

Fiduciary responsibility refers to a relationship of trust or obligation where a party in power is charged with the obligation to act on behalf of and in the interests of another, more vulnerable party.

Imprinting is the term used to describe the institutionalization of practices and beliefs within an organization. Significant events, such as founding conditions or radical changes, are said to leave an imprint on an organization's strategy and practices.

Institutional investors aggregate funds from individual investors and then invest collectively. Mutual funds and retirement funds are common institutional investors. Because they represent such large sums of money, these investors can be powerful actors in corporate governance.

Institutionalization is a term coined by Philip Selznick (1957) and refers to the process of infusing an organization with value, over and above the tangible value of its assets.

Interlocks exist when multiple board members sit simultaneously on the boards of different companies. By creating reciprocal interdependence among the board members, interlocks are thought to mitigate independence.

Leader–member exchange (LMX) refers to a body of academic research focusing on the dyadic relationships between leaders and their immediate followers. At the crux of this work is the understanding that leaders relate differently to different followers and that the nature of these relationships is key to leadership effectiveness.

Moral hazard occurs when decision makers are separated from the risks associated with their decisions. In the principal–agent relationship, for instance, the agent has the bulk of the decision-making discretion and yet the principal bears the bulk of the risk of bad decisions.

The **top management team** is that small group of managers at the highest levels of the organization who make the majority of the strategic decisions and control the firm's operations. The CEO is typically the leader of the team.

QUESTIONS FOR REVIEW

1   Imagine a world where Hugh McColl and NCNB had never existed. How do you suppose the U.S. banking industry would be different than it is today?
2   What is strategic leadership and what is its connection to the larger framework of strategic management?
3   Why have scholars concluded that defining and measuring leadership is so complex and so ambiguous? How would you describe effective leadership?
4   What are the four dimensions of leadership discussed in this chapter? Can you find examples of real leaders who have been successful in these four challenges?
5   What is institutionalization and why is it important to strategic management and organizational performance?

6 What is corporate governance and why is it important to distinguish between publicly and privately held firms in discussing governance structures?

7 How can executive compensation help to align the interests of managers and owners? Why is it necessary to incentivize managers to behave like owners?

8 What is meant by the independence of the board of directors? What are some common indicators of board independence?

Companion Website

For a chapter review outline with links to videos and other valuable web resources, please visit the *Strategic Management* website: www.routledge.com/textbooks/amason.

References

Chapter 1

Andrews, K. R. (1987). *The Concept of Corporate Strategy*. Homewood, IL: Irwin.

Chandler, A. D. (1962). *Strategy and Structure: Chapters in the History of the American Enterprise.* Cambridge, MA: MIT Press.

Gilbert, D. R., Hartman, E., Mauriel, J. J., & Freeman, R. E. (1988). *A Logic for Strategy.* Cambridge, MA: Ballinger Publishing.

Hofer, C. W., & Schendel, D. (1978). *Strategy Formulation: Analytical Concepts.* St. Paul: West Publishing.

Hoskisson, R. E., Hitt, M. A., Ireland, R. D., & Harrison, J. D. (2008). *Competing for Advantage* (2nd ed.). Mason, OH: Thomson/South-Western.

Mintzberg, H. (1987). The Strategy Concept I: Five Ps for Strategy. *California Management Review*, 30: 11–24.

Ohmae, K. (1982). *The Mind of the Strategist: The Art of Japanese Business.* New York: McGraw-Hill.

Porter, M. E. (1985). *Competitive Advantage: Creating and Sustaining Superior Performance.* New York: Free Press.

Chapter 2

Abrahams, J. (1999). *The Mission Statement Book: 301 Corporate Mission Statements from America's Top Companies.* Berkeley, CA: Ten Speed Press.

Amason, A. C., & Mooney, A. C. (2008). Icarus' Paradox Revisited: How Strong Performance Sows the Seeds of Dysfunction in Future Strategic Decision Making. *Strategic Organization*, 6: 407–34.

Audia, P. G., Locke, E. A., & Smith, K. G. (2000). The Paradox of Success: An Archival and a Laboratory Study of Strategic Persistence following Radical Environmental Change. *Academy of Management Journal*, 43: 837–54.

Basch, M. (2003). One-Time Gains and One-Time Losses: These Practices Sometimes Make it Hard Getting to the Bottom Line. *Florida Times-Union*, April 21, p. FB-12.

Collingwood, H. (2001). The Earnings Game: Everyone Plays, Nobody Wins. *Harvard Business Review*, June: 5–12.

Green, Paula L. (2002). Chainsaw Al May Discover the First Cut Was Not the Deepest. *Global Finance*, October.

Hilzenrath, David S. (2001). Sunbeam Accused of Fraud: SEC Says Dunlap, Others Overstated Revenue. *Washington Post*, May 16, p. E01.

Jones, P., & Kahaner, L. (1995). *Say It and Live It: 50 Corporate Mission Statements that Hit the Mark.* New York: Doubleday.

Lindenburg, E. B., & Ross, S. A. (1981). Tobin's "q" Ratio and Industrial Organization. *Journal of Business*, 54(1): 1–32.

Miller, D. (1990). *The Icarus Paradox: How Exceptional Companies Bring About their own Downfall.* New York: Harper Business.

Perfect, S. B., & Wiles, K. K. (1994). Alternative Constructions of Tobin's q: An Empirical Comparison. *Journal of Empirical Finance*, 1: 313–41.

Weber, H. R. (2002). Coke Drop Earnings Guidance: Soft-Drink Giant Says Move Puts Emphasis on Long Term. *Associated Press*, December 14. *Cincinnati Enquirer*: www.enquirer.com/editions/2002/12/14/biz_coke14.html (visited October 25, 2010).

Chapter 3

Castrogiovanni, G. (1991). Environmental Munificence: A Theoretical Assessment. *Academy of Management Review*, 16: 542–65.

Corey, M. (1990). The "Blunders" Making Millions for 3M. *Business Week*, July 16, p. 118.

Hedberg, B. L. T., Nystrom, P. C., & Starbuck, W. H. (1976). Camping on Seesaws: Prescriptions for a Self-Designing Organization. *Administrative Science Quarterly*, 21: 41–65.

Hunt, D. E. (1987). *Beginning with Ourselves in Practice, Theory, and Human Affairs.* Cambridge, MA: Brookline Books, pp. 4, 30.

Miller, D. (1990). *The Icarus Paradox: How Exceptional Companies Bring About their own Downfall.* New York: Harper Business.

Mintzberg, H. (1987). Crafting Strategy. *Harvard Business Review*, 65: 65–75.

Pascale, R. T. (1984). Perspectives on Strategy: The Real Story behind Honda's Success. *California Management Review*, 26(3): 47–74.

Post-it Note History (n.d.). www.3m.com/us/office/postit/pastpresent/history.html (visited May 2, 2004).

Quinn, J. B. (1980). *Strategies for Change: Logical Incrementalism.* Homewood, IL: Irwin.

Chapter 4

Abell, D. F. (1980). *Defining the Business: The Starting Point of Strategic Planning.* Englewood Cliffs, NJ: Prentice-Hall.

Abernathy, W. J., & Clark, K. B. (1985). Innovation: Mapping the Winds of Creative Destruction. *Research Policy*, 14: 3–22.

Boulding, K. E. (1956). General Systems Theory: The Skeleton of Science. *General Systems: Yearbook of the Society for the Advancement of General Systems Theory*, 1: 11–17.

Bourgeois, L. J. (1984). Strategic Management and Determinism. *Academy of Management Review*, 9: 586–96.

Button, K. (2002). Empty Cores in Airline Markets. Paper presented at the fifth Hamburg Aviation Conference, Hamburg, Germany, February.

Cheah, H. B. (1990). Schumpeterian and Austrian Entrepreneurship: Unity within Duality. *Journal of Business Venturing*, 5: 341–7.

Child, J. (1972). Organizational Structure, Environment, and Performance: The Role of Strategic Choice. *Sociology*, 6: 2–22.

D'Aveni, R. A. (1994). *Hyper-Competition: Managing the Dynamics of Strategic Maneuvering.* New York: Free Press.

DeGross, M. (2001). Kroger Knocks Harris Teeter out of Atlanta. *Atlanta Journal-Constitution*, June 26.

Eldredge, N., & Gould, S. (1972). Punctuated Equilibria: An Alternative to Phyletic Gradualism. In T. J. Schoph (Ed.). *Models in Paleobiology* (pp. 82–115). San Francisco: Freeman, Cooper, & Co.

Federal Reserve Bank of San Francisco (2004). *Banking Consolidation*. Economic Letter, June 18.

Gersick, C. J. (1991). Revolutionary Change Theories: A Multilevel Exploration of the Punctuated Equilibrium Paradigm. *Academy of Management Journal*, 16: 10–36.

Nelson, R. R., & Winter, S. G. (1973). Toward an Evolutionary Theory of Economic Capabilities. *American Economic Review*, 63: 440–9.

O'Neill, T., & Hymel, G. (1994). *All Politics is Local and Other Rules of the Game*. Holbrook, MA: Bob Adams.

Porter, M. E. (1980). *Competitive Strategy*. New York: Free Press.

Schumpeter, J. (1934). *The Theory of Economic Development*. Cambridge, MA: Harvard University Press.

Sjostrom, W. (1993). Antitrust Immunity for Shipping Conferences: An Empty Core Approach. *Antitrust Bulletin*, 38: 419–23.

Tushman, M. L., & Anderson, P. (1986). Technological Discontinuities and Organizational Environments. *Administrative Science Quarterly*, 31: 439–65.

von Bertalanffy, L. (1950). The Theory of Open Systems in Physics and Biology. *Science*, 111: 23–8.

Chapter 5

Andrews, K. R. (1971). *The Concept of Corporate Strategy*. Homewood, IL: Dow Jones-Irwin.

Bach, G. L., Flanagan, R., Howell, J., Levy, F., & Lima, A. (1987). *Microeconomics* (11th ed.). Englewood Cliffs, NJ: Prentice-Hall.

Barney, J. B. (1991). Firm Resources and Sustained Competitive Advantage. *Journal of Management*, 17: 99–120.

Bowman, C., & Ambrosini, V. (2000). Value Creation versus Value Capture: Towards a Coherent Definition of Value in Strategy. *British Journal of Management*, 11: 1–15.

Christensen, C. M., Raynor, M., & Verlinden, M. (2001). Skate to Where the Money Will Be. *Harvard Business Review*, November: 72–81.

Peteraf, M. A. (1993). The Cornerstones of Competitive Advantage: A Resource-Based View. *Strategic Management Journal*, 14: 179–91.

Porter, M. E. (1985). *Competitive Advantage*. New York: Free Press.

Priem, R. L. (2007). A Consumer Perspective on Value Creation. *Academy of Management Review*, 32: 219–35.

Timmons, J. A. (1999). *New Venture Creation: Entrepreneurship for the 21st Century* (5th ed.). Boston: Irwin/McGraw-Hill.

Wernerfelt, B. (1984). A Resource-Based View of the Firm. *Strategic Management Journal*, 5: 171–80.

Chapter 6

Edwards, C. (2006) AMD: Chipping Away at Intel's Lead. *Business Week*, June 19.

Hill, C. W. L. (1988). Differentiation versus Low Cost or Differentiation and Low Cost: A Contingency Framework. *Academy of Management Review*, 13: 401–13.

Hofer, C. W., & Schendel, D. (1978). *Strategy Formulation: Analytical Concepts*. St. Paul: West.

Parnell, J. A., & Wright, P. (1993). Generic Strategy and Performance: An Empirical Test of the Miles and Snow Typology. *British Journal of Management*, 4(1): 29–37.

Porter, M. E. (1980). *Competitive Strategy*. New York: Free Press.

Priem, R. L., & Butler, J. E. (2001). Is the Resource-Based View a Useful Perspective for Strategic Management Research? *Academy of Management Review*, 26: 1–22.

Teece, D. J., Pisano, G., & Shuen, A. (1997). Dynamic Capabilities and Strategic Management. *Strategic Management Journal*, 18: 509–33.

Chapter 7

Baum, J., & Korn, H. (1996). Competitive Dynamics of Interfirm Rivalry. *Academy of Management Journal*, 39: 255–92.

Berger, P., & Ofek, E. (1995). Diversification's Effect on Firm Value. *Journal of Financial Economics*, 37: 39–65.

Gimeno, J., & Woo, C. (1996). Hypercompetition in a Multimarket Environment: The Role of Strategic Similarity and Multimarket Contact in Competitive De-Escalation. *Organization Science*, 7: 322–41.

Henry, D. (2002). Mergers: Why Most Big Deals Don't Pay Off. *Business Week*, October 14; www.businessweek.com/magazine/content/02_41/b3803001.htm.

Hughes, A., & Singh, A. (1987). Takeovers and the Stock Market. *Contributions to Political Economy*, 6: 73–85.

Jensen, M., & Ruback, R. (1983). The Market for Corporate Control: The Scientific Evidence. *Journal of Financial Economics*, 11: 5–50.

Karnani, A., & Wernerfelt, B. (1985). Multiple Point Competition. *Strategic Management Journal*, 6: 87–96.

Nielsen, J. F., & Melicher, R. W. (1973). A Financial Analysis of Acquisition and Merger Premiums. *Journal of Financial and Quantitative Analysis*, 8: 139–48.

Peterson, K. (2004). Comcast Deal Gives Microsoft Entry into Cable T.V., *Seattle Times*, November 9.

Porter, M. E. (1987). From Competitive Advantage to Corporate Strategy. *Harvard Business Review*, 65: 43–59.

Rosen, R. J. (2006). Merger Momentum and Investor Sentiment: The Stock Market Reaction to Merger Announcements. *Journal of Business*, 79: 987–1017.

Rowley, I. (2006). Way, Way Off-Road. *Business Week*, July 7.

Rumelt, R. (1974). *Strategy, Structure and Economic Performance*. Cambridge, MA: Harvard University Press.

Servaes, H. (1996). The Value of Diversification during the Conglomerate Merger Wave. *Journal of Finance*, 51: 1201–25.

Williamson, O. (1975). *Markets and Hierarchies, Analysis and Antitrust Implications: A Study in the Economics of Internal Organization*. New York: Free Press.

Chapter 8

Allison, G. T. (1971). *Essence of Decision: Explaining the Cuban Missile Crisis*. Boston: Little, Brown.

Amason, A. C., & Mooney, A. C. (2008). The Icarus Paradox Revisited: How Strong Performance Sows the Seeds of Dysfunction in Future Strategic Decision Making. *Strategic Organization*, 6: 407–34.

Burns, T., & Stalker, G. M. (1961). *The Management of Innovation*. London: Tavistock.

Chandler, A. D. (1962). *Strategy and Structure: Chapters in the History of the American Industrial Enterprise*. Cambridge, MA: MIT Press.

Chandy, R. K., & Tellis, G. J. (2000). The Incumbent's Curse? Incumbency, Size and Radical Product Innovation. *Journal of Marketing*, 64: 1–17.

Cyert, R. M., & March, J. G. (1963). *A Behavioral Theory of the Firm*. Englewood Cliffs, NJ: Prentice-Hall.

Demirag, I. (1995). Short-Term Performance Pressures: Is There a Consensus View? *European Journal of Finance*, 1: 41–56.

Drucker, P. F. (1966). *The Effective Executive*. New York: Harper & Row.

Duncan, R. B. (1974). Modifications in Decision Structure in Adapting to the Environment: Some Implications for Organizational Learning. *Decision Sciences*, 5: 705–25.

Dutton, J. E., Fahey, L., & Narayanan, V. K. (1983). Toward Understanding Strategic Issue Diagnosis. *Strategic Management Journal*, 4: 307–23.

Ferreira, N., Kar, J., & Trigeorgis, L. (2009). Option Games. *Harvard Business Review*, 87: 101–7.

Fiol, C. M., & Lyles, M. A. (1985). Organizational Learning. *Academy of Management Review*, 10: 803–13.

Foster, R. N. (2003). Corporate Performance and Technological Change through Investors' Eyes. *Research Technology Management*, 46: 36–43.

Fredrickson, J. W., & Iaquinto, A. I. (1989). Inertia and Creeping Rationality in Strategic Decision Processes. *Academy of Management Journal*, 32: 516–42.

Ghemewat, P. (1991). Marketing Incumbency and Technological Inertia. *Marketing Science*, 10: 161–72.

Hedberg, B. L. T., Nystrom, P. C., & Starbuck, W. H. (1976). Camping on Seesaws: Prescriptions for a Self-Designing Organization. *Administrative Science Quarterly*, 21: 41–65.

Kahneman, D., & Tversky, A. (1979). Prospect Theory: An Analysis of Decision under Risk. *Econometrica*, 47: 263–91.

Lawrence, P. R., & Lorsch, J. W. (1967). *Organization and Environment: Managing Differentiation and Integration*. Boston: HBS Press.

Luehrman, T. A. (1998). Strategy as a Portfolio of Real Options. *Harvard Business Review*, September–October: 89–99.

McGrath, R. G. (1997). A Real Options Logic for Initiating Technology Positioning Investments. *Academy of Management Review*, 22: 974–96.

McGrath, R. G. (1999). Falling Forward: Real Options Reasoning and Entrepreneurial Failure. *Academy of Management Review*, 24: 13–30.

Miller, D. (1992). The Icarus Paradox: How Exceptional Companies Bring About their own Downfall. *Business Horizons*, 35: 24–36.

Mintzberg, H. (1987). Crafting Strategy. *Harvard Business Review*, 65: 65–75.

Nelson, R. R., & Winter, S. G. (1982). *An Evolutionary Theory of Economic Change*. Cambridge, MA: Belknap Press.

Pascale, R., & Athos, A. (1981). *The Art of Japanese Management*. London: Penguin Books.

Peters, T., Waterman, R., & Phillips, J. R. (1980). Structure is Not Organization. *Business Horizons*, 23: 14–26.

Rhoades, D., & Stelter, D. (2009). Seize Advantage in a Downturn. *Harvard Business Review*, 87: 1–8.

Scherpereel, C. M. (2008). The Option-Creating Institution: A Real Options Perspective on Economic Organization. *Strategic Management Journal*, 29: 455–70.

Schumpeter, J. A. (1942). *Capitalism, Socialism, and Democracy*. New York: Harper & Bros.

Teece, D. J., Pisano, G., & Shuen, A. (1997). Dynamic Capabilities and Strategic Management. *Strategic Management Journal*, 18: 509–33.

Tversky, A., & Kahneman, D. (1981). The Framing of Decisions and the Psychology of Choice. *Science*, 211, January 30: 453–8.

Chapter 9

Frankel, J. A. (1997). *Regional Trading Blocs in the World Economic System*. Washington, DC: Institute for International Economics.

Ghemawat, P. (2001). Distance Still Matters. *Harvard Business Review*, September: 1–10.

Sandberg, W. R. (1986). *New Venture Performance: The Role of Strategy and Industry Structure*. Lexington, MA: Lexington Books.

Schumpeter, J. A. (1942). *Capitalism, Socialism, and Democracy*. New York: Harper & Bros.

Stinchcombe, A. L. (1965). Social Structure and Organizations. In J. G. March (Ed.). *Handbook of Organizations* (pp. 142–93). Chicago: Rand McNally.

Vesper, K. H. (1980). *New Venture Strategies.* Englewood Cliffs, NJ: Prentice-Hall.

Chapter 10

Avolio, B. J. (2005). *Leadership Development in Balance: Made/Born.* Mahwah, NJ: Lawrence Erlbaum.

Boeker, W. (1989). Strategic Change: The Effects of Founding and History. *Academy of Management Journal*, 32: 489–515.

Diesnesch, R. M., & Liden, R. C. (1986). Leader–Member Exchange Model of Leadership: A Critique and Further Development. *Academy of Management Review*, 11: 618–34.

Dvorak, P., & Scannell, K. (2009). Investors Take Note: New Bill to Target Boards, "Say on Pay." *Wall Street Journal*, 96: B2.

Enrico, R. (with Kornbluth, J.) (1986). *The Other Guy Blinked: How Pepsi Won the Cola Wars.* New York: Bantam.

Fama, E. F., & Jensen, M. C. (1983). Separation of Ownership and Control. *Journal of Law and Economics*, 26: 301–26.

Fredrickson, J. W., Hambrick, D. C., & Baumrin, S. (1988). A Model of CEO Dismissal. *Academy of Management Review*, 13: 255–70.

Graffin, S. D., Wade, J. B., Porac, J. F., & McNamee, R. C. (2008). The Impact of CEO Status Diffusion on the Economic Outcomes of Other Senior Managers. *Organization Science*, 19: 457–74.

Hambrick, D. C., & Mason, P. A. (1984). Upper Echelons: The Organization as a Reflection of its Top Managers. *Academy of Management Review*, 9: 193–206.

Heifetz, R. A., & Laurie, D. L. (2001). The Work of Leadership. *Harvard Business Review*, 75: 124–34.

Judge, T. A., Woolf, E. F., Hurst, C., & Livingston, B. (2008). Leadership. In J. Barling & C. L. Cooper (Eds.). *The Sage Handbook of Organizational Behavior* (pp. 334–52). Los Angeles: Sage.

Kimberly, J. (1979). Issues in the Creation of Organizations: Initiation, Innovation and Institutionalization. *Academy of Management Journal*, 22: 427–57.

Pfeffer, J. (1977). The Ambiguity of Leadership. *Academy of Management Review*, 2: 104–12.

Selznick, P. (1957). *Leadership in Administration: A Sociological Interpretation.* Berkeley: University of California Press.

Wooldridge, B., & Floyd, S. (1990). The Strategy Process, Middle Management Involvement, and Organizational Performance. *Strategic Management Journal*, 11: 231–41.

Yukl, G. (1989). Managerial Leadership: A Review of Theory and Research. *Journal of Management*, 15: 251–89.

Index